The 1929
KELSEY
QUILTERS

The brave sisters, who found a safe place to worship, and
raise families in the Church of Jesus Christ of Latter-day
Saints, and the faithful missionaries that served them.

BEVERLY BURNETT HAMBERLIN

PRISTINE
PRESS AND MEDIA

The 1929 Kelsey Quilters
Copyright © 2025 by Beverly Burnett Hamberlin

ISBN
978-1-964804-52-1(Paperback)
978-1-964804-51-4 (eBook)
978-1-964804-53-8 (Hardcover)

Dedicated to Clara Dickason, Lela, Vaughn, Joye, Fayrene, Julia, Moroni, and Myrtle Lindsey Hamberlin.

The 1929 Relief Society Quilters, "The Kelsey Kids" the faithful missionaries Reva Dalton Topham and Thurza Ellsworth Boyle.

Also, to my dear friend Ann Pomeroy Barney, who encouraged and supported me.

PROLOGUE

What is a quilt? Is it just pieces of fabric stitched together to keep us warm? Is it meant to be something beautiful to cover a bed, or is it meant to comfort us?

It's like a puzzle with hundreds of pieces that fit together to make a design. It is really kind of like life itself.

How well and strong the stitches that hold it together are and how you protect it determines how it will endure the wear and tear of life.

The selection of the fabric we use determines if it will be pleasing to the eye and how it will feel to the touch.

The pattern or design will reflect what the creator is trying to represent. There is usually a theme to the colors and pattern.

If our life were to be reflected in a quilt, what would it look like? What if each piece represented what happened to us over our lifetime? Would even the worst of trials and the hardships we endure be part of a beautiful pattern? When put together, would we see how it has strengthened our testimonies of Christ? Would the service we give to others and our sacrifices for the Lord be the focal point of our design?

Isn't a quilt just a little bit like all of us coming together to warm the hearts of our brothers and sisters and comfort the sick and needy?

The Kelsey quilt is so many things to me. I see the faces of all the sisters who came together in almost the same way at about the same time.

They all heard the message of the missionaries in the Southern states and were touched by the spirit when so many others listened to that same message and did not believe it.

They came from Alabama, Arkansas, Florida, Georgia, Illinois, Louisiana, Tennessee, and Mississippi. Each one experienced persecution from their neighbors, family, and friends, which caused them to want to go where they could be with other members who believed as they did. They wanted to worship as they chose.

The Lord provided a way for them to all come to the same place to find refuge from their feelings. Not just luck brought them all to Kelsey, but rather the Lord's plan. He guided them with the help of the missionaries and provided a way for them to come together in a little safe colony to build up His kingdom and to help each other.

The trials these sisters went through to come together gave them the strength and courage to raise families to serve the Lord. The posterity from this one little colony has spread throughout the world.

TABLE OF CONTENTS

The 1929
Kelsey
Quilters

Beverly Burnett Hamberlin

The old Ault store complete with gas
filling station. 1915 Kelsey.

Myrtle with daughters Fayrene and Joye coming
home from the Kelsey school and Bennion
Hall at the top of the hill in 1934.

CHAPTER 1

A Ghost Town

Embrace Your Sacred Memories, believe them, write them down. Share them with your Families. Trust that they come to you from Your Heavenly Father and His Beloved Son.

—*Neil L. Andersen*

Kelsey, Texas, is now just a ghost town that most people have never even heard of, yet it played a massive role in the history of the Church of Jesus Christ of Latter-day Saints from about 1894 until the early 1930s. It became the mother colony for many of the Mormon converts of the Southern states by 1905.

Newly converted Saints from the Southern states fled their homes because those around them, including family and friends, would not let them worship in peace.

The Church had reopened the Southern States Mission for the first time in over forty years in some places after the murder of Parley P. Pratt in Arkansas.

People all over the South were accepting this new religion, but the mobs and nonbelievers were hard at work trying to stop the "Mormons," as they were called then.

In the 1890s, Wilford Woodruff was the prophet and president of the Church. People thought the Church was all about plural marriage and worshipping Joseph Smith. Stories spread like wildfires about the

Church. Stories like they would steal your wife and daughters and they were not Christians but worshiped Joseph Smith.

When President Woodruff issued the declaration that ended plural marriage, he hoped to end that, but the hatred for the Mormons continued.

The persecution was often instigated by the ministers of other churches, who felt the Mormons were stealing their members. They didn't understand that Jesus Christ was the foundation of the Church and Joseph Smith was only the means of restoring it.

In November 1902, Abraham Owen Woodruff, a member of the Quorum of the Twelve Apostles, was sent to east Texas. He was to assist President James G. Duffin in laying out a townsite on land owned by James Edgar. Elder Woodruff planned the town, but President Duffin then carried out the plans and encouraged the new Saints to build up the Church where they were instead of migrating to Utah. President Benjamin E. Rich was called to serve in the Southern States Mission in 1903.

The Church of Jesus Christ of Latter-day Saints called missionaries to Kelsey to help set up a school. The missionaries came to teach Sunday school and regular school. Many of them kept journals that told which missionaries served and when. These journals are fascinating and can be found in Church History, FamilySearch, and Ancestry.

Missionaries started handing out little pamphlets telling new converts about Kelsey, a place where Saints could come from all over the South. More families came, and their children grew up and married children from the other families, and they stayed in Kelsey.

There are countless stories about what went on in the Southern states and the amazing missionaries who left their homes and families to teach the Gospel. They endured so much, to the point of risking their lives at times.

The Hamberlin family often told the story of Osmer D. Flake baptizing their grandfather, James David Hamberlin, in the muddy Mississippi River in the middle of the night. They described how their family and friends persecuted them, telling them they had stolen their religion. After years of researching, I have found many different accounts of what went on back then. Still, the Hamberlin family did sell their crops in the fields and started on a long and dangerous journey to Snowflake, Arizona, in 1900 because that's where Osmer D. Flake was from.

The Lord found a way to build up his kingdom in this little colony in Kelsey, and I am so thankful for all they sacrificed to live this strange new religion.

At first, there was plenty of rich farmland for all those who came to stay. Salt Lake was very aware of the situation facing these new Saints who had sacrificed so much and had come to a new place in dire need of a new beginning.

The post office opened in 1902, and in 1910, the Marshal and East Texas Railway added a fifteen-mile stretch of track from Kelsey through Gilmer to connect to the main channel when they started clearing trees for logging. This provided a way for the farmers to get their produce and cotton to market.

The Kelsey Academy, a public school staffed by Mormon missionaries, opened in 1911.

The early Saints built homes and furniture. They built stores, a brick kiln, three sawmills, a shingle mill, a cotton gin, two blacksmith shops, and a grist mill.

They planted cotton, corn, fruit trees, and everything else they needed. They raised pigs, chickens, and cattle. They opened and ran dairies to supply fresh milk for their families and surrounding farms. Farming and working for the railroad formed the lifeline for the Saints, so when the railroad shut down in 1917, the farmers had to find other ways to get food to market. Then the Depression came in the 1930s and times were hard, forcing men to find work elsewhere. Many men and older boys went to Freeport, Texas, to work in the sulfur mines. Some even to the oil fields.

Today, Kelsey is a ghost town or a dispersed rural community, with most of the population being descendants of the original Mormon settlers. There are no longer any schools, churches, or places of business. However, the history of Kelsey will long be remembered in the hearts and minds of the posterity of these 1929 quilters.

This is a story that I believe had to be told, even though I didn't think I would be able to do it justice. I could not have written a single page without the Lord's help.

I trust I will include everything that needs to be heard in this story. I have grown from hearing the histories written by and about them and have learned love each one so much. They may touch your life in some way, as they have mine.

I had no idea when I began this story what the end would be. As I get to the end, it isn't clear yet, but I realize now that we never understand the beginning of our lives until we reach the end.

Each day that I researched these sisters, one clue would lead me to another, and some days, it took me down roads that I got lost on and would have to turn around and start again down a different path.

I would wake up some mornings thinking about people or things for no apparent reason. I found myself reading something repeatedly and still not knowing what to do.

These stories might encourage others to record their own stories of life experiences or motivate them to read the histories written by and about their ancestors.

The day I first met the Kelsey Hamberlins. Fayrene
Bonebrake, Julia Bryant, Moroni Hamberlin, Joye
Grubbs, and Myrtle Lindsey Hamberlin in 1981.

The well in Myrtles backyard that had been the
only source of water in the early years when they
came to Texas. Now just a reminder of the past.

CHAPTER 2

The Quilt

Four days before Christmas 2018, I received the call that Mary Cannon Hamberlin, an aunt of my husband, Jim, had passed away in Salt Lake City, Utah. She was eighty-six and not in excellent health, but it came as a surprise to me. When I got the call from her daughter, Debra, I felt terrible that I could not go.

Mary had been my aunt for over fifty years. I had attended Glenn's funeral seventeen years earlier when he died of cancer. Glenn and I worked together on family history research in the 1980s, and we both loved the temple. Glenn had worked for many years in the Salt Lake temple as an ordinance worker.

My first thought was of the sweet reunion they would have. Glenn is the youngest brother of my father-in-law, Doyle Carlos Hamberlin. We had lost Doyle in 1973. Mary is the great-granddaughter of George Q. Cannon and Elizabeth Hoagland.

I reflected on the time I visited with them as I attended BYU Education Week with three sisters from my ward. We took a side trip to Salt Lake City because I had an appointment with J. Richard Clarke, who at the time was a member of the Seventies over the Family History Department. It was about some temple work I wanted to do on my Thomas Jefferson line. It was just across the street from the temple, and Glenn was going with me for moral support. I was very nervous.

When I arrived at the temple, fasting for my meeting with Brother Clark, my heart was beating so fast, similar to the feeling of needing to bear your testimony while unsure what you would say. Shortly after the session started, I got this calm, peaceful feeling when I looked up and saw Glenn.

I hadn't realized he would be serving in the temple that day. When he saw me, we both smiled. I knew he loved me, and so did Heavenly Father. Love is so much stronger and more intense in the temple. We can feel Christlike love in his house, like no place else.

Glenn came to the Celestial Room when the session ended and hugged me. I will never forget that sweet feeling of the spirit that day. He then invited my three friends and me to go home after our meeting and have dinner. Then he called Mary and told her he had invited us for dinner. She was always such a gracious hostess and on such short notice. That afternoon, Mary prepared a delicious hot meal on the spur of the moment.

They lived in a ward in Salt Lake with Dallin H. Oaks, and for my birthday one year Glenn sent me an autographed book of Pure in Heart by Dallin H. Oaks that had not one but two signatures, with a "Best wishes, Beverly."

When Glenn died in 2001, I flew to Salt Lake alone, spent several days with Mary, and visited with her kids. I went with them to the viewing and funeral. I knew I would miss him. I kept in touch with her, but not like I did with Glenn when he was alive.

Debra told me, when she called, that they had been cleaning out Aunt Mary's house to sell when they made a surprising find. It was a quilt that none of them had ever seen before. It was neatly folded over a strong hanger and was covered in plastic. As they pulled away the covering, to their surprise, they found twenty-two quilt blocks that had not been sewn together.

Where did the quilt come from, and why did they not know it was there? Taking a closer look, they discovered that each of the blocks in the quilt, and those not sewn together, had the same eight-point star pattern in different fabric colors, but each had a different name embroidered on it.

Debra said they knew none of the names except Clara Hamberlin, but I might want to have it if I did. I couldn't believe they would give it away. I told her I would love to have it if she was sure they didn't want to keep it. Why were they giving it to me? I kept asking myself that question.

Glenn and Mary had made trips back to Kelsey, I am sure, because he was born there. Their kids were too young to remember any of the family there. I know they had been in touch with his family in recent years because the Kelsey family talked about Glenn to me. I decided the quilt had to belong to Clara Dickason Hamberlin, Jim's grandmother and Glenn's mother, because Clara lived with Glenn and Mary after her husband, Percy Alton Hamberlin, died in 1952 in Salt Lake.

When I married my husband, James Wesley Hamberlin, in 1965, his grandmother, Clara, lived in Phoenix, Arizona, with her son, Melvin, and his wife, Evelyn Hamberlin. That was when I first met Clara, but she was sick most of the time and bedridden. I never saw her go anywhere.

She also didn't like my mother-in-law, Olive. At least, that's what Olive told me. I was told not to tell her anything about what Olive did or said. That kept me from ever really getting to know her. I would later regret never hearing Clara tell me about her early life. I missed out on getting to know her.

Why did Clara never tell anyone about a quilt she kept in the back of a closet, or why did the twenty-two blocks never make it into a quilt? Did Mary know her story? If she did, why didn't she ever share it with me? Didn't they both know how much it would mean to me and others in the family? The secrets of the past will forever haunt me. I had to keep digging. Clara had taken this one to her grave, I feared. She lived to be ninety-two and died in 1982, long after I was deep into family history, and I had missed my chance to know what she was thinking.

A few days later, much to my surprise, when I came home from working my ordinance shift at the Mesa temple, I found I had received a large box with the most perfectly preserved quilt. Not a stitch was broken anywhere that I could see. It had a soft blue fabric on the backside. Twenty-four of the twenty-five blocks each held the name of a sister. One block had "R.S. Kelsey." I thought it must mean the Relief Society of Kelsey. Surely not someone's initials. Some sisters added a date of 1929, Kelsey or Gilmer, on their quilt blocks. Two of the orphan blocks said, "To my teacher." One added her mailing address to the quilt. Gilmer is a little town close by and is also in this community.

The names as they are written on the quilt are listed below, along with their FamilySearch number, full names, and how old they were when they made the quilt blocks.

Audrey Bryant	KW8P-5BN	Audrey Bryant Means	16
Laura Bryant	KWCJ-FHM	Laura Pauline Bryant Strausburg	18
Vera Wade	KWZL-6RW	Vera Esther Wade Russell	18
Loretta Burnett	KW8Q-H5B	Loretta Mae Alexander	19
Wilma Dotson	KWCN-9S3	Wilma Daisy Dotson Henderson	20
Carrie Hamberlin	KWN2-M8V	Carrie Lamarshand Dilley	22
Emma Wade	KWZF-Z2V	Emma Smoot Dixon	23
Rusie Futrell	KWZ4-D34	Rusie Susie Bessie Dawson	24
Ethel McKnight	KWCF-2YJ	Ethel Viola Burnett	34
Docie Knight	KWZK-L1D	Ella Theodocia Sanders	35
Viola Grantham	KWCN-9S3	Iva Viola Ennis	37
Ava Dixon	KW8P-57S	Ava Christine Ellett	38
Clara Hamberlin	KWCV-KY8	Clara Annie Dickason	39
Viola Perry	KWDC-9T1	Viola Green	41
Emma McKnight	KWC4-QLT	Emma Elizabeth Dickason	41
Abbie Lindsey	KWZB-PL3	Abbie Buckley	43
Ida Dotson	KWZ9-XKM	Ida Crook Hobby	52
Sis. Whitehead	KWZN-R4D	Mary Lucinda Tefteller	58
Berta Wade	KWZM-95P	Berta Adelaide Leake	60

Bea Shore	KW8L-NCM	Beatrice Jane Vice	63
Winnie Green	KW8K-VZN	Eleanor Winifred Ellett	68
Kittie Ellett	KWC7-X26	Martha Catherine Green	68
Belle Cummins	KWCN-RTS	Isabelle Josephine Crouch	70
Florence Bailey	KWJN-KPX	Amanda Florence Shirley	70

Lamar and Myrtle Lindsey Hamberlin on
their wedding day, 1917 Kelsey

Back: Vaughn, Otis and Lela. Seated: Joye
and Fayrene Hamberlin. 1941, Kelsey

CHAPTER 3

A Travel in Time

I had the opportunity to visit Kelsey three different times in the 1980s. The first time was with my mother-in-law, Olive Hamberlin, a widow, and I took her to Longview, Texas, to visit her sister, Ava Nell Powell, her niece, Patricia Holley, and her aunt, Sally Hooks. Sally was the half sister of Olive's mother, Crystal Irvin Hefley.

Sally had helped me find many family names for Olive's ancestors with dates and places for my research, and I wanted to meet and talk to her.

Jim and I had lived with his grandmother, Crystal, when we first were married. She needed our help, and we were able to save enough money to put a down payment on our first home.

Crystal had told me many stories about her family that I didn't write down because I had not yet learned the importance of family histories. She told me that, before she was born, her father had taken a wagon to town for supplies in Caney County, Oklahoma, and never returned home in 1889. They thought he had been killed by Indians that had been uprising in the area. Crystal's mother, Mary Olive Stone, later married Joseph Barbee, and Crystal had ten younger half siblings. Crystal died in 1974, but on my trips to Kelsey, I met and visited with two of Crystal's half sisters, a half brother, and their families.

Olive took me to see some of the places of her childhood, like the town square in Gilmer, where she had met Jim's father, Doyle. The kids from Kelsey often went there on Saturday nights to the dances and hung out around the square. That was where Doyle had courted her. I loved just listening to her and being there with her. She was not a member of the Church, and he knew his parents would disapprove, but he was adventurous and in love, so he married her anyway. They drove to Louisiana and married when Doyle was nineteen and Olive was only seventeen.

Doyle was such a good man, and I always admired him. I didn't understand why It was so important that he liked me and I had his approval. But he was the first member of the Church I had ever met who held the priesthood and had a testimony of the restored Gospel. There was just something about him I couldn't put my finger on. He died so young that my kids never knew him. He was only fifty-six when he died of cancer, but he had such a strong testimony of the Mormon Church, yet he never said anything to me about it or tried to convert me. I realize now how hard it can be to share our testimonies with our family an the people we sometimes love the most. Often, it is easier with strangers. Olive was not baptized until twelve years later, when she was twenty-nine and expecting her third child, Alan.

Olive and I went to Gilmer, looked at the house she grew up in, and drove around the area. As I passed an Exxon gas station, I noticed the sign that read, "Otis Hamberlin owner." I stopped and asked the man inside if Otis was there, and he told me Otis was out to lunch but would be back soon. We went back later, and Otis was so happy to see us. He called his mother, Myrtle Hamberlin, and his sisters, Fayrene Bonebrake and Joye Grubbs.

They invited us all to dinner the next day in Kelsey. What if I had not seen the sign? Sadly, Olive had not kept in touch with Doyle's family after he died. She would never have thought to look for them because she hadn't seen them in over forty years. She knew who Myrtle was but didn't know her or her children. I don't even know if Olive went to church in Kelsey. If she had, she would have known the sisters in the quilt.

Was it by chance that I made this powerful connection to this little ghost town that day? I think not. I was so excited that day to find them, but I never dreamed that I would be writing about this quilt forty years later.

The next day, I took Olive, her sister, Ava Nell, and her niece Patricia, and we met the Kelsey branch of the Hamberlin family.

They treated us like royalty and cooked us more food than I had ever seen. There were fried chicken, roast beef, potatoes, gravy, vegetables from their garden, fried okra, and fried green tomatoes. Then they served us cakes and pies of every variety for dessert. We were stuffed!

Moroni showed me how to cut a small slice of each pie so I could try them all.

There was so much family to meet and get to know. I loved hearing all about them and listening to their Texas accents. I took my tape recorder and recorded for a while, but we were all so excited, and everyone talked at once, making it sound like a lot of noise.

Myrtle was the widow of Lamar Hamberlin, Jim's great-uncle. Lamar is the brother of Percy Alton Hamberlin, Jim's grandfather. Her kids were first cousins of Jim's father, Doyle. Otis, Fayrene, and Joye all remembered Doyle from their childhood.

Fayrene Hamberlin Bonebrake dedicated her life to preserving the history of Kelsey, as did her sisters, Vaughn and Lela. They and the quilt motivated me to start writing this story. They don't have a block in the quilt, but they are a big part of the threads that hold it together.

I also met Moroni and his wife, Cornelia Jones Hamberlin, and his sister, Julia Hamberlin Bryant, that day at Myrtle's home, and they remembered Doyle as well. I never met Victor Carl or Lamar, Doyle's uncles, or his father, Percy, who came to Kelsey with their parents in 1904 after the family was baptized in Mississippi. I know they would have known and served with all the 1929 quilters. I had no idea that I would get to know how their lives intertwined. Myrtle's daughter, Lela, had died of cancer before my visit, and her second daughter, Vaughn Rowley, was sick and wasn't there.

Vaughn was the one who did so much of the research on the Hamberlin and Lindsey family lines. I saw and spoke with Vaughn in the hospital the next time I visited Myrtle, Fayrene, and Joye. She was bald from her cancer treatments and hooked up too many tubes and machines, but her face lit up when she spoke of her ancestors.

It was a short and sweet visit. We shared some of the stories we remembered about our family and the many hours of searching for records and treading through cemeteries. I had researched the Hamberlin line also but it was before FamilySearch or computers, so I couldn't see their research results until I met them.

She called all the grandpas Papa, no matter how far back they were on the pedigree chart. That was so endearing to me, showing how much she loved them and knew they were family, not just names on paper. We laughed and cried together, and then I never saw her again. I found something written about her after she died that says it all.

"Her light and influence reached beyond the veil to the ancestors she loved. She exerted much of her life and resources collecting information and stories that are invaluable to all of us without the convenience of computers and media available to us today. She painstakingly researched, recorded, and disseminated vital data for us and future generations. Many spiritual experiences strengthened her faith in the divinity of the Gospel of Jesus Christ and the life hereafter."

What a great tribute to Vaughn. I know someday we will meet again. She loved them all so much, just as I do. That is what happens to you when you get to know your ancestors.

I only took my kids to Kelsey once, and they got to see Moroni Hamberlin, the stake patriarch. He showed them where he gave patriarchal blessings and told them how he prepared for each one with fasting and prayer. As you might expect, they were much more intrigued by the well in Myrtle's backyard that I was afraid they might fall in.

It was no longer the primary water source for the family but a reminder of the past, as was the old schoolhouse where their grandfather, Doyle, had gone to school when he was their age. It had meant so much to the Hamberlin family; they bought it when it closed and still owned it when I was there. It was like traveling in time to drive the old country road that had once been just clay dirt between Kelsey and Gilmer.

Myrtle told me she walked to work at the laundry in Gilmer where she and her sisters worked and returned home daily. This was the same road traveled so many times by the "Sisters of the Quilt," as I had started calling them."

From my first visit, I felt like I had been drawn into the past like a time traveler. I felt a presence I could not explain. As I began to put this story together, I could already tell that all the puzzle pieces were falling into place, but I had no idea what the complete picture would be. I could hardly wait to see.

CHAPTER 4

The Orphan Blocks Go Home

When I first looked at all the blocks that were not in the quilt, only a few were familiar to me. The names I recognized in the quilt included Clara Hamberlin, Jim grandma. I knew Carrie Hamberlin and the Lindseys because that was Myrtle's maiden name, and I recognized Bryant because I had met and exchanged letters with Julia Bryant and Myrtle in the 1980s.

But then one of the orphan blocks was Cornelia Hamberlin. A name I knew because I had taken photos of her and Moroni. I had a sweet picture of Moroni and my three kids when he gave us a tour of where he gave patriarchal blessings. I have since met a lot of people who received their patriarchal blessing from Moroni.

I was so confused about what I should do with blocks that had names I did not recognize embroidered on each one.

What was I supposed to do with them? I couldn't imagine sewing them together with new fabric when the fabric they had used was almost a hundred years old. Then who would want it, and what would anyone do with it? At that time, I didn't know anyone who knew all of them; I didn't know for sure. I almost always see everyone in a family group sheet, so naturally I wanted to know who they were and how they fit together. The questions disturbed me so much that I finally just prayed that I would know what to do with them.

It didn't take long before my prayers were answered, and I knew exactly what I was supposed to do with them. The answer was so simple. Why didn't I think of it on my own?

Maybe because we need to always ask for the Lord's help but be careful what you pray for because sometimes we don't always want to do what the Lord wants us to. But I have since learned that if we try, we can do anything the Lord asks of us if we seek his help.

I needed to find out who they were and then send each orphan block back to a family member who would enjoy and appreciate it.

That sounded simple enough. I soon learned that this would take a lot of work because I had to find out who they were first, then find the family members and deliver them.

It turned out to be the most gratifying adventure I had ever experienced before. I had so much help getting them to family members. The people who received the orphan blocks were amazed when they got them. One of the women who helped me thanked me for letting her be a part of it. One said that delivering the blocks was like children going home to people who loved them. They brought tears of joy to all who received one. I got so many thank- you messages and heard beautiful stories of how people felt when they saw them.

They shared them at their book clubs and with their quilting friends. They brought so much joy to a lot of people. It was so amazing.

The following is a list of the names I sent home to living relatives, as they appeared on the orphan blocks, the FamilySearch ID number, and their age when they made the blocks.

If you want to see the quilt blocks or know if you are related to them, you can go to FamilySearch and enter the ID number, opening a window into their lives.

Faye Dixon	KWZL-XVM	Oleatha Faye Dixon	11
Bee Lindsey.	KWC1-F4D	Jesse Beatrice Lindsey	11
Bee Bell	KWC1-LRN	Evelyn Beatrice Bell	14
Velda Smith	KWZC-DKH	Velda Maleese Smith Bowers	16
Zelma Alexander	KWCP-6H6	Zelma Fern Lindsey	19

Ruth Ellett	KWZ1-VJQ	Ruth Marie Sanders	26
Cornelia Hamberlin	KWZX-R7N	Cornelia Jones	26
Joe Simmons	KW8B-FKQ	Dolly Jo Muckleroy	29
Myrtle Jones	KWZ2-P66	Leona Myrtle Jones Woodward	29
Med Buckley	KWZ3-PHM	Mary Medomosille Ault	30
Ethel Bradshaw	KWCK-216	Ethel Letha Wade	32
B. Bell	KWC1-F4D	Blanche Lindsey	37
Ethel Davis	LWJR-LVZ	Ethel Mae Bailey	37
Loretta Dixon	KWJ6-8V9	Etta Loretta Shore	38
Alice A.	KWZF-DGR	Cora Alice Shore Alexander	40
Manie Farley	KWJZ-1F2	Mary Manie Collins	43
E. Henderson	KWCQ-W2Q	Carrie Effie Dove Hunter	43
Daisy Jones	KWZH-35G	Daisy Green	47
Ida Futrell	KWNF-XXL	Ida Adella Irwin	51
Minnie B. Dixon	KWZN-GSP	Minnie Belle Luna	58
Joe Smith	KWJX-MB6	Mary Josephine Martin	71
Sallie Davis	LWJR-LVZ	Sarah Frances Cagle	81

Clara Dickason and Percy Hamberlin,
wedding day 1911, Kelsey.

CHAPTER 5
A Monumental Puzzle

I had to find out who the names on each block were. Because the quilt was created in 1929, I decided to take the 1930 census of Kelsey Upshur, Texas, and start looking. Some names were a lot harder than others. They often used a part of their name or a nickname.

It was like a giant puzzle, and I do love a good one. What a great mystery it turned out to be. It reminded me of a puzzle where someone had removed half of the pieces and put them somewhere else. The funny thing was some of the pieces fit in other puzzles I had already been working on for years and couldn't find the missing pieces. As I write this, I am still solving little mysteries daily.

I started by making a family tree for each of the sisters who had made a block in the quilt or an orphan block. I worked each tree until they connected to someone else's or fit into my Burnett tree. I started with Jim's grandmother, Clara Hamberlin, who was already in my Burnett tree.

It is the Burnett tree because I was born Beverly Juanell Burnett on February 17, 1947. I get a little obsessed with numbers sometimes. I have seven letters in each of my names, and seven is my number. I look at the numbers in everything I do. For some reason, numbers and dates have always fascinated me and seem to stick in my head.

The Percy Hamberlin family just seemed to disappear in the 1930s. They do not show up on any census. No Percy, Clara, or children can be found in Texas or anywhere. I had never looked very closely at the 1930 census. I knew they lived there in 1930 because they were still there in 1940, and Jim's older brother, Doyle, was born in Gilmer, Texas, in

1939. Sometimes the census taker misses a house. Maybe no one was home that day.

When I found Carrie Hamberlin on the 1930 census, I knew she was married to Percy's brother, Victor Carl. I was amazed to see the pages full of the names I needed to find. There they were like little pearls that I just had to gather up and string together so my journey began.

Our home teacher for the last thirty years or more, Ron Compton, was a very close friend of my husband, Jim. And over the years, Jim and Ron had hunted and fished together.

They planned a big trip to Mexico every February to fish for bass. Then they filled out hunting permits for deer, elk, and sometimes buffalo in the spring.

Ron, his wife, Lisa, and their whole family are very dear to our hearts. They have been close to us over the years, as we have sent out missionaries, had weddings, and welcomed grandchildren. Ron is an attorney, and I once did some family history research for him to find a client's descendent who received some money. I also made Ron a family tree on Ancestry called the Compton tree. I had cleared some names for him to do temple work. Now with Ordinance Ready, anyone can learn to find their family names on FamilySearch.

One night, I was looking for a name on an orphan block. I thought that it said Ned Buckley. I was unsure whether it was male or female, but it was a Buckley in Kelsey, so I started a Buckley tree. I began adding the Buckleys, who lived in Kelsey in 1920 and 1930. Then I found that because some of the Buckleys had already been added to another tree on my computer, it switched trees on me. I did not realize that until suddenly I saw that I was in the Compton tree.

What was going on? It took me a few minutes to figure out Ron's mother was Mar Jo Buckley. She was born in Texas but not Kelsey or Gilmer. Her last sibling to be born in Gilmer was in 1933. Her mother or Ron's grandmother was Mary Medomosille Ault, who married Arthur Morris Buckley. I realized she was the Med Buckley I was looking for. The stitching looked like an "N" instead of an "M."

Med and her family had lived in Kelsey in 1920, but in 1930, they had moved to Freeport, Texas, because her husband, Arthur, a carpenter by trade, was working in the sulfur mines, along with many others from Kelsey. Work for the young men in Kelsey in the early 1930s was scarce after the railroad shut down.

I could not believe that Ron's grandmother Med made a quilt block in 1929 with Jim's grandmother, Clara, and it was the very one I was now holding in my hands. When we figured this out, we were all so excited.

Lisa had the orphan block framed. They gave it to Mar Jo, Ron's mother, for Mother's Day 2019. Imagine the surprise of getting a gift from your son made by your mother ninety years ago and fifty-three years after her mother's death. Ron was not born until 1957, after his grandmother Med had passed away.

As I dug deeper, I found that on the 1910 census, Jim's great-grandfather, James Dickason, and Ron's great-grandfather, Joshua Ault, are on the same page. Med Ault was ten years old, and Clara Dickason was nineteen.

That meant that they had known each other for over twenty years when they made the blocks. The quilt block Clara had kept hidden in a closet for almost ninety years was in perfect condition. Why did she do that and not use it like everyone else? Did she save it just for me to find? I wondered why anyone would hide twenty-two blocks that didn't belong to you instead of giving them to someone to finish. Who was the teacher that the quilt was to be for?

My husband, Jim, was very supportive of my work on the quilt research. Jim said he thought they had sent it to the right person. He knew I wouldn't quit until I found out who they were. Maybe he thought I was a little bit obsessive.

Jim had a small, malignant mole removed from behind his left ear in November 2020. Then by February 2021, he was not feeling well. I tried to get him to see the doctor, but he said he had an appointment on March 13 with his doctor.

By March 8, he decided to go to the ER. They would not let me go in with him because of COVID. I dropped him off and waited in my car for him to call. They kept him that day and ran tests to see what was up.

They found a large tumor on the liver. They put him on heavy pain medications, and I could only see him during visiting hours. He slept when he could and did not want me to sit there and see the pain he was in. I was never able to see or talk to the doctors. Jim only told me what he wanted me to know, I guess. We knew it was terminal, but I thought we had a little time.

They sent him home after nine days of blood work, a liver biopsy, and other tests, with an appointment in a few days. He said they would figure out how to treat him as soon as they could get the pain under control.

When Jim returned home from the hospital on Wednesday, the first person he called was Ron. He wanted to get his will and legal documents in order. Ron came on Thursday night, spent over an hour with him, and had a good visit. Jim wanted me to show Ron the old photos of his dad, grandpa, and other ancestors that I had made appear to move with an app on My Heritage. Jim thought it was so amazing to see the faces of his ancestors, whom he had never met, move. He wanted to see his dad, Doyle, who had died forty-eight years ago.

The next day, on Friday afternoon, Jim was in so much pain that my daughter, Courtney, and I decided to call for an ambulance, even though he did not want to return to the hospital. Suddenly, Courtney looked at me and said, "Mom, he's gone." I couldn't believe it happened that fast. Just then, the doorbell rang. I ran to the door, expecting the paramedics. When I opened it, there stood Ron, with all the legal papers signed and notarized.

I will never know how he did that so fast and complete as Jim had wanted it done. So in March 2021, Ron spoke at Jim's funeral. After the services, along with some of Jim's hunting and fishing buddies, they fried up Mexico bass for all our friends and family. The Relief Society provided the rest of the food. Ron still ministers to my needs, bringing his wife, Lisa with him. He handled all my legal papers and took good care of me.

I am so thankful that because of the quilt, they could know a little about their connection in Kelsey and how their families intertwined. I researched the sisters for two years before Jim's death. I have learned so much more in the past years since his death. The quilt inspires me each day to keep going and finish my work here. The research on the "Sisters of the Quilt" is never-ending. I find more pieces to this puzzle every day. So many beautiful histories were left behind. Their stories were like mana from heaven to me, strengthening my testimony daily.

Each time I found a sister and saw her face and found her husband and family, my love for them grew. I feel like I will get to see them all someday. It is so amazing to hold something made so long ago and to be able to feel the love that was put into it.

I had known for years that another family in my ward, Shane and Jamie Pritchett Dawson, had come from Kelsey, but I hadn't looked at their family tree. When I started searching for the sisters, I found that Rusie Futrell, one of the quilters, was a Dawson, and her father was William King Dawson, Shane's great-grandfather. Rusie was Shane's great-aunt, and the funny thing was that William King's first wife, Sophronia Mary Irwin, was the niece of Jim's great-grandmother, Julia Irwin Hamberlin. That solved the question of how we were related to the Dawsons. Many of Shane's relatives were related to the Hamberlin family, and now they are in my tree.

When I started reading Kelsey's histories, I found that one of the first families to settle in Kelsey was the Bodines—the grandfather of Jerry Bodine in my ward. Jim had been Jerry's home teacher for the last five years before Jim's death. Jim never knew that Jerry's grandfather lived on the same country road and knew his great-uncle, Victor Carl Hamberlin. Jim loved visiting the Bodine family and had always taken them fresh bass whenever he and Ron had gone fishing in Mexico. All three of them came from Kelsey.

Jerry's grandfather is John Jay Bodine, born in 1888 in Texas.

The following story came from John's personal history of living in Leon County, Texas.

On a spring morning in 1899, two LDS missionaries known as "Mormons" came to our home at about 10:00 a.m. Mother gave them seats on the front porch and went to the field to get Father. We had been hearing about what the Mormons were preaching, and just a few days before that, I remember hearing them say they would like to meet them. Father (William Thomas Oliver Bodine) spent the rest of the day asking questions, discussing religion with them, and helping notify the neighborhood of their meeting at the church we all attended that evening.

They held several meetings that week, and I will never forget the thrill that came to me when they would sing. I especially remember one song, "We Thank Thee Oh God for Prophet." Another one was "Ere You Left Your Room This Morning, Did You Think to Pray." He also really liked "Mormon Boy."

The following Sunday night after the meeting, John's father stood up and announced that he was going to be baptized and invited them all to come down to the creek. Only a few people came to see him baptized on March 6, 1898. The missionaries left the next morning, returned about three weeks later, and baptized his mother, Matilda Elizabeth Click, on April 4, 1898.

During this time, the Baptist Sunday school got all worked up and went to pieces, and persecution began to set in. My father's brother, James, came to see him and informed him that he did not want any more to do with him. When the people learned that the Mormon missionaries had returned, they made up a mob and sent word that they were coming to our home to get them.

My parents prevailed on them to stay and said they would be protected. The mob came that night, and my father met them at the gate with his gun in his hands, ready for action, and warned them to stay outside and not enter his property, and if they did, it would be at the peril of their lives. They built a bonfire by the side of the road, a few hundred yards away, and created a disturbance, cursing and swearing most of the night. My father stood guard all night with his gun, ready for action, in order to protect the missionaries.

The mob leaders were called Christian people and good citizens in the community whom my father knew and had dealings with. The missionaries were not molested, and after a day or two, they left without being able to hold any more meetings in that part of the country.

When John's parents were baptized, the mission was called part of the Southern State Mission. Later it became the Southern Western States mission, and James G. Duffin was the president of it. They had headquarters in Independence, Missouri.

John was baptized at the age of thirteen in 1902, along with his brothers. He was very happy and excited about the church.

When President Duffin came and stayed at their house for a district conference in the area, about eighteen or twenty missionaries came.

One missionary came, who had been mobbed about two weeks before that, and the stripes still showed on his back where the mob had whipped him. John said, "The mission president talked to my parents about them going west to Utah. He told them of a safe place in Upshur County, Texas, called Kelsey, that had been set apart as a gathering place for the Saints and thought it would be good if we moved there. But he said we should use our own judgment, and if we decided to go west, it would be with his endorsement. After considering it, my father decided we would go to Kelsey, Texas, and he began preparation to move our family. This was a great disappointment, as I had been all set to go to Utah, and I had told my parents that if I ever got old enough, I would go anyway."

John's life history is excellent reading, as is almost all of them. He stayed in Kelsey until his mission call to Louisiana for one year and was set apart in 1907 by none other than Samuel O. Bennion as one of the first three missionaries sent out from Kelsey.

I couldn't believe that the quilt was connected to four families in my ward. That was only the beginning of this monumental puzzle. Their stories have changed my life.

Another piece of the puzzle I recently found is that a sister on my ordinance shift in the Mesa temple told me her mother, Ethel Verine Smith, served a mission in Kelsey in 1928.

I couldn't believe she had been called to teach English I and II, American literature ancient history, and home economics at Kelsey High School. She loved teaching, but the home economics class was challenging because she had not taken any college classes on food preparation. She said, "I got by with what I knew about the food groups, a balanced diet, and tried to teach them to cook without so much bacon fat and grease." Good luck with that!

Ethel's daughter, Jane Lambert, said Ethel often talked about Kelsey when she was growing up. The same sisters who made my quilt made two small quilts for her at the end of her mission. One was yellow, with no names, that she called her "sunshine quilt." The other had the sisters' names, but she had worn it out long ago and had no pictures. She did have a picture of the "sunshine quilt" that was pretty worn. I haven't found a quilt from 1929 that was in perfect condition like the one I have, probably because no one else had hidden theirs for ninety years. From the many histories I have discovered, it seems they made quilts for everyone. Everyone they cared about that is.

Maybe there are still family treasures and quilts waiting to be found if we just keep looking.

Ethel didn't write much about the sisters in Kelsey, but she did say that the people of Kelsey, Gilmer, and Enoch were very good to them, and the student activities were fun. She led me to another clue because her companion was Reva Dalton for a very short time in May 1928.

That name I had seen on the "Kelsey Kids" Facebook page not long ago. Reva had kept a journal of her year in Kelsey teaching at the same school as Ethel. Only Reva was there; I just realized in 1927 for a short visit to a conference. Then again, in 1929, to teach at the Kelsey school. I didn't read the journal until I got to almost the last sister, Manie Farley. I couldn't believe I had nearly missed a big part of the story, even though every day I prayed that the Lord would help me to know what he wanted me to say about the sisters.

The next morning, I woke up very early after reading the journal and wished I could start with a different approach. Instead, I will just start editing like crazy and pray it will make as much sense to you as it does to me.

Now I have so many endearing little notes about them that make me love them even more. It also has caused many more tears to fall because my heart is full of their tender moments.

I see now that two more sisters played a significant role in this little colony. They were Reva Dalton and Thurza Ellsworth Boyle, two selfless missionaries who gave up their time to serve and teach these women the eternal principles of the Gospel daily. They spent time in their homes working, eating, laughing, and even mourning with them. They truly loved them.

Reva's daily notes in her journal were the frosting on the cake. After researching and studying their families for years, I knew who she was talking about each day, and I got to hear how they lived without electricity and running water and with cars that you had to hand crank to start.

Belle Cummins, the midwife and often
called the Growing Woman.

Standing: Samuel Crouch and Elizabeth Bearce.
Seated: Belle, Joseph Petty, and Martha Crouch.

CHAPTER 6

Curiosity as Big as Texas

When I first started to research the names, I was just curious, but personal stories of their lives changed everything. They came alive to me. I knew I had to share them so they would never be forgotten.

The first story was about "Belle Cummins," or as I soon discovered, her name was Isabelle Josephine Crouch. She was born in Bell Rock, Texas, in 1859. I found her family on the 1860 census in Burnet, Texas.

Her father, James Rice Crouch, was twenty-three, and her mother, Tempie Armenia Petty, was only eighteen. Belle also had a two-year-old sister, Martha. The following year, a brother, Samuel, was born in 1861, and then a sister, Mary Lee, was born in June 1863.

The Civil War would change everything. Belle's father enlisted and went to war. Food was hard to come by just to feed their family. Then her sister, Mary, died in September 1864. Her father died on February 5, 1865, at twenty-seven, just a few months before the war ended.

Her mother married one of her cousins, William "Billy" Petty, on November 19, 1867. Billy died shortly after the marriage. Almost immediately, Tempie married another cousin, Nathan Petty, on January 29, 1868. Then a different cousin shot and killed her husband, Nathan, because he was said to be in love with Tempie too. So much bloodshed went on at that time. Then in September of the same year, their son, Joseph Aden Petty, was born shortly after Nathan died. Belle was only about ten years old at the time all this happened. Now she has a new baby brother to help take care of, and by now, she was no stranger to senseless death and sickness. She had lost so many from her own family.

In 1873, her mother was married, for the last time, to Charles Bierce in Caldwell, Texas. They had a daughter, Adeline, in 1875, and a son, John Bierce, in 1878. I don't know what happened to Charles, but Belle said, in an interview with Joey Smith's grandaughter, that when Belle was first married to William Hector Lee in 1878, her mother was a widow for the fourth time.

Heck, as Belle called him, was very handsome and a great horseman. She was so proud of him and said, "He was the love of my life." He had courted her for over a year and had asked her if she would marry him. Then when she was nineteen, he got up the nerve to ask her mother for permission to marry her. When her mother said yes, he ran to find Belle, who was picking cotton in the field, to tell her. Belle told her granddaughter that they immediately planned the wedding three days later. They had a big wedding feast, with turkey cooked outside over an open fire and wedding cake baked to perfection, at the home of her widowed mother.

Heck's family just loved her, and she was very happy. She had two sons, Brunson Lester Lee, born 1880, and Chester Arthur Lee, born 1883. Then Heck's brother got into some trouble with the law. There was not much real law at that time in Texas. A lot of mob hangings were going on. Heck feared for his brother's life, so he helped him escape from a certain death in a Texas jail.

Then Heck and his brother became wanted men, and Heck had to leave Belle and his family alone, with a promise to send for them as soon as he could get settled. Heck had never learned to read or write, so Belle never received any news from him. She must have felt helpless and alone, not knowing where or how he was. Then finally word came from Heck's sister, telling Belle that Heck had gotten sick with pneumonia and died in 1884. Belle was twenty-five and all alone with her sons.

Knowing she would need help to raise them, she married Samuel Banks Grover, a man thirty-one years older than her. She said he was a good man and knew he would be kind to her boys, so they married in 1886. They lived in Gonzales, Texas.

The next several years brought them two daughters, Maggie Arminta and Olive Belle, and another son, Leonard Crouch Grover.

One day in 1897, a letter came inviting them over to Mr. Reed's home in Delhi, Caldwell, Texas, to hear some Mormon elders preach. They had been holding meetings there for several weeks, but the Grovers hadn't heard them preach.

There was quite a bit of excitement going on over these preachers and their sermons, and she wanted to hear them. For some reason, Grandpa Grover couldn't go to this particular meeting. Granny went anyway, invited the two elders to her home, and held cottage meetings. The spirit of the message must have touched her. The meetings continued for several weeks; many neighbors, family, and friends attended the meetings, and some were baptized. Belle and Samuel were baptized in June 1897, then her son, Chester, in October, and the girls, Maggie and Olive, in November.

But friends and family who did not join were not always so kind and accepting of the choices that they made. They were so persecuted they did not know what to do. Then just when you think it could not get any worse, her husband got sick and died in January 1898. Her son Brunson had married a young lady named Katy Elizabeth Johnson.

He had a son, Wesley Hector Lee, in February 1899, only to have his wife burn to death in a house fire in December, leaving him with a ten-month-old baby for Belle to tend.

She carried on, firm in her belief in Jesus Christ, with just a few visits from the elders who passed through now and then with a message, but there was no place to attend church or any members nearby. She must have had a strong testimony of the Bible and the Book of Mormon. This continued for years until the elders brought a new message that Kelsey, Texas, had been designated as a gathering place for the Southern converts to the Church of Jesus Christ of Latter-day Saints.

Belle arrived in Kelsey during the cold of winter in November 1902. She had her family, her son's new wife, a grandchild with only twenty-five cents, a team of horses, and a wagon to her name. On Christmas Day, one of the horses died; on New Year's Day, the other broke his neck and had to be put down. As difficult as her trials were, Belle found herself in a new place where she could be with others who believed as she did. She found the comfort she sought as she began a new way of life with a new religion.

Belle married George Washington Cummins shortly after arriving in Kelsey. He had been baptized in December 1900 and was her son, Brunson's, new father-in-law. Brunson had married George's daughter, Lona Elizabeth Cummins, in April 1902, after the death of his first wife, Katy. Now his father-in-law was his stepfather.

In 1910, the census says Belle was a widow, but George didn't die until 1913, according to his death certificate. At the time, he was eighty, and she was fifty-one. Whatever the reason, she was alone again, yet with her youngest son at home and her married kids close by, Belle made the best of it. She became the most sought-after woman in the colony.

Belle had learned so much from her life experiences about caring for and nursing the sick and dying. She is listed on the birth certificates of my father-in-law, Doyle, and his brothers, Ancel and Glenn. Probably the other brothers too, but no medical person was listed on theirs. She not only quilted with the sisters in the quilt but delivered many of their babies.

I soon learned to recognize Belle's signature as I looked at the colony's birth certificates. She delivered most of the babies born in the colony for many years. Because all aid was refused to the Mormons, doctors declined to go to them in times of sickness. Therefore, if someone became ill, they would call Sister Cummins, and she would always ask them to try to get a doctor first, but their efforts were usually in vain.

This condition existed for many years. "Belle was a very gifted midwife, and I say gifted because that's how she termed it. Her grandmother before her also has a marvelous record as a midwife. Granny has a record to be proud of because in those dark and trying days, she delivered over a hundred babies, never losing a mother, and only delivered two stillborn babies. Speaking of this as a gift, she says she knows it to be, for she was called to help those people, and she was badly needed."

Lacoleon Smith Means, the granddaugther of Joe Smith, also one of the quilters said, "Belle was called the growing woman. She was responsible for mixing and dispensing various home remedies such as berry wine (to be used only for healing of the sick) and a leaf tea tonic concocted from herbs she grew herself." Sister Cummins named her tonic Liver Regulator, but Kelsey citizens knew it by its more popular name, "Scrapegut."

Belle was even asked to dress and prepare the dead for burial.

But like most of us, she must have learned that death is a part of life everyone must go through. The blessings that come from preparing loved ones for burial can be bittersweet.

Belle's daughter, Maggie Arminta, married Luther Kennedy Bailey, the son of Florence Bailey, a quilter. That puts her in the Bailey tree. Her grandson, Boyd Luther Lee, married Victor Carl Hamberlin's daughter, Effie Ziella Hamberlin. That connects Belle to the Hamberlin tree. Her granddaughter, Maurine Lee, married Arthur Cecil Ault, Ron Compton's great-uncle. That puts her in the Compton tree. What a tangled web we weave!

I imagine she made many quilts over the ninety-three years of Belle's life, and I am so thankful to have just this one. Not only does it have her signature, but the stitches she placed there to hold together this quilt and a new colony of Kelsey, what I wouldn't give to hear her tell her stories about all she experienced. I wonder if I would have listened when I was young.

The Saints had so many things to overcome. They had to all work together and help each other. They would often sing, play games, and dance. They planted gardens for themselves and their neighbors. They worked together for the common good of the community. They had church services and the spirit of the Gospel of Jesus Christ. They created a gathering place of peace and safety for their families.

These amazing sisters had all gathered together in this tiny colony and shared their love for Heavenly Father and the Gospel with each other. They had no idea of the impact their lives would have on so many people worldwide, maybe even in your life if you look closely.

I found one history written by Belle's granddaughter, Sidna Lee Loe, on FamilySearch, submitted by her great-granddaughter Katie Lee Bishop, and another great history in The Upshur County Texas 150 years of Progress book. And that book had stories submitted by family members. Many of the other family stories in the book were submitted by Fayrene Hamberlin Bonebrake.

Back: Percy, Jim, Flossie. Front: James D., Lamar, and Julia Irwin Hamberlin. 1900, Mississippi.

Victor Carl Hamberlin and his new wife, Carrie Dilley Hamberlin.1928, Kelsey.

Carrie Lamarshand Dilley Hamberlin. 1924, Kelsey

Letha Irwin Hamberlin, the daughter of Victor
Carl and Effie Erwin Hamberlin, 1939.

CHAPTER 7

Mississippi to Texas

The meaning of death has not changed. It releases a spirit for growth and development and places a body in the repair shop of Mother Earth, there to be recast, remolded into a perfect body, an immortal, glorious Temple, clean, whole, perfected, and ready for its occupant for eternity.

—*Spencer W. Kimball*

The first members of the Hamberlin family to convert to the Church were James David Hamberlin and Julia Helen Irwin.

They were married the first of 1874 in Yazoo County, Mississippi, where they were both born and raised. Their oldest son, Victor Carl, was born at the end of the same year. Alma, a daughter, was born in 1876. Within six years, they buried four young children. Lena was born in September 1878, and Josie was born in July 1880. They both died within eighteen days of each other in October 1880. Hettie Ina was born in February 1882 and died eighteen months later in 1883. In the same place in December 1884, little William Moses was born, died on the same day, and is buried in Sunflower Valley. In 1886, when Percy was born, only twelve-year-old Carl and ten- year-old Alma lived out of the six. They had moved back to Satartia, and so Percy, along with the following three children: Flossie, born in 1888, James David in 1890, and Lamar in 1893.

They lived in the river bottoms because the soil was richer, and the babies died of malaria. They moved to Sharkey County, and a terrible flood struck during their residence in Sunflower Valley. They lived in a large two-story house, and the water reached the first floor's ceiling. The family was forced to the second floor. Wild hogs and turkeys came up on the porch of the second floor and used it as a refuge from the elements, while deer came to the pasture and grazed when the waters were receding. The deer were so hungry that they sometimes ate from the hands of the children. When Lamar was about eight months old, a great epidemic, probably influenza, struck the valley. People were hard-pressed to care for the sick and bury their dead. Julia Irwin lost nine members of her family.

Their daughter, Alma, died when she was seventeen. She had gone to a dance with friends on a warm February night in 1894. Everyone was having a good time when a blizzard suddenly appeared, and everyone hurried home in the freezing cold night air. Alma contracted the disease and died a short time later.

Victor Carl, the oldest, married his cousin, Effie Irwin, in 1896. When the Mormon missionaries came through Yazoo in 1898, many were curious and wanted to hear about this strange new religion. Elder Jardine was preaching to a group, including James, Julia, and some others when a mob came with rifles. Surprisingly, they put down their guns and listened. Afterward, they told him it was a good sermon but to leave the county and not return, or they would "tar and feather" them.

James's family was converted then but not baptized as the elders were forced to leave at gunpoint. The mob that chased the missionaries out included members of their own extended family.

It wasn't until February 1900 that Elder Osmer Flake and his companion crossed the muddy, big, black Mississippi River after dark for a prearranged baptismal service that was held by lantern light at Cove Hole in James's gin field. Twenty-nine converts were baptized that night, including James and Julia, Victor Carl and his wife, Effie, Percy, and Flossie. Victor Carl then rowed the elders back across the river to safety.

After that, things were never the same because of persecution and hard feelings about the religion. Their families told them they stole their religion because they had done the baptisms secretly in the middle of the night.

Elder Flake encouraged them to come to Snowflake, Arizona, where he was from. James sold his crop in the field for $500 and started west with his family in two covered wagons in 1900. Six weeks later, they arrived in Glen Rose, Texas. They camped on James's half brother, John Hamberlin's, farm while they picked cotton.

Moving on to pick new fields, they settled in Kaufman County, Texas. They were very excited when the Mormon missionaries found them there. James had managed to convert some of his neighbors, who were then able to be baptized along with Jim Jr. and Lamar by Elders Woodland and Rigby.

Lamar said, "The elders told us of the little Mormon colony called Kelsey and encouraged us to go there. In 1904, we went about seventy-five miles to the Kelsey July 24 celebration by mule-drawn wagons. We liked what we saw and forgot about Arizona."

They moved to Kelsey in November 1904. Lamar said, "Jim, Percy, and I drove the cows. It was a beautiful place with clear running water. There were very few homes in Kelsey then." The Mormons were the Edgars, Bodines, Buckleys, Dixons, Hunters, Cummins, and Lees.

"We camped in our wagons for six weeks on Coon Creek. Our first neighbors were the Belle Cummins family. Unable to find a house in Kelsey, Dad rented a farm nearby, but we went to church and other activities in Kelsey until 1910 we moved nearer to the church." Victor Carl and his wife, Effie Irwin Hamberlin, came to Kelsey with their first three sons.

The oldest was Martin Alonzo, born in 1897, who married Ercel Sanders. Ercel's sister Ruth Ellett made an orphan block, and Docie Knight made her block in the quilt. Their stories come later, as the families start to weave together to create a strong community. Lorenzo Tracy was born in 1900 and had married and moved to Salt Lake City by 1930.

Moroni, born in 1902, was the baby in 1904 when they arrived in Kelsey. He was an outstanding leader in Kelsey his entire life. It was such a sweet experience for me just to meet him. He died in 1986 at eighty-three and is buried in the Kelsey Cemetery. In 1905, Moroni had a brother, Sidney, who lived just a few months over one year.

Victor Carl and Effie had their first daughter, Julia Amanda, in 1907. Julia lived in Kelsey all of her life, married Carl Bryant, and raised a family of her own. The Bryant family played a big part in building this community, and their story is later. I visited with Julia and Moroni in Myrtle Lindsey Hamberlin's home several times on my visits there.

Victor Carl and Effie had eleven children before Effie died in 1926. All their children, but one, grew to adulthood, married, and had families.

Their son, Scyril Berwis Hamberlin, married Sibyl Estelle McKnight in 1936 and had a son, Larson Edwin Hamberlin, in 1938. Sibyl's father is John McKnight, and her mother is Ethel Viola Burnett, whose block is in the quilt "Ethel McKnight." The names in these stories will weave together like a piece of fabric or, you could say, fit together just like a puzzle.

The only children of Victor Carl I ever met were Moroni and Julia, but they made a big impression on me from the first time I saw them. They loved Kelsey and never moved away their whole life.

James David Hamberlin was their grandfather as well as my husband's great-grandfather. They knew him well and said he was a jolly, fun-loving man. He was a good farmer and raised some of the county's best crops of cotton, corn, and sweet potatoes. The Gilmer Mirror noted on February 11, 1909, "Mr. J. Hamberlin brought in some of his long-staple cotton seed for sale." James also raised milk cows, pigs, and chickens for family use.

James's children all settled in Kelsey for some years. Percy Hamberlin married Clara Dickason. Clara is the one who had the quilt in her closet.

Flossie Hamberlin married Arthur Lindsey (Myrtle's brother), and Jim Jr. married Pearl Bamburg.

When Lamar married Myrtle Lindsey in the Kelsey church on July 4, 1917, they had over four hundred guests. It was the Fourth of July, so I think that explains the large attendance. Then many danced all night at the reception hall. Over the years, July was a big month for celebrating, especially the fourth and twenty-fourth.

While dating, Lamar and Myrtle often went to the Kelsey dances and church or baptisms. Their first date was riding in the buggy from a baptism to the church. Myrtle quit school to care for her sister, Maude, who was sick and lived near the Hamberlin family. Their notes to each other read things like "Light the lamp in the window if I can come over tonight" or "Leave the shade up if you can go to the dance." The Kelsey school and church activities were the highlights of their lives. James and Julia's children all had an interest in and appreciation for Kelsey, even though some moved away.

James's youngest son, Lamar, told of walking, as a seven-year-old, beside the wagon when his family came to Texas. In Marshall, Texas, he and Jim Jr. were sleeping in the wagon beside a church where the adults slept the night of the Great Galveston Hurricane of 1900. They were frantic the next morning when they woke and found the wagon was gone. Amazingly, the parents found it blown across the cemetery with the boys still sleeping inside. Lamar said, "Dad rented a cabin on Christmas Eve in Kaufman County, and Papa bought a box of five hundred vanilla wafers. We often laughed about the Christmas we had five hundred cakes for dinner. Thoughtful missionaries and great friends made that for happy years."

He tells of the 1908 tornado in Kelsey that demolished sixteen houses. "The Ennis house was torn up, and a large bed held the roof off the family till we got there. We tore planks off where they could get out." Lamar stated that in 1915, Kelsey had 675 members. There were four stores, a three-chair barbershop, a railroad depot, a cotton gin, a shingle mill, and three sawmills. He and his brothers helped build the school, church, and railroad.

James David Hamberlin died of lockjaw in 1925. Julia lived among her children, and she died in the home of Lamar and Myrtle in 1926. She was buried beside James in the Kelsey Cemetery.

Lamar added that they always blessed the food before eating, and he never remembered going to bed without prayer.

This story is taken mainly from one that Fayrene, Lamar's daughter, gave me years ago and she later submitted to the Church History Department. The first time I met Fayrene, it was like I had always known her. We talked for hours each time I visited her. We knew all of the same people from our research. The more I researched this quilt, the more her name came up. So much of the history is there because of her. She spent her whole life trying to preserve the history of Kelsey and the people in the colony.

I never dreamed in the eighties, when I spent time there, that I would be given the task of putting this history into a book because of a quilt that I can't get out of my head. The Lord does work in mysterious ways.

Clara Hamberlin is the only person who knows what she intended to do with the quilt she had concealed so nicely in the back of her closet.

If I would have been closer to her when she only lived across town from me, I would have had all the answers to my questions. I think now that the Lord knew I would have to do this, and he put me in the right place, but I just missed my chance and now I get to do it the hard way. Thank goodness he is here to help me do this. I wonder how often we miss an opportunity the Lord puts right in front of us, and we don't recognize it.

William and Emma Dickinson Mcknight With son Edward "Dewey and daugther Erma Blynn. 1915 Kelsey, Texas

John Wesley and Sarah Virginia Roberts Dickason Wedding day 1877, Louisiana.

CHAPTER 8

A Louisiana Love Story

Even in our deepest trials we can feel the warm embrace of the Savior's love as we trust him and accept his will.

—*John A. McCune*

Clara's Father, John Wesley Dickason, was born in 1856 near Baton Rouge, Louisiana, and lived there until he was fifty- four when he moved his family to a small colony of members of the Church of Jesus Christ of Latter-day Saints in Kelsey, Texas. He was a child during the Civil War. His father was a farmer, like most men at that time in Louisiana. John was a farmer all of his life.

John and his future wife, Sarah Virginia Roberts, grew up within thirty miles of each other, but that was a great distance to travel in those days. We don't know how they met, but they were both twenty- one when they married in December 1877. They lived and farmed with John's family for the first few years. Their first child was born a year and a half after the wedding.

They rented farmland nearby that included a small house and began farming independently. Months later, this baby girl died in January 1880. The swampy, rich, bottom farmland was very hard on the health of babies and small children. Their son John Wesley died at fifteen months in 1885. Susie Maggie was born in 1884 and later married John Jackson Barksdale. Sarah Virginia died at eighteen months in 1888.

Emma was born in 1888 and married William McKnight. "Emma McKnight" has a block in the quilt. Then came Clara in 1890, and she married Percy Hamberlin. "Clara Hamberlin" has a block in the quilt. She is the one who had put the quilt and all the orphan blocks in the closet. If the quilt had been made for her, would she have had a block in it? I wonder.

The last daughter, Mary Estelle, married Benjamin Franklin Bailey, the brother of Ethel Bailey. Her family stayed in Kelsey until the 1940s.

This was taken from a story written by a great-grandson, David Lindsey, who also shared their love story.

A glorious event came to the Dickasons' family in 1897. Missionaries from the Church of Jesus Christ of Latter-day Saints came to Louisiana. Missionaries had not come that far south in the prior forty years.

John, Sarah, and their family were some of the first in Louisiana to meet the missionaries and be converted to the Church. John and Sarah had ten children, and four of them had already died at this time. They were ready to hear about the glorious message of the Gospel and eternal families. John and Sarah and their twelve-year-old daughter, Susie Maggie, were baptized on June 15, 1897. They were an important part of the local church organized in Louisiana.

The Dickasons continued to live in this area until 1909, when they heard of a community established in Kelsey, Texas, as a gathering place for members of the Church. They desired to be in a community where there were many others of the same faith and where they were not constantly persecuted. In 1910, they sold everything they could and then moved with their children to the little Kelsey community.

Love Story

Growing up, I often heard my mother, Ruth Cobb Lindsey, speak fondly of her great-grandparents, John and Sarah Dickason. She said they were her picture of a perfect couple and marriage. When you were in their presence, you could tell they loved and respected each other. To be in their presence was to feel loved and appreciated. Their children loved to be with them and to learn from them. Their grandchildren and great-grandchildren always enjoyed going to Grandma's house.

In July 1919, John and Sarah were able to travel to Salt Lake City and be sealed as husband and wife for time and all eternity. In January 1948, at the age of ninety-one, after seventy years of marriage, John and Sarah Dickason died within six days of each other in Kelsey. They are together now for eternity.

The 1910 census puts them living in Gilmer on Kelsey Road, the same road on which Ron Compton's grandma, Med Ault Buckley, lived. John and Sara continued to live in and farm near Kelsey until their deaths.

Out of the ten children, only four of their daughters reached adulthood. Susie Maggie Barksdale died in Kelsey the year before they died in 1947 and is buried beside them.

Emma Elizabeth Dickason was born in 1888, just three months after the death of her older sister. She was living in Kelsey until after 1950, according to the census. She married William McKnight in 1911 in Kelsey.

Emma's first son, Edward Dewey, was born in 1912. His teacher was Reva Dalton. When I looked at his birth certificate, I noticed his name was actually Edward Doyle, but everyone always called him Dewey. He was on the high school basketball team in 1828. He never married. He died at forty-two from contusions and lacerations of the brain due to falling with epileptic seizures. I don't know when they started for him, but I had an older sister, Sandra, who died at twenty-six following a seizure. She had fallen in the shower at a health spa in San Diego and suffered second and third-degree burns over 90 percent of her body. Her seizures started in her teens.

Emma also had a daughter, Erma Blyn, who was fifteen and still in high school when Emma made the block in the quit. Erma was valedictorian in high school and worked and saved money to attend the University of Texas.

Erma and her friends spent a lot of time with Sister Dalton. She married Weldon Green of Thatcher, Arizona, in 1943, and together they served in the Church and in their community. They raised their family in Safford, Arizona. In 1952, they had a two- year-old daughter, Sharon Ann Green, drown in an irrigation ditch by their home.

It seems every time I read about a sister, it brings back my childhood memories. When I was about two and a half years old, two days after my brother, Randy, was born in 1949, my mother was in bed, and my grandma was hanging clothes on the line. My sister Sandra and I, along with some neighbor kids, were throwing sticks in the irrigation ditch in front of our house on Alma School Road in Mesa, Arizona. Everyone had a bridge to go over the ditch for their driveway. I threw in my stick and ran down to the next house to catch it, but as I reached for it, I fell in, and my dress got caught under the bridge on a nail.

When I didn't come up, my sister Sandra ran to the house for help. They called the fire department, and when they arrived, I had been in the water for over eight minutes, and they knew that I had drowned and possibly washed down to the head gate. Then suddenly, I just popped up, and my mother and grandmother both jumped in before the firemen could. They said I was gray from not breathing but had no water in my lungs. I have often wondered why it was that I lived and so many children I know of drowned.

At that time, we lived with my grandpa and grandma Whitlock. It was on the edge of town and across the street from the experimental farm. Their next-door neighbor was Annabelle Garner White. She is the mother of Wilford "Whizzer" White and grandmother of Danny White of the Dallas Cowboys. My stepbrother, Dick Mansperger, was director of player personnel for the Dallas Cowboys in the 1960s and 1970s.

In the late 1980s, my mother, my aunt Ethel, and I returned to look at our old house, and Annie still lived next door. She told us she had always wondered what became of Martha, my grandma. She then told us she remembered the day I fell in the ditch and how worried she had been. Annie told me her baby girl had fallen in that same irrigation canal and drowned when she was one year, two months, and two days old. Her name was Betty Juanita, and I am Beverly Juanell. She was born ten years and ten days before me. I told you I had a thing with numbers. Why did I not drown that day?

When I was the only one in my family to join the Church and got into family history, I decided it was up to me to do the research for my ancestors. Maybe that was my purpose in life. Then as time went on, I was sure of it.

Emma must have been a considerable support to her daughter at the loss of her baby because Emma had lost a baby girl, Willie Faye, in 1918, who didn't even live three months. Erma Blyn lived to be ninety-nine and was married for sixty-seven years. She has lots of posterity.

William and Emma had a son, Delbert Dickinson McKnight, in 1921. He married Thurza Colleen Burnett, the daughter of Donnie and "Loretta Burnett," who had a block in the quilt. That ties me back to the Dickasons, and Jim's grandmother, Clara. Loretta had named Thurza Burnett after Thurza Ellsworth Boyle, the 1929 missionary in Kelsey.

Emma's daughter, Maurine McKnight, married Victor Carl Hamberlin Jr. It looks like everyone is connected to someone else in this one quilt.

Emma's younger sister, Clara Annie Dickason Hamberlin, is my mother-in-law's mother-in-law. The one person I wish I knew better, but I was afraid to talk to her when she was alive.

My grandma Whitlock died when I was fourteen. She had lived with us off and on for years. My mother was the baby of thirteen children, so she lived mostly with us, or we lived with her. I have known her all my life and never asked her anything about her childhood or early years. I just thought she had always been old.

Now that my grandkids look at me that way, I feel awful that I never heard Clara talk about how she felt about life and love. What had her childhood been like? Now I will never know because no one wrote it down.

Clara was born two years after Emma in Baton Rouge, Louisiana, in 1890. She was baptized when she was eleven and always loved learning about the Gospel. As she got older, she was a Primary teacher and held many church callings. She married Percy Hamberlin when she was twenty-one and he was twenty- five. By then, she had been through the loss of seven siblings. Myrtle told me she was sickly and took to her bed a lot of the time. I wondered if she thought maybe she would die like all of them had.

Percy cared for her, did much of the housework, and helped her all he could. They had five healthy boys: James Artie (1912), Ancel Enos (1915), Doyle Carlos (1917), Melvin Rodger (1920), and Leland Glenn (1922). She always said she liked boys best, just like Olive, my mother-in-law, said when she had four boys. I know my daughter, Courtney, wishes she had a daughter. But Courtney has five boys just like Clara. How strange is that?

Why did Clara never tell anyone about her quilt? Was she saving it for a granddaughter or someone special she cared about that never came? Did she forget she had it? The questions still drive me crazy. I am thankful that I have had the good fortune to have had the quilt for a while, at least long enough to find out about the quilter's connections. I want to make sure it is put in a safe place. Maybe the Heritage Foundation of Kelsey would be the perfect home if they had room. It does need to be in Kelsey.

Percy and Clara lived in Kelsey for over thirty years. They moved to Salt Lake City in the early forties. She was a widow at sixty-one after having buried a son, Ancel, when he was forty-four. He died of a brain tumor in 1949 in Mesa. Ancel named his first child, a daughter, Fayrene. She was one of my husband's first cousins, whom I met in Mesa. She did not know about her dad's cousin she was named after until I told her about my trip to Kelsey.

Clara's son, Doyle, Jim's dad, died just before Christmas in 1973. Clara then lived another nine years and died of cancer in 1982. Clara was always strong in the Gospel. She is the only one I know who received two patriarchal blessings in her lifetime. She wasn't happy with the first one. It must not have told her what she thought it would. Years later, she got another one that said almost the same thing. Then maybe it told her more than she first thought. Myrtle and Clara were sisters-in-law, but they were never very close. Perhaps it was just a family competition. I don't know of anyone who was Clara's friend in Kelsey. As I said, my mother-in-law, Olive, never got along with her. Olive also said Clara didn't care about any of their family except her own sons.

My mother often told me my grandmother Burnett only liked my sister, Sandra. I believed her, so I never worried about trying to change her mind. Later I realized that Sandra was the oldest of my siblings. My grandmother cared for her as a baby as she did the rest of us, but we didn't remember because we were too young. Sandra was six when my brother was born, and she loved staying with Grandmother Burnett for days. Sandra sent her birthday and Christmas cards. She wrote her letters and showed her love. My grandmother showed her more love, but that didn't mean she didn't love all of her grandchildren the same.

The Lindsey Family, 1912, Kelsey.

William Jasper Lindsey and Martha Mull's children,
in order of birth and who they married.

1– Arthur– Flossie Hamberlin
2– Pleasant– Julia Sanders
3– Maude– Thomas Bradshaw
4– Sarah– William Chevalier
5– Blanche "Bee"– Charlie Bell
6– Sadie– James Henry
7– Geneva– Merrill Bennion
8– Lillie– Archie Lindsey
9– Myrtle– Lamar Hamberlin
10– Connie– Thomas Denton
11– Don Carlos– Vera Dixon
12– Irene Ethel– Stanley Carter
13– Parley– Vera Cook
14– Mamie– Myron Fox
15– Raymond– Mildred Myers
16– Hubert– Dorothy Miller

CHAPTER 9

The Lindsey Matriarch

Martha Emma Christina Lucinda Mull was born in 1867. Her husband, William Jasper Lindsey, was born in 1860. They were born in Alabama. They married in Shelby, Alabama, in 1886. Martha, or Mattie, was the last child of Henry Mull and Eleanor Leach.

Mattie was left an orphan at an early age, and she and her brothers had to go and live with different families. Mattie worked for one family who demanded she care for their numerous children and do most of the work caring for the baby throughout the night. She got very little sleep and such rough treatment that she felt she could not live under the circumstances. Knowing they would not let her leave, Martha tied her clothes in a rag, waited until all were sleeping through her clothes over her shoulder, and ran away. She walked all night.

This time, Martha found a job working for a woman with eight children and eight borders. She did all the cooking, dishwashing, washing, and ironing for nineteen people and sometimes cared for the children. At night, she made bread and set it on the oven door to rise while she ironed. All this she did for $4 per month plus her room and board. She considered herself fortunate that these people permitted her to attend school during the winter. Mormon missionaries were in the area, and several families, including William Jasper and Mattie, were baptized. They had to break the ice for their baptism in November 1887.

Shortly after being baptized, Billie and Mattie boarded an immigrant train to Salt Lake City, Utah, to be near the church.

Mattie was an example to all of us through her life of service and just plain good works. I want to be like her when I grow up. There are many books written about her life and family. This was taken from the Lindsey Book#1.

One of the Lindsey books contained a tribute by Arlene B. Jones

Everyone's Grandma

It was Sunday morning ten years ago in a small east Texas town where I first saw the outstanding singer of a small congregation. The fact that she enjoyed singing was apparent. Her voice was exceptional for an elderly woman. The tone was clear and true. She sang as high as the younger voices but just a trifle slower.

I noticed her coal-black hair drawn back and up in a high bun. Her time-crumpled face had a kindness and goodness about her that was to be pictured in the frame of my mind always. Crow's feet stretched for a smile around her dancing black eyes, and you could feel the warmth of her heart in her song.

Her cotton dress had sleeves to the elbow and a ballerina-length skirt. Her only jewelry was a wide wedding band and a gold watch pinned to her dress above her heart. At another glance, I noticed her sheer nylon hose and comfortable oxfords.

When I became acquainted with the pleasant singer after church, I found she was known as Grandma Lindsey. Such a kind, sincere remark she made to me. "I'm glad you decided to come to Texas and make your home here."

Later my friend Albertine answered my questions about Grandma Lindsey. "Almost everyone is related to her. We're not, but we all call her Grandma because of our sincere admiration for her." (Albertine Simmons

Fowler, the daughter of Dolly Jo Muckleroy or "Jo Simmons," a quilter, was related to Grandma but didn't know it.) I learned more about Grandma Lindsey having had sixteen children who grew to maturity which was an accomplishment in itself. I know all of the fifteen now living. One daughter died after having four children. To know Grandma is to understand the orderly way in which she set out to cook, sew, and mend for a large family. Managing the home became easier as the children grew old enough to be helpful in these tasks.

The water for household use was drawn with a rope and bucket from the well on wash day. The water was heated outside in a big washpot where the clothes were boiled after being rubbed on a washboard.

The many past experiences of this well-loved individual, Grandma Lindsey, have given her qualities worthy of emulation and the honor of being called grandma by hundreds.

Her granddaughter, Fayrene Hamberlin Bonebrake, said that having practically no formal education was of remarkable mental ability; she quarreled with no one, nor did she indulge in idle gossip. Although she did not seek to antagonize, she was frank in her beliefs and opinions. Indeed, she could say more without words than most people. In May 1953, Mattie fell ill and, for several days, suffered greatly. Thirteen of her children gathered around her, and two were on their way to her side when she peacefully passed away as an infant yields to slumber. Mattie was buried in the Kelsey Cemetery beside her companion of fifty-four years.

Thus ended the lives of two people who clung to the precepts of their religion through much adversity, who firmly believed that no labor was too hard, no sacrifice too great if it might make of their children honest, upright men and women.

Back: Zora, Luther Kennedy, and Joseph. Front:
Florence, Shirley Erskin, James Duran, and
James Arthur Bailey. 1900, Mississippi

Ethel Bailey Davis. 1927, Kelsey

CHAPTER 10

Her Sister's Keeper

Amanda Florence Shirley's orphan quilt block reads, "Florence Bailey." She played a significant role in the new little colony. She was converted to the Gospel in 1901 in Mississippi. She was forty-three years old. She and her family then moved to Utah to be close to the church, where they were sealed as a family. They stayed long enough to learn much about the church's teachings before going to Kelsey to help the new converts.

At first, I thought they were called to serve a mission, as many others had been at that time. But if they were, it was a very long mission. It seemed they never left for long, even when they tried. The Lord always brought them back to Kelsey. They spent over thirty years there. What was it that always drew them back? Was it the weather, good friends, or their love of the land?

Florence made a significant impression on her younger sister, Ethel Shirley, who wrote the following history of Florence, which I found on FamilySearch.

My reason for writing this sketch is that I feel our family sketches would not be complete without something being said about the useful life of the older girl in the family, and I also feel no one in the family appreciates her qualities better than I do or has had a better chance to prove them than I have.

She is some eighteen years older than me, and I lived at her place a good deal after she married and while I was yet a child. She and her husband were just as kind and thoughtful to me as if I were their child.

Amanda Florence was born near Poplar Creek, Montgomery County, Mississippi, in 1858, the daughter of Johnathan Travis Shirley and Rebeca Jane Thrailkill.

She was the second child in a family of fifteen children. The oldest child, a boy named James, died at the age of two years. The next five children were all girls.

Florence was of medium size and medium complexion, with hazel eyes and jet-black hair that was a mass of curls until she was old enough to wear braids. I have heard my mother say that the hairstyle when Florence was a grown-up girl was to bob up all of the hair except one or two curls and lay them over the shoulder. Her hair, being so curly, would lend itself very readily to this style, which she wore a good deal.

Before Florence was old enough to go to school, the war between the states was declared, and Father was taken away from the family consisting of a mother, grandmother, and four little girls. She can well remember those dreadful days when she and her mother were all that were able to work to support the family. Being the eldest girl, she would naturally have to help care for the younger children. She was very serious and thoughtful and took responsibility very young. No doubt, her earliest recollections would be of helping her mother take care of little girls.

I have heard my mother say that when Florence was seven years old, she was all the help she had in sickness and other times until the other girls were old enough to help. School facilities were meager during the war and for some years after, but the girls did receive some schooling.

When Florence was about ten, the family moved to Attalla County, Mississippi, and took up a homestead claim. Florence was very industrious and did much to help build a new home. The oldest girl would have to take the lead in many things. Soon after they moved to the new home, Mother's health failed, and she had a paralytic stroke. This left the children motherless except for the care the older sister could give them. She proved a true mother.

I have been told that in all the years she lived there, taking charge of the home when Mother was unable and helping to build up a new home, and with all the deprivation she was called to endure, she never complained or found fault with her lot. She grew to womanhood on this homestead and married James Duren Bailey at twenty-three, a young man who had grown up in the same locality.

I was a child about five years old when my sister, Florence, married. I can remember her taking me home to stay a week or two at a time to try to improve my health.

I can also remember, to some extent, the void left in our lives when she married, for the third girl, Adella, married a couple of weeks after Florence did and only lived a few months after she married. The second girl, Selena, a beautiful young girl about eighteen, had died only about three years before. We were then bereft of our three oldest girls. We had three other girls about grown up, but nevertheless, we missed the three older ones.

Florence and her young husband lived on their little homestead for three or four years, then decided to move to Louisiana for a while. But they did not like the country very well and returned the following year. They bought a piece of land and built a comfortable home in the old neighborhood where they were reared.

They lived there for some fifteen years. I dare say they spent some happy years there, near all their relatives. Their three younger children were born here, making them six children in all. Their oldest child died in babyhood. They were permitted to rear the other five, four boys and one girl, to adulthood. The youngest was ten years old when they left their home in Mississippi.

Their children have been a credit to them, all living honorable and useful lives. While living in their home in Mississippi, the parents and the children took an active part in the community. They were a highly respected family wherever they lived. In the spring of 1901, this family heard the Gospel of Jesus Christ preached by one having been commissioned to preach. They were deeply impressed with the story of the restored Gospel. They received a strong testimony that it was true, and they gladly accepted it, although at that time, it was a very unpopular religion with their friends and acquaintances. However, that did not deter them from taking upon themselves the cross of Christ.

They hoped to better their condition both spiritually and financially by moving west. By the end of October 1902, they had sold all their property in Mississippi and started west, searching for a new home.

After looking around for some time, they located in Boxelder County, Utah. They bought a home with farmland, farm animals, and machinery. After one year's experience in the high altitude and severe winter, they decided to go back South again, but not to Mississippi. They thought there were better farming lands in other places.

For a few years, they looked around to see where they could be the best satisfied. The children were all grown up by this time. They desired that their grandchildren should have the best advantages the country afforded for education and social development. Also, they must consider their spiritual uplift.

Finally, they bought a home and farmland in Upshur County, Texas, there being a good many Latter-day Saints people in that locality. There, they rested from their trials for a while and enjoyed many happy days with friends and relatives who were there or came to visit.

I visited there one winter, from December until April, and spent a very pleasant winter in their home, in that balmy atmosphere. I found they had been able to build them a nice home and had been sending their children to school. Two of the boys were teaching school at the time. I think they were greatly blessed financially, as well as otherwise. They were out of debt and with as much of the comforts of life as anyone in the neighborhood.

They all had good health then, and their children were marrying and locating around them. I found they were living on a very high plain, spiritually. They were taking an active part in all the church activities, Sister Florence being one of the presidents of the Relief Society, a women's organization that takes care of the poor or sick or ones needing help. She was continually doing good. She endeared herself to the people in the community through her acts of charity and hospitality. Among her other acts of charity was her help when I was left a widow with six little children to support. Their home was a home that everyone loved to visit. It was in the fall of 1911 that I visited their place. A few more years and they were leaving this nice, comfortable home.

By the year 1916, two of the boys had gone west and obtained positions in Salt Lake City. The daughter and her husband wanted to try their luck in Ogden, Utah. The two married boys in Texas were thinking of going to Arizona, so the father and mother decided to go with them.

They sold their land in Texas and moved to Arizona. They bought a tract of land and raised a very successful crop. They realized a large income on that year's crop but decided that the climate was too hot and sold all of their land and stock for cash. They then left Arizona and came back to Utah. The father and mother had to return to Texas, as their land had been turned back to them, but the boys were located here permanently with their families. The people who bought their land could not pay for it, but in the year's work in Arizona, they had realized enough to pay for all the trouble of moving.

In this, we can see how the Lord blessed them. Throughout all the years since they joined the Church in 1901, they had paid a strict tithing to the church, one-tenth of all they gained, and were many times better off than when they began paying.

They must have been an honored and respected family wherever they lived. They have lived happy lives because they adhered to the principles that bring happiness. They have lived very strictly the laws of honor, morality, and religion, and through their adherence to the principles of governing a happy life, they have been blessed with a family of honorable children and plenty of this world's goods.

Throughout all the years from 1918 to 1932, sister Florence and her husband made regular trips, every two years, from Texas to Utah, and sometimes as far away as California, to visit their children and friends who lived so far away. I always looked forward to their visit as a treat and laid aside everything else to visit with them.

For the last six years, Sister Florence has not felt like taking long trips to visit, and I have not seen her since

1932. She is well past the eightieth milestone but is still able to take care of herself and her home.

Just lately, I received a letter from her in which she expressed some thoughts regarding her past life. She said the thing that had borne her up through all the trials of life was her faith in her religion. Her faith in the Gospel of Jesus Christ has never failed to comfort her in times of trial.

She, like everyone else, has had her trials. She buried her oldest child in babyhood and her third son after growing to manhood, filling a good mission for his church, married, and was well established with a nice home and family in Salt Lake City, and was taken out of this life by accident in his youth.

We wish her many years of usefulness in this life before she goes to her well-earned rest in the kingdom prepared for the faithful children of our Heavenly Father.

This story about Florence that her sister tells helped me get to know her and how she served her whole life. Her grandchildren said she was an ardent hostess in welcoming and assisting missionaries in her home. She was very quiet, always neat in home and appearance, very gentle, kind, and above all, a "lady."

At some point, they did move to Ogden, Utah, where she lost her husband in August 1945 and died in October 1946, four months before I was born. How I wish I could have known her in her youth.

It gets tricky now because her niece, Ethel Mae Bailey, was born in 1892 and was the daughter of William Bailey and Augusta T. Shirley, so she was also her husband's niece. Ethel married Thomas Ellis Davis.

I have an orphan block that says "Ethel Davis" and another block that says "Sallie Davis." I believe it was made in honor of "Sallie Cagle Davis," who died in 1929 when the blocks were made. They are a close match in color and fabric, and the handwriting and embroidering are the same. Ethel and Sallie were not members of the Relief Society or the Church.

I am sure the same person made them. I still have these two blocks because I haven't yet figured out who to give them to! The only one in the quilt I could connect them to was "Florence Bailey." I was so sure someday I would know who gets them that I kept them to see.

Today, I realized that Ethel's brother, Benjamin Franklin Bailey, is the husband of Mary Estelle Dickason, Clara's youngest sister who didn't have a block in the quilt. I will have to wait and ask Clara; she is the only one with all the answers.

Ethel's daughter, Hazel Lauren Davis, married Travis Preston Futrell, the son of Ida Irwin and James Edward Futrell.

Hazel and Travis grew up as neighbors. They walked to the same school and attended church together. Momma Davis went with them during their courtship; she carried the lantern if it was night. They were married in 1931 by President Green.

Hazel joined the Church after her marriage. They worked in the Church all their lives. Travis served as the song leader, ward clerk, and teacher. Hazel also taught Sunday school and Primary for many years.

Travis had a brother, John Whitaker Futrell, who married Rusie Susie Bessie Dawson ("Rusie Futrell"). That connects them to the Dawsons and the Comptons in my ward and puts them in my family tree. The Dawsons also came from Mississippi at about the same time as the Hamberlin family in 1904.

The obituary of Ethel Davis says she was eighty-six years old and had lived in Kelsey for fifty-seven years. She was a housewife and a Methodist. She never joined the Church, but her mother and brother were members.

Kelsey was good to the Davises and the Bailey family. Even though the Baileys joined the Church, none of the Davis did, even though they raised their families in the community, participating in church activities.

Ethel's daughter, Hazel, must have done the temple work for her parents after their death. I noticed in the obituary also that the services were held in Kelsey, where she was laid to rest in the Kelsey Cemetery.

J. C. Wade and Emmons Bryant conducted the officiating. Emmons is the brother-in-law of Julia Hamberlin Bryant. He was a bishop and a stake president. She was loved by the ward and family members that lived there. Her husband had family in the Church also. I am so thankful for temples that make it possible for families to be together forever, even after death.

Florence Bailey's son Luther Kennedy Bailey, married Maggie Arminta Grover, the daughter of Belle Cummins, in 1907, after they all came to Kelsey. That connects Belle's and Florence's trees.

Florence had another son, James Arthur Bailey, who married Kittie Green Ellett's daughter, Katy Oletha Ellett. "Kittie Ellett" has a block in the quilt, and so does her daughter, Ava Ellett, who married William Thomas Dixon. Her block reads, "Ava Dixon," and matches her mother's block. They are my favorite color, red. I knew right away I was going to love them.

My mother never joined the Church when she was alive. She had told me she wanted a Mormon funeral, which she got. I was able to do her work the following year, in 2000. She could have had so much more joy if she had done it herself.

She was a good mother, and I was able to seal my whole family together in 2013 after the death of my father, Marvin Forrest Burnett. He was a born-again Christian, a good, kind, and honest man, and lived to be ninety. By then, all of my siblings were gone too.

When my older sister, Sandra DeFreese, died of burns she suffered at a health spa in San Diego when she was twenty-six, she had two little boys, Charlie, five, and Bobby, two.

My brother Randy died from complications of his wounds in the Vietnam War when he was thirty-eight and had a wife, Shari, with cancer, a son, Travis, eleven, and a daughter, Jessica, six.

Shari lived twelve years with ovarian cancer and died in 2000. Travis later died at the age of twenty-nine of brain cancer.

My sister Charlett never was able to have hildren of her own. Being nine years younger than my oldest sister, Sandra, she spent considerable time caring for nieces and nephews. Sandra always called her "Honey," so when the kids couldn't say "Aunt Charlett," they all started calling her "Aunt Nee." It was an endearment she cherished and refused to be called anything else. She died of cancer in 2009 at the age of fifty-six.

Four generations, standing: Verl Gardner Francis, Mattie Sherman Armstrong, and Arthur Odell Ellett Sr. Seated: Mattie Ellett Francis, (baby) Verline Francis, Kittie Green and Isaac William Ellett.

Back: Faye Dixon, her brother Maurice and his wife, Dorthella Boyack Dixon.Front: Mother Ava Ellett Dixon, son Richard Jewkes, niece Martha Dixon,son Dale Jewkes and father William Dixon, 1944.

CHAPTER 11

Far Above Rubies

*Who can find a virtuous woman? for her price is
far above rubies.*

—Proverbs 31:10

Kittie Ellett was born Martha Catherine Green in 1861 in Calhoun, Alabama, during the Civil War. Her father, Charles Green, came from Denmark several years before the war had started. He had a job making saddles for the Confederate Army, so he most likely did not have to fight.

Charles had married a girl from Philadelphia who died six months after the wedding. He had changed his name when he came to America, so he is very hard to trace.

Then he married Martha Catherine Craig in Harris, Georgia, in 1858. The following year, they had a son, George Franklin Green. They had moved by then to Bedford, Tennessee. Two years later, they had a daughter they called Kittie. They lived in Calhoun, Alabama, with the Civil War going strong.

Charles lost his second wife, Martha, leaving him with a four- year-old and a two-year-old. Kitty's mother was only twenty-five when she died. Kitty's dad then did what most men did in those days. He married again to a young relative of her mother's, Mary Elizabeth Pike.

When Kitty married Isaac William Ellett, she had eight half siblings. They married in December 1880 in Madison, Alabama. Her dad and Mary had five more children over the years, giving her fourteen half siblings and just one brother, George.

I learned much about Alabama's history when I sent out my oldest son, James Doyle Hamberlin, on his mission. He was called to the Birmingham, Alabama, mission, and the first place he was sent to was Huntsville in Madison County. He had one experience there with a man in a car on the street pointing a gun at Jim and his companion as they approached the door of someone's house. But then suddenly the car drove off. It shook them both up at the time.

None of Kittie's family except her brother, George, ever left Alabama or joined the Church, yet she had a strong testimony and raised her children in the Gospel.

Her husband was never a member, and I wondered if he supported her in her church activities and callings. She was baptized in 1897 when she was thirty-six. Like so many sisters, she never got to attend the temple for herself.

I wondered who joined when she did. Was it a neighbor or a friend? When missionary work resumed in Alabama, the Southern States Mission was created. Opposition was widespread in the 1880s, with some even asking Alabama's governor to force the missionaries from the state. They still tarred and feathered people sometimes there.

Kitty's obituary said she died of old age, but her death certificate said she had been sick for a long time with colon cancer. She had been visiting her daughter, Katie Bailey, in Spanish Fork when she became ill and had been with her for over a year. Katie's husband was the son of Florence Bailey.

Kitty's husband, Isaac, lived ten years after her death and died in Mesa while living with their other daughter, Ava Dixon. When I saw that, I realized they had lived right down the street from me in 1949, when I was two.

Arizona must have been too hot for them because Ava and her family soon returned to Kelsey. Arizona is too hot for most people, except for us natives.

Kittie's son, Arthur Odell Ellett Sr., was born in 1883 in Alabama. He became a schoolteacher and Senator in Spanish Fork, Utah.

The next son, William Walter Ellett, was born in 1888 and died in an accident at seventeen.

The third son, Albert Hayden Ellett, was born in 1898 and became a judge in Salt Lake City.

The fourth son, Robert Owen Ellett, was born in 1901. He stayed in Kelsey and married Ruth Marie Sanders, who signed her orphan block "Ruth Ellett." Ruth's sister, Ercel Maud Sanders, married Victor Carl Hamberlin's son, Martin Alonzo Hamberlin. Ruth's brother, Benjamin, married Ruby Pearl Ault, Med's sister and Ron Compton's aunt.

Ruth's sister, Ella Theodocia Sanders, married Frederick Homer Knight. And she has signed her orphan block "Docie Knight."

Ruth's youngest brother, Joseph Milton Sanders, married Brunson Lee's daughter, Gracie Belle Lee. I think that made Ruth related to everyone in Kelsey. I sent Ruth's block to her daughter, Ruby Nell Ellett Gratch. Ruby said, "I cried when I saw my mother's handwriting." Ruby loved seeing the frail little block her mother had made before Ruby was born. Ruth's family moved to Orange County, California, before 1950.

My first great-grandchild is Ruby, and she was three when I found Ruby Ellett Gratch. I saw that my granddaughter, McKenzie, who had named her daughter Ruby, looked so much like Ruby Gratch when Ruby was young. Over the years, Ruby has shared many stories about all the people in Kelsey she remembered. She had dated a Hamberlin in her youth. She has Hamberlin cousins in Kelsey. Ruby was living in San Antonio, Texas, where my grandson, Elder James Ridge Hamberlin, served his mission in 2019.

Kitty's daughter Ava Christine Ellett married William Thomas Dixon, who was baptized in 1903 along with his family. His mother is Minnie Dixon. Ava was married in 1914 in Kelsey and sealed to her husband in Salt Lake City two years later. Her quilt block reads "Ava Dixon."

Ava joined the Church in 1913, FamilySearch says, which would have been the year before she married. She might have been baptized sooner. She was one of the few quilters who was able to go to the temple.

The new converts in the early years were blessed dramatically because of their faith. I believe the Lord knew that a time for going to the temple often would come to later generations. We are so blessed today to have so many temples and to have them so close. Now most of the members are close enough to attend a temple at least once.

Ava and William Dixon had two children. A son, Harold Maurice, and a daughter, Oletha Faye, were baptized at eight. Harold Maurice died in 1970. He was fifty-five, had a wife and three children, and retired from the Texas Border Patrol in Longview, Texas. Maurice was well known to the sister missionaries of 1929. Sister Dalton refers to him often in her journal. He was fourteen at the time.

Ava's daughter, Faye Dixon's orphan block, was sent to her daughter, Stanla Sue Shulps. Sue was a big help to me in getting the orphan blocks home. She helped me find Ruby Ellett Gratch. I got to know Sue pretty well with all of our phone conversations. We not only shared a love of family, but we both loved Elvis and his music.

I hadn't planned to be there when I returned to Kelsey in the summer of 2023. I was on a trip to McAlester, Oklahoma, to visit my only living stepbrother, Royce, and his wife, Joyce Jackson, on my dad's side. I realized from the "Kelsey Kids" Facebook page they were having a little get-together of the old-timers at the Heritage Center in four days at the Kelsey Cemetery.

Everyone I knew there was in the cemetery. I had talked to Sue a few weeks before, and she told me she was trying to get a place and move back to Memphis to be close to the temple and Elvis. She returned to Kelsey to care for her younger sister until she died. I had offered to have her stay with me until she could move. I had never seen her face before, but I felt good about her. We talked a long time about her sister, Kim, and I knew how she missed her.

I felt impressed to ask her if she could help me find relatives and where they lived in 1929. She told me she sold all her furniture, didn't even have a bed, and was sleeping on the floor, or I could stay with her. I told her I could get a motel, but I soon learned there was "no room in the inn." There was no inn, motel, or other place I could have stayed. I felt that was where I needed to be so I decided to go on Thursday. On Wednesday, Sue called and said she got a bed and wanted me to stay with her in Big Sandy. My prayers were answered. We spent five days and four nights together. She showed me everything and took me to church in Gilmer, where the old Kelsey first ward still meets. I saw many people I had just heard about.

We visited Genice Bryant and Moroni Hamberlin's son Keith and his wife, Beth. I had never met any of Moroni's kids. Then we went to see Wendy Tefteller, and I gave her the quilt blocks for Ethel Davis and Sally Davis. Wendy showed me the clippings she started from Ethel's plants—her mamaw. I knew I would find a home for them that I felt good about.

Sue felt like a sister to me, and I will always be grateful to her. She went with me to the Heritage Center on Sunday, and we took the quilt for some of the relatives to see and heard them tell stories about their ancestors. She has now moved to Memphis, and I know where everything is in Kelsey. Both of our prayer were answered.

Sue's mother, Faye Dixon, was married five times and had children from four different spouses. Sue was her second youngest child, and she has contributed so much to their history, as did Dana Larry Myers, her older half brother, whom they called Derge.

Derge said, "All of Ava's grandchildren called her Ma. She was pretty strict, and she spoiled us all. If you didn't do what she told you, she made you get your own switch. And she would use it on you and say, 'You hear me now?' She would say it over and over again.

Every Saturday, Ma would go grocery shopping. That was the only day Ma didn't cook. She always had bologna or pickle loaf sandwiches, potato chips, and root beer or orange soda from thirty- two-ounce bottles. On Sunday, Ma would cook either pot roast or fried chicken."

He knew all of this because, for a time, when he was young, he lived in Ava's home with his mother, Faye, and his siblings. He had many happy memories of his grandpa too.

We never really appreciate the importance of what grandparents do when we are young. My dad's mother died after I was married when she was ninety. My mother's mother died when I was fourteen. But I think about them all the time and the beautiful memories I have of them.

Eleanor Winifred "Winnie" Ellett and
George Franklin Green. 1925 Kelsey.

Tom and Viola Green Perry with children
Leroy, Floy and Horace. 1918 Kelsey

A birthday party in Lamar, Texas, 1895 for Viola Ennis
Grantham. Parents, Calvin Richard Ennis, and Ida
Dora Layton with brother Carling and their dog. Center
is Viola, brother Hurk, and maternal grandmother,
Amanda June Betterton Layton on the right.

CHAPTER 12

The Methodists

When messengers are sent to minister to the inhabitants of the earth, they are not strangers, but from the ranks of our kindred, friends and fellow beings and fellow servants, in like manner our fathers and mothers, brothers, sisters, and friends, who have passed away from this earth, having been faithful and worthy to enjoy these rights and privileges may have a mission given to them to visit their relatives and friends upon the Earth again, and bringing from the divine presence messages of love of warning, every proof and instruction to those whom they had learned to love in the flesh ...

—Joseph F. Smith

Kittie's older brother, George Franklin Green, married Eleanor Winifred Ellett in 1881 in Madison, Alabama. Her block in the quilt says "Winnie Green." I found their conversion story had been submitted on FamilySearch, written by a granddaughter, Betty Jo Lindsey Bailey.

My grandparents, George F. and Winnifred Ellett Green, were staunch Methodists. George was a deacon in the church, and they were happy with their religion.

They owned and operated a small grocery store in Kern, Texas, with the help of their son, Robert. One night, Grandpa dreamed two men dressed in dark suits, white shirts, and derby hats with books under their arms came to see him. He was so impressed with the dream that he told Grandma and Uncle Robert about it. Grandma didn't pay any attention to the dream.

The next day, Uncle Robert was on the porch and saw the men that Grandpa had dreamed about. He recognized them from Grandpa's description of the dream. He called Grandpa and said, "Your men are here." They introduced themselves as Mormon missionaries. Grandpa was so impressed with their message; I guess he was ready to be baptized then. Grandma was another story. She about hit the ceiling and was sure Grandpa had lost his mind. Things didn't improve, and Grandma just couldn't see it. Finally, Grandpa said if it was going to cause that much family problems, he would forget it. By now, Grandma decided she would read "that book" and see what had hold on him so strong. Of course, she read when he wasn't home. She too was soon ready to be baptized.

They were baptized on May 10, 1908. George was forty-nine, and Winnie was forty-seven. They were sealed in the Salt Lake temple in 1913.

They moved to Kelsey when it was still a new colony. The church leaders called them to go to Kelsey and they helped to set up the branch there. George was called to be the branch president of Kelsey from October 1918 until September 1932. He was the branch president during the time the quilt was made.

The first wedding he was asked to perform was for a young couple, Robert Simmons and Dolly Jo Muckleroy ("Joe Simmons"), on July 23, 1919.

Winnie was another one of the few sisters who was able to travel to the Salt Lake temple and take out her endowments.

Before I was baptized into the Church of Jesus Christ of Latter- day Saints, I was a Baptist, and I didn't have to change anything I already believed; I just added upon it.

When they were sealed in 1913, George and Winnie, along with their eleven-year-old son, Leon, and were able to seal their four sons and a daughter who had died as infants to them in the Salt Lake temple.

Leon later married Med Ault Buckley's sister, Ada Ault, and they raised their family in Kelsey close to Winnie.

Winnie's son, Robert, born in 1886, married Etta Jones, the sister of Stuart Jones, who had married his sister, Daisy Green, born in 1882. Their kids are all double cousins. Winnie was very busy with grandkids as she supported her husband in his callings and served in her own. She died three years after she made her block in the quilt at the age of seventy-one.

I can't imagine the heartache that comes with losing five babies. She must have been a strong woman, but the Gospel gave her a lot of joy, and knowing they could be together again forever gave her strength. Winnie is buried in the Kelsey Cemetery with her husband and three of her children.

Her daughter Viola Green was born in Madison, Alabama, in 1888. When she was five, her mother lost a baby boy, Woodfin, who was only two years old. The following year came a little sister, Irene.

By 1897, they moved to Navarro, Texas, where her father started farming. That same year, her mother lost a baby girl, Katie, who only lived a few days. And she lost two baby boys, John, in March, and Earnest, in November 1898. In March 1900, George Jr. was born. The boys, all three, were born and died the same day.

Viola married Tom Harrison Perry in Navarro in 1906 when she was eighteen. In 1907, she had a daughter, Emily Christina, and then in 1910, a son, Horace Milton. Emily Christina died in 1912. She was four years old. Viola was baptized into the Church of Jesus Christ of Latter-day Saints two months later with her sister Daisy Jones. Viola's husband, Tom, never joined the Church. Her son, Horace, later married Florence Bell Lindsey, the granddaughter of Myrtle's sister, Blanch Lindsey, who has an orphan block.

Viola named her next son Bennion Leroy, born in 1915. The whole town loved President Bennion and named the high school gym after him too. Bennion Leroy married Docie Knight's daughter, Erma Blyn Knight. Docie has a block in the quilt.

She had a daughter, Floy Irene, two years later in 1917. Floy married the son of Sister Grantham from her first marriage, Joseph William Mitchell. That ties us all to the Grantham tree.

Viola's husband, Tom, had owned and operated a dairy farm and a small store across from their home in Kelsey that sold things like grain, milk, bread, and eggs. When the Depression hit in the thirties, people couldn't afford to buy. He became depressed like so many. Struggling to feed his family, he left Viola to care for everything. Her oldest son had already gone to Freeport to work in the sulfur mines.

She managed the best she could for a few years, and in 1937, she hired a young man to run the dairy. His name was Charlie Odell Gage. Two years later, they were married. In 1940, the census said Viola was fifty and Odell was twenty-five. That is a significant age gap, but all the family loved him. He was baptized in 1941, and they were married for forty years. She lived to be ninety, and he was sixty- four when she died. He lived to be ninety and died in 2006.

Most of this story comes from Ruby Ellett Gratch, whose mother is Ruth Ellett, who has an orphan block.

Sister Grantham, who shared grandkids with Viola Perry, was Iva Viola Ennis. She was born in 1892 in Lamar County, Texas. She has a block in the quilt.

She joined the Church in 1906, two years after her parents. She is the daughter of Calvin Edward Ennis and Ida Dora Layton.

On the 1910 census, she is seventeen and divorced, but later she married Joseph William "Jodie" Mitchell in November 1910 in Lamar,

Texas. That is where they lived when their daughter, Beatrice Othello, was born—her first child.

She moved to Oklahoma and had two little boys named William Shelton and Welton "DC." When the boys were four and one, her daughter Beatrice died in 1917, just days before her sixth birthday.

Two months later, she lost her husband, Jodie, in Oklahoma. The boys were born in McCurtain County, Oklahoma. I am still looking for information on Viola. Where did she go, and what did she do? She had the Gospel also, so somehow, she made her way to Kelsey.

Maybe missionaries came by and told her about a safe place. Her parents were members, so perhaps she went home to Texas, and they told her about Kelsey.

In 1922, she married James Edward Grantham in Kelsey. In December 1923, they had a son, Edward Ennis Grantham. Her husband was sixty-eight, and she was thirty-one, the birth certificate says. But his headstone says he was sixty-one when he died a year and a half later in 1925.

In 1930, she was a widow again for the second time. This time, she had a lot of support from her ward family. Then she married for the last time twenty-eight years later to Benjamin Welch Thompson, and she is buried next to him in the Kelsey Cemetery. She lived to be seventy-five. Viola (Sister Grantham) experienced many hardships in her lifetime, but I believe she must have gained strength in the Gospel, and I'm glad I have a piece of her history in my quilt.

I get very excited when researching the lives of these sisters, as you can probably tell. I am the first member in my family to join the Church and have researched since 1979.

The spirit of Elijah is powerful today, and it's still turning the hearts of the children to the fathers. As I look at their families daily, I find more connections to my own. We are all one big family that belongs to a Heavenly Father, and we should always remember that.

Stuart and Daisy Green Jones, wedding day 1902, Kelsey.

Cornelia Jones, and Patriarch Walter
Moroni Hamberlin.1982, Kelsey.

CHAPTER 13

Living to Be One Hundred

Faith in God includes faith in his purposes as well as his timing. We cannot fully accept him while rejecting His schedule. We cannot worship Him but insist on our plans.

—Neal A. Maxwell

Daisy Eleana Green was the firstborn daughter of George and Winnie Green. Her orphan block reads "Daisy Jones." She was born in Crossroads, Madison, Alabama, in 1882. I have seen photos of her face when she was young, beautiful, and first married to Earnest Stuart Jones in 1902.

She came with her family to Navarro, Texas, when she was only fifteen in 1898. Earnest Stuart and Daisy have five daughters, including Cornelia, who married Walter Moroni Hamberlin—Doyle Hamberlin's cousin.

Addie Mae, who married James Jefferson Ault, the brother of Med Ault Buckley, Ron Compton's grandmother.

Mary Winnie married Myron Bryant, the brother of "Laura Bryant" and "Audrey Bryant," both having made blocks in the quilt. Daisy was also the sister-in-law of Julia Hamberlin Bryant, Moroni's sister.

Mildred, who married Victor Leroy Lindsey, was not only related to Myrtle Lindsey Hamberlin but was also the nephew of Ruth Saunders Ellett and cousin of Ruby Ellett Gratch, who looks like my granddaughter, McKenzie. Just another side note: McKenzie's husband, Todd Benson Riding's, mother is Kellie Flake, and Osmer D. Flake, the missionary who baptized the Hamberlins in Mississippi, is Kellie's great uncle—her grandfather's brother.

Mildred's daughter, Betty Jo Lindsey, married Meldrum Bailey, the grandson of Susie Maggie Dickason, Clara Hamberlin's sister.

Don't worry. We never have to keep it all straight. That is why computers were invented. We just have to know that we are all brothers and sisters.

Cornelia Gladys Jones was born in 1903 in Navarro, Texas, the oldest of five girls. She married Walter Moroni Hamberlin in 1924. Moroni is the son of Victor Carl Hamberlin and his first wife, Effie Irwin. Cornelia had an orphan quilt block: "Cornelia Hamberlin."

I am glad I could see and visit with this sister and feel her spirit in life. Not much is written about her, although she was baptized at ten, a year after her mother joined the Church. Her father never joined but supported her mother in all her callings. Moroni and Cornelia were such a big part of the history of Kelsey. They raised two boys and a girl. I have never seen a photo of Cornelia smiling, but I have when I saw the light of the Gospel in her face as we visited.

She played the piano for almost all the events she attended. She was active in the Relief Society and Primary organizations. She loved the Church and was a hard worker. She supported her husband as patriarch of the branch. I sent her block back to her family.

I have researched Daisy and her family, read her obituary, and see her face in photos at one hundred. She was a good woman and a great mother.

Her granddaughter wrote and posted her history on FamilySearch in 1997.

Daisy Eleana Green Jones

A Women of Faith and Great Determination Written by Nelda Lindsey Sellers and submitted By Betty Jo Lindsey Bailey

Mama Jones was a very strong and capable woman. She served for many years as the Relief Society president. She didn't have a car as we do today, so she had to walk as she went all over the Kelsey community taking care of people. This meant she often left her family at home to "fend for themselves" while she was taking care of others. Since Papa Jones wasn't a Mormon, it must have been especially hard for him to let his wife go help others when this meant additional work for him to take care of their family. Mother said she never heard Papa complain about Mama being gone so much. She truly believed in being her "brother's keeper," and Papa was very selfless in allowing her to do so.

Mama Jones died a month before she turned 101. Although she was living in a nursing home in her final years, she was mentally alert and continued to read her scriptures faithfully. In the last few years, she wasn't able to walk by herself. She would either hold on to you or get around in her wheelchair. But that didn't slow her down. She continued to help those around her.

In 1977, when Mama was ninety-five years old, her daughter, Mary Winnie Jones Bryant, had cancer and was seriously ill in a Dallas hospital. Mama worried about Mary Winnie and mentioned several times she wanted to see her one last time. Others felt Mama shouldn't go because she was too old, and it would be too hard on her. Betty Jo and I talked about it and decided if it were our daughter, we would feel the same way. We told Mama that we would take her. She was so excited. Mother and Irene also went with us. I will never forget how touching it was when Mary Winnie saw Mama. Although they were both old, it was "mother and daughter together again" as they talked and held each other for what they knew was the last time on earth. We always felt Mary Winnie was holding on because she wanted to see her mother again before she died. Mary Winnie passed away a week later. Needless to say, Mama experienced no ill effects from the Dallas trip.

Jim and Cora Alice Shore Alexander 1905.

Charles and. Bea Shore about 1945, Kelsey

Cora Alice Shore Alexander. 1925, Kelsey.

Loretta Mae Alexander and Donnie Odell Burnett.

1930 Kelsey basketball team. Coach on left is Lloyd Hunker, and coach Curtis woods on right. Front row: Rawleigh Alexander, Andrew Bender, Dewey McKnight, Aubrey Means, and Johnny Means. Back row: Kyle Whitehead, Alfred Aaron, Johnny Ault, and Mose Whitehead. Identified by Erma McKnight in 3020 at age ninety-five.

CHAPTER 14
A Hill of Yellow Daffodils

Bea Shore became a name I will never forget, and I can't wait to meet her someday. She was born Beatrice Jane Vice in 1868 in Illinois. Her father, James Milton Vice, came from Kentucky, and her mother, Harriet Michaels, was born in Illinois. Bea had a lot of brothers and sisters. Her mother was either the second or third wife of James Vice; no one was sure, but she was the last.

Her mother, Harriet, died when Bea was seven. I couldn't find any sources to prove it, but her family said she had a little sister and a baby brother when her mother died. That would have been very hard for her father. Ancestry records say the baby brother died four years later in 1879, and the father died in 1881. I don't know where she and her sister went, and I can't find them in 1880. That does explain maybe why she was married at the age of fourteen. Bea had grown up in Illinois, where she married Charles Hamilton Shore in 1883.

They had a son, John Henry, in 1886, and daughters Cora Alice, in 1889, and Etta Loretta, in 1891. They were blessed with twins, a boy and a girl, in 1894. Roy Lee and Floy Beatrice both only survived a short time, and they both died in 1894.

Charles and Beatrice had a store for a while in Illinois and later sold it and bought a farm where they grew corn and cotton. They enjoyed the simple life on the farm.

The Shores decided to move to Kansas but didn't like it there.

Alice said the only things she remembered about Kansas were living in a two-story house with four bedrooms upstairs and that the wind blew through the house, making weird noises; it sounded like the whole house would topple over. So they moved to Waco, Texas.

In 1900, the census lists them with their three kids and says Charles was a saloonkeeper, but that could mean anything. Then in 1910, he returned to farming, and all their kids were married and gone.

They had been married twenty-seven years when Charles got a job as a traveling auditor with the Raleigh Medicine Company. Bea said, "While traveling on a train for the company in about 1915, Charles met two missionaries and became interested in their message of salvation through our Lord and Savior, Jesus Christ."

Charles then invited the missionaries to visit their home. After much prayer and a thorough investigation of the Church, he and Beatrice were baptized into the Church of Jesus Christ of Latter-day Saints in May 1916.

Later that year, they moved to Kelsey and bought land high up on a hill overlooking the little community. Everyone called it "Shore Hill," and is still called that today. The people of Kelsey remembered it because every spring, the entire hill would be covered with yellow "daffodils." Even now, over a hundred years later, a few can still be seen, so they say.

The Shores ran a grocery store in town, and they grew to love the good people who came to live there. Today, I went to my grocery store, and right up front was an extensive display of yellow daffodil bulbs. I bought a big bag and planted them in pots in front of my house. I can't wait to see them come up in the spring, and I will think of Bea Shore. You can be sure!

They lived good, honest lives in those days. Back then, a gentleman's word was his bond. The people in the community were like one big family, and they said when someone was sick, in need, or had a home burned, no one had to be asked or given a special calling. The entire community helped out. It was known by all as a safe place to live and raise a family.

Beatrice Jane was known for her biscuits and gravy and just plain good cooking, along with her beautiful handiwork, including tatting, crocheting, quilting, and embroidering.

When I married Jim, my mother-in-law, Olive, taught me to make biscuits and gravy with hash browns and eggs I fixed it every morning for my family for over twenty-five years. I thought everyone ate that for breakfast. I guess they did in Texas! I was glad that Bea's family remembered that she had made it for them. My sons learned to make it for themselves when they left on their missions. It was probably what they missed most about home.

In her later years, Bea had hick white hair, and most people called her "Granny Shore." Everyone loved her, her family recalled.

Charles died in Apr 1947 and Bea in December 1950; both are buried in the Kelsey Cemetery. Their posterity is still a big part of Kelsey and helps preserve its history even now.

Cora Alice, the first daughter, made an orphan block, writing her name as "Alice A." She then added, "Kelsey." It took a while and a lot of studying to realize she was married to James Buford Alexander, and she must not have wanted to write "Alexander" out, and "Kelsey" was where she lived.

Jim met Cora Alice at a party, and then she said they kept company for about a year and married when she was sixteen in December 1905. Alice married Jim and had three children when she and her two oldest children, Bill and Loretta, joined the Church of Jesus Christ of Latter-day Saints in Limestone, Texas. She was baptized by Elders Thomas K. Gunnell and Alonzo Hamberlin in 1917. Alonzo is Victor Carl's son who served his mission in Texas.

Jim and Alice Alexander visited Alice's parents in Kelsey, where many people of their same faith had settled. They liked the community's people so much that they bought a farm and moved there in the fall of 1918. Jim was baptized before the end of that year. They were staunch Church members and always had strong testimonies of the Gospel. Two years later, she was sealed to her family in the Salt Lake temple.

Coleen Burnett McKnight wrote,

Alice was busy canning vegetables, fruits, pickled hog's feet, juices, jellies, and jams. She made a lot of clothes for the children, quilted, crocheted, knitted, and embroidered many articles over the years.

In the fall, they parched peanuts and baked sweet potatoes. The family enjoyed being together for taffy pulling and making popcorn balls. Alice made homemade ice cream often, and the kids took turns sitting on the old quilt on top of the freezer outside by the house while Papa Jim turned the hand crank. As they ate ice cream and told stories, laughter filled the house, and one by one, they would get up to get a sweater and then run back to eat more ice cream. Jim would wake everyone up in the middle of the night to finish eating the ice cream in the days before the electric refrigerator. No one minded but looked forward to this as it was a family tradition.

Jim and Alice both loved music and passed this on to their children. Jim played the French harp and harmonica, and Alice played the violin and the piano. Willie played the saxophone, and Loretta and Norma played the piano. Rawleigh and Imogene just loved to dance. The entire family loved to dance, but Mama Alice was rather shy about it. She said Papa cut up too much! The children still dance to this day.

Jim was a farmer before he went into the dairy business with his son-in-law. There was always plenty for the family to share with relatives and friends. Each year, they killed hogs and calves that were stored in the smokehouse. Wood was cut and stacked for fuel. The barns were filled with hay, peanuts, popcorn, etc. They always had fresh milk, buttermilk, and butter.

Alexanders opened their home in 1928–29 to the sister missionaries Eva Dalton and Sister Stewart. The sisters became very attached to the whole family. Reva was very energetic and outgoing. She loved the Gospel and grew to love the people of Kelsey and the surrounding areas. Reva brought a lot of good culture to a town with no electricity. She taught them to love learning and to get an education.

Even though she died before I was born, I couldn't stop the tears when I read her history on FamilySearch and realized that she didn't live ten years after she served her mission. Still, I was so thankful for her service and her testimony. My heart ached for her husband and children.

I have been there when children in my own family were left motherless, and I have recognized the Lord's hand in their lives. I know all things are for our good.

Alice's block went to Kimberly Barney Burch, the granddaughter of her son, Rawleigh Alexander. I found her through her contributions in FamilySearch. Kimberly is a quilter herself and loved her great-grandmother's block. Kim helped me get the blocks to living relatives. I sent her six blocks, and she knew who to send them to. She is the one who told me how hard it was to mail them because it felt like sending your children out into the world. She shared their stories in her quilting group. She wants a quilting reunion of the blocks and to meet in Kelsey someday. Kimberly now lives in Louisiana.

Alice had a daughter, Loretta Mae, named after her sister, Etta Loretta. Loretta Mae was born in Limestone, Texas, in 1909. She married Donnie Odell Burnett the year before she added her block to the quilt along with her grandmother, Bea Shore. Loretta's block was signed "Loretta Burnett."

Coleen McKnight added, "The first time Donnie saw Loretta was when she was plowing. He stated that she was the woman he would marry, and he did. We have laughed over the years about this because, in time, Loretta said she didn't do windows and her hand didn't fit a broom or a mop."

Burnett is my maiden name, and Donnie was already in my Burnett family tree. Now I can connect the Shores and Alexanders to my tree. Donnie and Loretta's son, Donald Buford Burnett, was baptized when he was eight in 1937 and married a girl from Utah named Linnie Shirlene Wade. They lost a baby boy at birth on April 14, 1961. They named him Wade Burnett. His death certificate says he lived an hour and a half. How hard that must have been. But they were all sealed with their daughters and son, Wade, in the Salt Lake temple just three weeks before I had my stillborn son on September 1967. I didn't give my firstborn son a name. His headstone simply reads "Baby Boy Hamberlin." I just couldn't give a baby that I never got to see the name I had picked for him. Looking back, I would have named him "Burnett Hamberlin" if I had known then what I do today. Wade Burnett is buried next to his parents in the Kelsey Cemetery.

Loretta loved the sister missionaries who lived in her home and taught her school classes. She was close to Sister Reva Dalton and Sister Thursa Boyle, The missionaries who lived with the Alexanders in 1928–29 were Sisters Dalton and Stewart. The Boyle's home was close by. Loretta named her daughter Thurza Coleen Burnett after Sister Boyle in 1932. Her aunt, Loretta Dixon, had called her daughter Reva Eldeen Dixon in 1928.

Loretta Burnett had been sealed to her parents in the Salt Lake temple when she was about eleven but didn't receive her own endowment in the Atlanta, Georgia, temple until August 1983, after the death of her husband. That same year, Gordon B. Hinkley dedicated the Dallas, Texas, temple. It wasn't until after her death in April 1986 that she was finally sealed to her husband.

Donnie was the love of her life as a teenager. One of their life projects was to open and run an ice cream shop in Gilmer. I was told they made the county's best homemade ice cream. They had lots of practice because her parents had a dairy and were famous for making ice cream in the early years before electricity.

I often wondered what these new converts thought about taking that long trip to be sealed to their families. They had no idea what the Lord had in store for them. That one trip gave them a lifetime of blessings if they were faithful to their covenants. Loretta's granddaughter Heather was so sweet to tell me about her memories of her grandmother. Heather reminded me that she would have been expecting her father, Donald Buford, when Loretta made her block, making it even more special.

Heather said, "Loretta was a successful businesswoman, cook, mom, and grandmother. On a personal level, she is always in my thoughts daily. I have makeup and moisture routines that I do twice a day. Strictly Estee Lauder. And I wear her perfume too; she loved White Diamonds. She taught me always to keep my money in order and straighten the edges. She taught me how to shop too. I could write a novel."

Wen Burnett wrote, "My grandmother was one of the first female business mavericks of her day. When it was truly a man's world, she started her own business in the most manly of industries, the oil and chemicals industry. She fought her way through the sea of testosterone to make it an innovative and viable regional company in her formative years. That took a lot of courage, tenacity, and Texas resoluteness. She was a real firecracker but also extremely kind and generous. She would be worthy of a book."

I couldn't agree with them more, even though I have only skimmed the surface of these great ladies' lives.

Loretta Alexander Burnett had an older brother, Willie Hamilton Alexander. He married first Zelma Fern Lindsey just one year before Zelma made her orphan quilt block. Hers read, "Zelma Alexander" Kelsey Texas.

After looking at her history, I realized that she later married the widower of Med Buckley, the grandmother of Ron Compton.

Zelma Fern Lindsey became Ron's stepgrandmother. He remembers her, and she is buried in the Mesa Cemetery with others of her family. Her headstone reads, "Zelma F. Alexander." Zelma is the daughter of Mary Luton and Pinkney Lindsey, Jessie Beatrice Lindsey was born in

1918 in Kelsey. Her parents are John Bynum Lindsey and Mary Luton. "Bea Lindsey" is what her block says. She is the half sister of Zelma, and they also have a brother who is a Denton. They are cousins of Myrtle Lindsey Hamberlin. She was eleven years old and made her block for her teacher. She spent a lot of time with Sister Dalton.

Bea Lindsey married Wallace Harold Meyers in Dallas, Texas, when she was sixteen. She lived in Caddo, Louisiana, for a while, then back to Kelsey for the birth of her daughter Laquita Ann Meyers in 1936 and son Randy Meyers in 1941.

They moved to Mesa in about 1952, and she was a good friend of mine in the 1970s. I worked with her for a few years and knew her mother and brother, but I never knew she was born in Kelsey. Her husband was Dan Franks, and by the time I realized who she was, in 2019, they had all passed away.

Bea Shore's second daughter, Etta Loretta, was first married to a young man named Lynch Bell in 1908 and had two sons and a daughter by 1914. But that marriage was not to last. Lynch took the two boys and returned to his parents in McLennan County, Texas.

Loretta took her daughter and moved to Kelsey, Texas, with her parents, and they were baptized in 1919. Her two sons were not members of the Church and were raised by their dad.

Loretta then married Clyde Dixon, the son of Minnie Dixon, in 1924 in the Salt Lake temple and signed her orphan block "Loretta Dixon," then stitched the following: "Apr. 1929 Kelsey."

Her daughter, Evelyn Beatrice Bell, made a block that read, "Bee Bell, Apr. 1929 Kelsey". She embroidered a little pink flower on each side. The block matched the daughter she had named after her mother.

Beatrice lived with her mother and stepfather until 1930. She was married at fifteen to Alvoid Louis Iglinsky in Freeport, Brazoria, Texas, and had her first son in the summer of 1931. Her husband was working in the sulfur mines like others from Kelsey. They moved to Louisiana to work in the mines there for a while, and she had their second son in Sulfur Port, Louisiana. By 1940, they were back in Freeport. The census gave her age as twenty-five; she had sons Avoid Jr., nine, and Clyde Lee, five. Her husband was twenty-seven.

Ten years later, in 1950, she lived in Longview, Texas, and married Joe Terry Corley. They were married in January 1948. She drives a bus for the city, and Joe is a truck driver. Her son Clyde is fifteen and lives with them—no Avoid Jr. She married in the Methodist church in Longview, and her family came.

In the summer of 1958, she lost Joe in what the death certificate said was a drowning accident. They were swimming in the Gulf of Mexico at Surfside Beach just out of Freeport when he fell from the inner tube raft and failed to come up. The newspaper said he died from a heart attack. Whatever it was, it was a great shock to her.

She lived to be eighty-two and was a widow for thirty-nine years. Her obituary says she moved to Longview in 1942, probably when she divorced her first husband.

It also says she was a nurse's aide and a Church of Jesus Christ of Latter-day Saints member. She attended the senior citizen dances. She probably remembered her childhood in Kelsey; they say they had the best dances.

I sent their quilt blocks to her granddaughter, Sheronne Futrell Carlin, also the great-granddaughter of Ida Irwin Futrell, who is part of my husband's Irwin line and came to Kelsey from Mississippi. I am thankful I sent most of the orphan blocks to their new home before I started writing about the "sisters of the quilt." If I had known all I had learned about each sister, I would have been tempted to keep all of them. Then I would have missed the blessing of sending them home. And the chance to connect with the families that received them.

The Shore family tree now connects to the Burnett, Hamberlin, Compton, Futrell, Ault, Dawson, Dixon, and Lindsey trees.

Wilma Daisy Dotson

Flavius Carlyle Henderson

Back row: Gwendolyn, Carol, Glenna, and Flavius Jr. Front row: Wallace. Wilma, twins Sharon and Linda With Sandra in between, and Flave Henderson. 1952 Bannock, Idaho.

Alfred, Carl, Ida, and Wilma Dotson, Sevier, Utah 1919.

Flora Belnap and Carl Christopher Dotson's
wedding day was February 10, 1932.

William Robert Henderson and Carrie Effie
Dove Hunter. The first marriage performed in
Kelsey was performed at Sacrament Meeting.

Back: Robert, Lloyd, Flavius, and Amy. Front: Ollie Odell, Mark, William Carrie and Hester Henderson. 19 26 Kelsey.

CHAPTER 15
Wedding Bells Ringing

Carrie Effie Dove Hunter signed her orphan block "E Henderson." Effie was born in 1886 in Ellis, Texas, the first child of William Wesley Hunter and Minnie Yeaman. She married William Robert Henderson in 1904.

William and Minnie had both come from Illinois to settle in Texas. They married in 1884 in Ellis, Texas, and started their family. The first two were girls, Carrie Effie and Bessie Beatrice. A son, Joseph, was born and died in 1889. They had five more children after that: Roland Silas (1892), Hallie Melvina (1894), George (1895), Walter (1898), and Olive (1900).

Minnie died in 1905, leaving him with small children. Effie, being the oldest, would have been the one to care for the younger children.

William and Minnie had been converted to the Church of Jesus Christ of Latter-day Saints in 1900 and baptized with their oldest daughters Effie and Bessie. Their son Roland was baptized the following year.

Years later, in 1917, William Wesley Hunter traveled to Salt Lake City and did his and his beloved wife Minnie's temple work. He also did the work for his father and mother. He never remarried. Although he died in Salt Lake City in 1936, he is buried in the Kelsey Cemetery next to his eternal companion, Minnie.

Effie's husband, William Henderson, was born and raised in Mississippi. His mother was widowed, so it befell the young William to care for the family.

He felt he could do more to support his mother by joining the army, so he fought in the Spanish-American War and the Philippine- American War.

While he was in the Philippine campaign, he got hold of some Mormon literature and became somewhat interested in Mormonism but soon found that the Mormons were an unpopular people. He heard so much talk about the Mormons and their beliefs that he questioned whether any people could be that bad, so he was determined to investigate further.

After his release from the army, he wen through Salt Lake City, visited, and talked to some Church officials there. He obtained and read more of their literature, then returned to his home in Mississippi.

After returning to Mississippi, he was baptized into the Church. The elders who baptized him told Brother Henderson of a new Mormon colony founded in Texas where the Mormons throughout the Southern states were gathering to make their homes.

Brother Henderson desired that when he married, he would marry a girl of his faith. After learning that Kelsey was a gathering place for the Saints, he was determined to go there and find a wife. He came to Kelsey and met and married Effie Hunter, whose family had been among the first Mormon settlers.

Effie and William were the first Mormon couple married in Kelsey. As Brother Henderson expressed, "The little colony of Kelsey had existed about three years when the unpretentious, quiet little wedding ceremony was performed as the first number on the program at Sacrament Meeting, January 24, 1904." That was the first marriage to be performed in Kelsey.

This was taken from a history written by Fayrene Hamberlin Bonebrake and lots of research of facts.

A Letter from William Henderson, Midvale, Utah, August 30, 1954

To the Latter-day Saints and friends of Kelsey and Upshur County, it has been suggested that I write you a letter. It is hardly fitting that one in my humble station be so honored, but I will gratefully embrace the opportunity and send you a word. Latter–day Saints, more than any other people I know, are interested in the principle of eternal progression. It would be well if we did more about it. One does not have to occupy an exalted position in order to advance in learning in knowledge, wisdom, understanding, and intelligence. The poet who wrote the following lines would probably have never been heard of if he had not also himself labored as those whom he has depicted.

"The heights by great men reached and kept were not attained by sudden flight, but they, while their companions slept, were toiling upward in the night." This war against the powers of darkness is inevitable. It will continue. Wherever God gets a move in motion for the benefit of humankind, Lucifer, true to his evil way, will have his imps on hand, seeking a means to overthrow it. Those who have been in Kelsey all these years can look back into the past and know that this has been as true there as it has been here…

Before closing, I would like to add a few words of encouragement. The Saints have suffered they are learning wisdom from what they have suffered. The eyes of God are watching over his work there. I once heard a local elder there say that he did not believe the Lord concerned himself with such a measly little group as we were. My thick head had the truth beat into it long years before I left there that God is deeply concerned about the work and people there.

Effie and William's first son was born and died in January 1905. A small, simple headstone marks the spot where he is buried in the Kelsey Cemetery. I couldn't find any death certificate to tell me what happened to him. Did he even take a breath? I wonder. Imagine the grief they must have gone through at such a loss. Then to make matters worse, her mother, Minnie, died in June. Minnie was only thirty-six, so it must have been unexpected. Sometimes it is so hard to understand the Lord's timing. Effie understood that the Lord loved her and was comforted by the knowledge she had gained from this new religion.

The Lord blessed them in December 1905 with a second son, Flavius Carlyle Henderson. A son who brought them much joy. He served a mission at the age of twenty in Texas, where he served in the branch presidency.

Flave married Wilma Daisy Dotson, born in October 1909. Wilma was born in Ackerman, Mississippi. Her block in the quilt says "Wilma Dotson."

Wilma's personal history says her father, Alfred Dotson, was born in Louisville, Mississippi, and her mother was born in Braggs, Alabama. Her father had been married before, and when his first wife left him, she took all the children except two boys, the only half brothers Wilma ever knew. Alfred had several children in his first family who died very young.

He and his two sons had gone to Idaho to live close to his family, and while he was in Pocatello, Idaho, Bishop Del Hess's son came home from a mission in the Southern states. Her father, Alfred, asked the bishop to give him the name and address of some good Southern girls. He gave him the name Ida Crook Hobby. Ida's block is also in the quilt and says "Ida Dotson."

They corresponded for about a year and decided they liked what they read about each other, and he proposed to her. She accepted, and he visited Ida two weeks before the wedding. It was the first time they had met in person. They were married in Braggs, Alabama. They returned to Salt Lake City, where they were sealed for time and all eternity in the Salt Lake temple. They then moved back to Mississippi, where their three children were born.

First, Carl Christopher, then a son, James Cook, who was stillborn, and last, Wilma Daisy. Wilma was born in a log house.

The only transportation was a horse-drawn wagon in those days. Ackerman, Mississippi, is rural and far from the nearest town. They had a small farm there. It was hilly and very green. There was a spring at the bottom of a hill way off from their house. It is lovely there. They lived close to her uncle Burkett Dotson. He had a big farm with many cows, a barn, and machinery. Her aunt Lena sold cream and butter. She had a big barrel churn with a lid fastened on one end. Wilma accidentally touched the fastener and let all the milk spill on the floor. Aunt Lena was pretty mad at her.

They had to carry all their water from the spring. Her mama did all the laundry in the spring. She would heat the wash water in a big iron pot and scrub the clothes on a washboard. The white clothes were boiled in the pot with lye water. She made the soap by letting the water run through the ashes and making the lye from it. She made the soap by boiling meat, grease, and lye together.

There was a small stream that ran through the pasture. Wilma dearly loved to fish on that little stream. It was small enough to step across and deep enough to have small perch. One hole in the stream was big enough that Carl and Wilma were baptized into the Church of Jesus Christ of Latter-day Saints. It was cold when Carl was ready to get baptized, so her mother got a pot of hot water and poured it into the water so that the water wasn't so cold when Carl was baptized.

The traveling elders baptized them. The one who baptized Wilma was Carl E. Lundell. The traveling elders would come to her parents' home to do their laundry. Sometimes there would be six elders at a time. The house was so small that Wilma didn't know how they slept there.

When Wilma was very young, there wasn't an organized Church branch near them so that she couldn't attend Primary. The branch was far from their home in the fall of 1919.

When Wilma was ten, the family moved to Salina, Utah, where her father's brother lived. They lived in Salina for over a year. Her father was a carpenter and found some work while they lived there. Land was expensive, and he couldn't afford to buy, so they moved to Mesa, Arizona. While they lived there, he picked cotton for about a month.

He and Ida wanted their children to be with the Saints so they would have LDS people to marry, and they heard about some of their friends who had moved to Kelsey, Texas. He decided that was the place for them, so they moved there. The names of the friends were Tom and Mandy McKnight. They stayed with them until her dad was able to buy a farm. He bought it from a woman named Willie Dilly. (The mother of Carrie Hamberlin and the daughter of Joe Smith, both quilters). The farm had forty acres and a small house. Wilma was twelve years old when they bought the farm, and she said she was disappointed that the house was so small and unpainted. Her papa also purchased an old mare, a horse-drawn wagon, and what farming equipment Willie Had.

The closest neighbors were Fred Knight, Taylor Smith, and Victor Carl Hamberlin. They had children close to their ages, so they became very good friends. Toby Smith became her closest friend.

Wilma started school there in the fifth grade. Her first teacher was a missionary named Clarence Cottam. The Church sent missionaries from Utah and Idaho to teach school as part of their missions. Kelsey was the name of the branch where they lived.

Percy Hamberlin, Carl Hamberlin's brother, and Will McKnight were neighbors. Taylor Smith would coach plays in the branch. Wilma was in some of the plays. She had a lot of fun.

During her early childhood, Wilma had chronic appendicitis and couldn't eat tomatoes or anything with seeds. Her mother would make fresh tomato juice for her to drink. She said it tasted so good. After she was twelve years old, a friend of hers had her appendix rupture, and it scared them all so much that they had the doctor come and remove hers.

Dr. Daniels put Wilma on the dining room table and had her mother, Ida, administer the ether for him. He removed the bad appendix, and after a few days, she could go back to school. The following two years were uneventful.

They had berries on the farm: dewberries and blackberries. Wilma could pick a syrup bucket full of berries and walk up the old railroad track to Rosewood, and Mrs. McKinley would pay twenty- five cents a bucket for the berries.

Wilma grew into young womanhood and had several boyfriends— Roger Smith, Travis Futrell, and Claude Muckleroy—but the one she liked best was Flave Henderson. Flave and Wilma dated for a while and became engaged. While waiting for the wedding, Flave went to work in Oklahoma on a farm. The Great Depression was just starting, and most people had trouble finding work.

Flave and Wilma were married on June 7, 1930. They had the first formal wedding in Kelsey, complete with bridesmaids, a best man, a rehearsal dinner, and the whole shebang. Elder and Sister Boyle were serving on their mission, and Sister Boyle arranged the wedding. She knew how to do it right.

Virgil Means, a good friend of theirs, sang, "I Love You Truly." Her father gave the bride away. Branch President George F. Green performed the ceremony. One of their uncles remarked, "Whoever heard of practicing to get married." He thought it was pretty ridiculous. They had a nice reception with cake and homemade ice cream at her parents' home. They went to Gilmer for their honeymoon. That was all they could afford.

After Ida Dotson became a widow at fifty-nine, she lived with her son and his family Carl and Flora Belnap Dotson in Bannock, Idaho. In 1946, her address was the same as theirs, but it looked like she had a little apartment in the rear for a while. I believe she stayed with them for the rest of her life. She lived to be ninety-seven.

Her obituary says she had two living children, eleven grandchildren, thirty-one great-grandchildren, and a great-greatgreat-grandchild. Also, she enjoyed genealogy research. I knew I liked her.

Wilma wrote her life story, but her granddaughter Sharon Kay Henderson Miller submitted it to FamilySearch. Sharon told me she was pleased to have her story shared with the quilters. I thought it was especially nice that Wilma's grandparents were the first couple to get married in Kelsey, and then Wilma and Flave had the first formal wedding with all the bells, whistles, and lots of frills.

They have a lot of posterity spread throughout the country, but so far, I can't connect them to others in the quilt. But I am still looking.

When I saw that she lived with her son and daughter-in-law, Flora Belnap, I realized I had known Flora's nephew, Wallace, better known as Wally Belnap, and his wife, Carol, since 1977. Even though I can't connect the Dotsons to any other families in the quilt yet, I can connect the quilt to a lot of my other good friends right here in Mesa. I want them to see how their relative connected to the quilt.

Berta Adelaide Leake Wade, 1900, Dekalb, Alabama..

Jasper and Berta Leake Wade along
with their dog. 1942, Kelsey.

Ethel Letha Wade Bradshaw, 1920, Kelsey.

Vera Mae Wade Russell Lofting, 1935, Kelsey.

Emma Smoot Dixon Wade, 1925, Kelsey.

CHAPTER 16

The Wade and Dixon Lines

Loretta Dixon's mother-in-law is Minnie Dixon, born Minnie Bell Luna in 1871 in Hickory Flat, Benton, Mississippi. Minnie was another example of these hardworking women. She made one of the orphan blocks.

In 1957, the Kelsey Relief Society did a special This Is Your Life program honoring Minnie for her years of service. It was the 115th anniversary of the Relief Society, and to surprise Minnie, they had all of her children except one son, who lived in Florida, come up on the stage.

Minnie is the mother of twelve children, thirty-seven grandchildren, fifty-six great-grandchildren, and three great-greatgrandchildren. At that night's dinner, they served a blue and gold three-tiered cake baked by the current Relief Society president, Myrtle Hamberlin.

Minnie was only able to attend school for a couple of months during the spring planting season and a couple of months during the harvesting. She had to work in the fields with her brothers.

Sometimes I forget they endured all their hardships without electricity or running water. With outhouses and a well in the backyard for their only water source.

Her obituary and the anniversary program in her honor told me a lot about her. She married Mathew Henderson Dixon Jr. at the age of eighteen. After the wedding, she rode to her new home side saddle on horseback. They lived in Mississippi, and they operated a cotton gin.

Mathew married Annie Jane Redfern in 1886 and had a daughter, Carrie, in 1887, who died after only a few months. Not long after the death of Carrie, his wife had also died.

When Mathew met Minnie, he was so bashful that he wrote her a note asking her to marry him. She obviously said yes because they were married in 1889. Minnie's first baby was a son, John, who died the same day he was born in January 1890.

I don't know if he ever took a breath, but I know what a sense of loss that would have been. Her second baby came in December 1890, and she named him Tazwell Jackson Dixon.

In April 1892, she had another son, named James Franklin Dixon, only to lose Tazwell in September 1892, just before he turned two. James Franklin died at only fifteen months old in July 1893. I could never even imagine what that must have been like for them.

Four months later, she gave birth to her first daughter, Annie Belle Dixon. What a joy that must have been to them, but I am sure they worried every day that they might lose her.

The following two sons were William, who married Ava Christina Ellett, and Clyde, who married Etta Loretta Shore. Both women made quilt blocks, but only Ava's was in the quilt. Loretta's was an orphan block.

The Dixons were so ready to accept the Gospel when the Mormon elders came to their home. Minnie and her husband were greatly impressed with this new religion. Mr. Dixon joined the Church in 1899, but one thing held Mrs. Dixon back. She had heard the Mormons had more than one wife. They had another daughter, Clara Lee Dixon, and another son, Benjamin, by 1901.

The elders gave them a little newspaper telling of a place in Texas called Kelsey, designated as a gathering place for the Latter-day Saints. Mr. Dixon wanted to move to Kelsey right away, and in those days, the husband led and the wife just followed.

They had a good home with plenty of the finer things in life. Many friends and family lived nearby, but they wanted to be where the Church was.

So in January 1903, they sold out, left what they couldn't sell, and came on the train to Gilmer, where the Edgars met them with wagons to bring them and all their household goods to Kelsey. It was six miles of bare and bleak countryside with a rutty road. She cried all the way. She stayed at Edgar's home, and brother Edgar told her if she stayed one year in Kelsey, no one could run her away.

When they arrived, there were only seven families in Kelsey: Jim and John Edgar, Bell Cummins, William Henderson, the Hunters (Effie), Stoker Lee, and the Bodine family. The Dixons made eight. When Minnie saw that the Mormon men had only one wife, she was baptized and joined the Church in August 1903.

She began to work diligently in all church activities, holding first a position as a Sunday school teacher, in which capacity she served faithfully for sixteen years. During that time, she reared nine children. She served eight years as Primary president and three as Relief Society president.

She visited and cared for the sick, helped lay out the dead, and dressed many babies.

Her daughter, Vera Mae Dixon, married Don Carlos Lindsey, the brother of Myrtle Lindsey Hamberlin, in December 1921.

Their daughter, Emma Smoot Dixon, married Byron Asbury Wade, whose mother was Berta Wade, and his sister was Vera Wade. All three women have a block in the quilt.

Minnie suffered greatly with the loss of her husband in 1921. At that time, she had several children who were dependent on her still at home. She showed great courage and remarkable faith in carrying on her church work and providing her family with a livelihood.

She was a gifted seamstress, and one winter, she helped Mrs. Leon Green make twenty-five quilts for people in the area.

She has weathered many storms of life. She was a widow for forty-one years, and in the twilight of a truly eventful life, her obituary says, "She gives us her life philosophy to think of others and serve them, trust in the Lord, be honest and fair in all dealings and live the very best you can." She did that and never left Kelsey for the rest of her life. She died at the age of ninety-one and never was able to attend the temple. Her work was not done until after she died in 1983 in the Ogden, Utah, temple, by her family.

Berta Wade is the next to have a block in the quilt. She was the first child born to Moses Asbury Leake and Charlotte Lucinda Wofford. They named her Berta Adelaide Leake.

She was born on the very first day of the year 1869, where her family had survived the devastation of killings and burning of property in Cartersville, Georgia, during the Civil War. It was the second marriage for both parents. Berta's mother, Charlotte's first husband, was killed in the Civil War, and she had two little girls, ages nine and ten. Berta's father was a widower with two little girls, ages seven and nine. After Berta came five younger brothers and two younger sisters, she had a large, blended family for love and support.

Berta married Jasper Carolina Wade in Chattanooga, Georgia, in 1890. Berta and Jasper lost their first baby, a girl, Pearl, who was only a couple of weeks old in 1891. Then came a son, Chester (1892), who married Lillie Amonette. The next were Clyde (1894), who married Carrie Dixon, Ethel (1897), who married James Bradshaw and had an orphan block that read "Ethel Bradshaw," Mamie Adeline (1898), who married James Braxton Futrell, Paul Wade (1900), who married Susie Amonette, Howard Wade (1902–1904), Jasper Wade (born 1904), who married Med's sister, Lola Ault, and Byron Asberry (1907), who married Emma Smoot Dixon, with a block in the quilt.

The youngest daughter was Vera Wade, and she had a block in the quilt. Vera married Ralph E. Russell at the end of 1929 and had a daughter, Berta, in 1930, and a son, Ralph, in 1933.

Then in the 1950 census, she was married to Cecil Lofting. They were married in 1940 and had a son, Cecil, in 1941. Ralph Russell was fifteen and lived with them.

After two failed marriages to men who never joined in her beliefs, she married Kenneth D. Boyd in 1979. Kenneth was baptized and joined in her faith. The Lord had other plans for her, and in 1982, she once more became a widow. She was a very active businesswoman and owned several stores at different times. She succeeded at work and kept busy with her family and Church.

Vera was a widow nineteen years and died in 2001 at the age of ninety. She lived a full and active life in the church.

Berta and Jasper's son, Byron Wade, was born in 1907 in Indian Territory that later became Vanoss, Oklahoma. In 1916, Jasper moved his family from Oklahoma to Kelsey.

There, Byron met Emma Smoot Dixon, and from the time they were twelve years old, they started planning their wedding. He finally married his sweetheart in 1927.

In 1928, Emma gave birth to their first child, a son, Delmar Byron Wade. He was born premature and only lived one day. They were later sealed in the Salt Lake temple.

So many sisters lost their first child at birth or when they were very young. This is something I have found that binds us all together in the Gospel. The times that are so hard and burdens so heavy, we have to turn to the Lord for comfort. It is in our darkest hours that we can feel his love the most if we remember to call on him and be grateful for his amazing sacrifice of giving his life for us. Christ has promised that he will never forget or leave us.

The joy we feel when all is well pales compared to the joy we will feel in the presence of Heavenly Father and his Son, Jesus Christ. His arms are always open to us if we will just come unto Christ.

In 1928, Byron and Emma moved to Oklahoma, Kansas, and then back to Oklahoma. They raised four sons and one daughter in what we sometimes call the mission field. Their son Arnold Lee Wade served as patriarch of the Oklahoma City Stake.

For many years, they held Sunday school and Sacrament meetings in their home. There were no other members where they lived. They often traveled many hours for branch meetings because Byron served as branch president in Blackwell, Oklahoma; Pratt, Kansas; and Ada, Oklahoma.

He served as a high councilor in Oklahoma Stake and Oklahoma South Stake District president in West Kansas. Byron was called to serve as patriarch of the Oklahoma South Stake in 1972 and was ordained by Elder Gordon B. Hinkley. He served as patriarch also in Shreveport Louisiana Stake and Gilmer Stake.

This was taken from memories of Tommie Wade.

Emma wrote much of her own history, saying that she enjoyed family history and temple work. Music, sewing, cooking, gardening, and canning. Her special interests were homemaking, church activities, and teaching the Gospel to her family.

Their son, Paul (November 17, 1900–May 6, 1991), wrote the following story about the conversion of his parents, Jasper and Berta Wade.

Dad had always been a very religious and visionary man. He was a student of the Bible, having previously been associated with both the Methodists and the Baptists, but they had been praying as much as five times a day for quite a while to find out which church was right.

One day, Dad was going into town on a wagon, and he saw a vision. This vision was like a movie. Before him, he saw a picture of their house and two men. One of the men picked up a chair, moved it to the window, and sat down. There was no sound, but across the picture was written, "These men will bring you the gospel of Jesus Christ." When he got home, he told Mom about the vision. He described which elder would pick up the chair and move it to the window. Dad told Mother to watch and see where they sat if he wasn't home.

One day, they were picking apples in the fall, and the sun was about a half hour before setting. As they were getting ready to go into the house, Dad saw two men coming up the road from the barn west of the house and said, "There they are now."

They went into the house. The one he saw in the vision picked up the chair, went by the window, and sat down. They sat in the house just like he saw them in his vision in daylight. Dad had many questions, and they 131 sat up late (till about two o'clock) that night talking about it.

The elders were Charles A. Howard and J. H. Stoles. Mother and Dad were baptized on May 26, 1901, and we were blessed after they were baptized. I was six months old when I was blessed.

Berta's daughter, Ethel Wade, married Thomas J. Bradshaw in 1920. Ethel had come to Kelsey with her parents in 1916. She was born in Alabama in 1897.

Tom's first wife was the daughter of William Jasper and Martha Lindsey, Maude, the sister of Myrtle Hamberlin. They married in 1906 and had two children before they came to Kelsey. Tom didn't join the Mormon Church until after his fourth child, Elvin, was born in 1915.

Soon after Elvin's birth, Maude became ill. She was in a lot of pain, and the doctors could not find the cause. Her condition steadily worsened, and her sister Myrtle came to help care for her before she died. Maude is buried in the Kelsey Cemetery.

Tom and the children then moved in with Maude's parents. The baby, Elvin, died during the flu epidemic six months after Maude's death. Later that year, Tom went to Salt Lake City and was sealed to Maude in the temple.

When he married Ethel in 1920, it was in the Salt Lake temple. Ethel then raised Maude's children as her own, and she and Tom had four more.

Shortly after her marriage, Ethel was called as Relief Society president. She worked in that organization for the rest of her life. She also served as branch organist and chorister. She served as a local and stake missionary and had many other callings.

Ethel recalled when the banquet was held to help raise money for the gymnasium, Bennion Hall. She said it was right after the Boyles came in 1928 or 29. It was really a big affair, and the church was filled. About thirty turkeys were picked, washed, and cooked in preparation for the occasion.

Tom and Ethel's home was often full of church officials. Mission presidents, historians, and others came. President Bennion also stayed at Wade's home, and once he brought Elder Talmadge, an apostle, and Ethel took care of him.

Ethel summarized her philosophy of life as follows: "If you want to be happy, help somebody." She then commented, "The Church will bring you through your sorrow." She always told her children, "Do the best you can, and the Lord will bless you." Tom died in 1965. Ethel died in 1983. When they died, they were still on their old homeplace in a new, smaller home.

Submitted by Fayrene Hamberlin Bonebrake

Mary Lucinda Tefteller Whitehead, 1893, Tennessee.

Dolly Joe Muckleroy and Robert Simmons
were married the day before the big July 24,
celebration in Kelsey, Upshur, Texas, in 1919.

CHAPTER 17

Sister Whitehead

Teffteller was a name I had never before heard and seemed to come out of nowhere to me. I was sure she wouldn't fit in any other family tree I had created. Mary Lucinda signed her block in the quilt "Sr. Whitehead."

She was the oldest daughter of Samuel Monroe and Elizabeth Lucille Whitehead Teffteller. That means her mother was a distant relative of her husband. She was born in Happy Valley, Blount, Tennessee, in 1873. She had ten brothers. Her only sister, Martha, died at the age of eight. Mary Lucinda was fifteen at that time.

The Teffteller family had been in Tennessee for over fifty years. Mary Lucinda married David Lafayette Whitehead in 1894, and he was also a native of Happy Valley. They had lived in the same place all of their lives.

Sister Whitehead's granddaughter, Grace Juanell Muckleroy DuRee, lived in my son Forrest's ward for a while, and she remembered the Hamberlin name from her ward list. She contacted me when she saw my post about the quilt on the "Kelsey Kids" Facebook page.

Grace is the only one I know who has the same middle name, except for my cousin Nora Juanell Whitlock, as I do. She said her father gave her that name, and so did mine. I took the quilt to her house and showed it to her and her husband. The next time I talked to her, she had lost her husband and moved to her daughter's house. She still lives close to me.

I loved talking to Grace about her grandmother, Mary Lucinda. Grace told me they lived in a narrow valley stretching about thirty-five miles between the Little Tennessee River and the Little Pigeon River.

At each end of the valley was a Baptist church and a cemetery. Anyone who went to church at all must have been Baptist. There was only one road that went all the way through the valley. They didn't get a lot of people just passing through.

When Mary Lucinda married David Whitehead in 1894, he was about five years older than her, but they had probably known each other their whole lives. For a short time, he was the mailman, and he went to Maryville once a week to get mail. He was the justice of the peace and was a farmer like his father.

The year their fifth child was born, in 1904, the Mormon missionaries came through the valley and baptized her husband, David. He was the only one in the family to join the Church. There were no members or meetings for him to attend on Sunday. How did he keep a testimony of the Church?

When the missionaries were in the area, they would stop and pay David Whitehead and his family a visit, sometimes leaving a message from the first presidency or just seeing if he needed anything. They often spent the night and visited with the family. The visits paid off after ten years when, in 1914, everyone eight or older family was baptized. That included Mary Lucinda, Fred, Lewis, Stella, Rhoda, and Cora Whitehead. It must have been a great day for him to have his family become members.

It wasn't until 1925 that they decided to leave the only home they had ever known to move to Kelsey, leaving behind the married children. Fred's, Lewis's, and Rhoda's spouses never joined.

Stella's husband was baptized later, in 1950. Then the next year, in June 1951, he took her to the Salt Lake temple, and they were sealed. They even took her father, David, and sealed all of the family that hadn't been sealed and had them sealed at that time. Stella died the very next year of breast cancer.

When David and Mary Lucinda left Tennessee in 1925, they took Cora, Ralph, Bill, Kyle, and Porter. They had buried a one-year-old son, David Andrew, in 1907. Cora was the oldest child at home with four younger brothers, ages nine through eighteen. Cora was born in 1904, so she was almost twenty-one. She left behind a longtime sweetheart and went with them to this unknown place to start a new life.

They bought forty acres with a large, two-story, six-bedroom house, and he planted corn. The family had a big vegetable garden, a peach orchard, and other fruit trees.

It must have been hard to leave married kids in Tennessee just when you started having grandkids. Mary Lucinda only lived in Kelsey for about five years.

Her closest neighbors in 1930 were her quilting sisters. Emma McKnight, who was Clara Hamberlin's sister, Ethel McKnight, who was a Burnett, Docie Knight who was a Sanders, Sister Whitehead's daughter, Cora, and son-in-law, Martin Muckleroy, lived next door.

But living in the home with her family was her brother, Columbus, better known as "Lum" Teffteller, with his wife, Jessie, and two kids.

Mary Lucinda Teffteller Whitehead was surrounded by family when she died in October 1930, just one year after she made her block in the quilt. Her death certificate says she had high blood pressure and a cerebral hemorrhage. It probably happened suddenly with not much warning. She was only sixty-two and is buried in the Kelsey Cemetery.

She now has lots of posterity that comes from Kelsey. She connects to the Hamberlin, Muckleroy, and the Lindsey trees. Her granddaughter Belita Muckleroy is married to Danny Grizzle.

Danny is related to almost everyone in Kelsey. His mother is Carol Denton, and her parents are Thomas and Connie Lindsey Denton. Connie is the sister of Myrtle Lindsey Hamberlin. Then Carol Denton's sister Mary Lula married Med Ault Buckley's brother, Bartholomew Ault, putting them in the Compton tree. The funny thing is his best friend all the way through school was Shane Dawson, from my ward.

Now I think almost everyone in the quilt fits into my tree. It's a good thing we have computers. All the names and faces of the sisters dance in my head at night when I sleep. I go to bed and wake up with them on my mind. I feel like I know them all, or at least I know a lot about them. This past summer, I met Dan Grizzle, his mother, Carol Denton, and his brother, Gary, in Kelsey.

Mary Lucinda's son-in-law Martin Muckleroy's sister, Dolly Jo Muckleroy, signed her orphan block "Jo Simmons." Her parents, Robert Muckleroy and Della Ophelia Knight, lived in Henderson County, Texas. They had Oma Mae and Dolly Jo, then the twins Claude and Maude. In the summer of 1904, while moving the family from Henderson County to Kelsey, Texas, they went out of their way to visit one of Della's sisters, who lived in Wills Point, Texas. A day or two after leaving Wells Point, traveling by a horse-drawn wagon, Della succumbed to pneumonia. Robert buried her in an unmarked grave beside the wagon road, and Robert continued to Kelsey and left his four children with some of his wife's relatives.

He then returned to the area where he grew up and found another wife, Lela Josephine Martin, whom he married in June 1905.

This was taken from a story by Allen Martin Muckleroy, a great-grandson of Robert and Della Knight Muckleroy.

Dolly Jo married Robert Sharp Simmons in 1919. They had their first daughter, Doris Fay, in 1921, then Albertine, born in 1924. Albertine didn't think she was related to Granny Lindsey, but she was. The last daughter, Blenda, was born on August 20 and died on September 21, 1931. She only lived for a month and a day.

Dolly and Robert were baptized in May 1909 and sealed in the Mesa temple in 1949. They were married for over seventy years, died, and are buried in the Kelsey Cemetery. He was ninety-two, and she was ninety-four when they died.

Mary Manie Collins and Marion
Farley, 1930, Brazoria, Texas.

CHAPTER 18

The Lone Star of Texas

The only sister I found who didn't even live in Upshur County was Mary Manie Collins or Manie Farley. It took me several years to figure out the Freeport sulfur mine connection with Kelsey.

When I found the only person in Texas with that name, I made her a Collins tree and connected her to FamilySearch. I discovered she was a Church of Jesus Christ of Latter-day Saints member, and I contacted the person who had put up pictures and information about her.

She is Laurie Seemann Howell, and she told me she had never heard of Kelsey, but Manie was her great-grandmother. Laurie lived in Newburg, Missouri, so I sent her the quilt block.

She had no idea how Manie connected to the sisters in the quilt. For the longest time, she was just a piece of the puzzle that didn't fit anywhere. I tried to fill in all the gaps I could, and Laurie joined the "Kelsey Kids" on Facebook. She told me that most of the Collins and Farleys had not stayed in the church like she had. The "Kelsey Kids" is where everyone posts memories of their ancestors who settled in Kelsey in and around the early 1900s.

I have been a member since 2010 and love looking at the history there. They sometimes put up old journal entries, family pictures, letters, and even quilt pictures—anything you want to share about Kelsey.

In 2022, Dale Topham put a note on Facebook that said he had found a journal from his grandmother Reva Dalton, dated 1927–1929, and would look up names for people. Laurie had him look for Farley, and he sent her a couple of entries that put them in Kelsey during those years, and that was the year of the quilt, so I knew I had the right Manie Farley.

Manie was the last sister to finish writing about it, so I looked at the journal. When I read the posting of Reva's grandson, Dale, I found he had recently added a link to it. It was amazing to read it, and I recognized who almost all of them were.

Her journal brought the whole community together for me to better understand their way of life. Their day-to-day activities and how they worked and played together. They took care of one another and served the community.

The church in Texas covered a large geographical area. Even though the Farleys and Collins were in Dallas and Freeport, they belonged to the Kelsey Conference or branch.

Mary Manie Collins was born 1886 in Newton, Arkansas. She married Alfred Barrett when she was fifteen in 1902 and had a daughter, Mary Francis Barrett, in 1903. When that marriage failed, she married Marion Constantine Farley in 1907. He had joined the Church in Arkansas in 1899 when his parents had. Manie didn't join until 1915, and they lived in Arkansas with two sons, Terry Littleton and James Toney; his family called him "Buncas." A daughter, Lucy, was almost two, and then they had a son, Marion, in 1915, who died in 1918.

Then a daughter, Ader L. Farley, was born and died the same day in May 1917. Then Lottie in 1922 and Willard in 1924, who completed their family. Manie lost her husband in 1938 and was a widow for twenty-eight years when she died in 1966.

James Toney (Buncas) and Lucy spent time with the Kelsey members even though they had to travel. Manie went to church with the people from Kelsey who had moved to Freeport for work. She lived twenty-eight years as a widow, and I know that had to be so hard. Her temple work was done after her death.

Rusie Susie Bessie Dawson Futrell, 1930, Kelsey.

Back: James Braxton. Front: John Whitaker, James Edward,
Ida Adella Irwin and Travis Preston Futrell, 1913, Kelsey.

Standing: William, Luther, Frank, Claude and
Myrtle. Seated: William King holding Rusie, Rena
and Docia Lewis Dawson. 1905, Mississippi.

CHAPTER 19

Rusie Susie Bessie

*Each trial in life is tailored to the individual's capacities
andneeds as known by a loving Father in Heaven…*

—*Howard W. Hunter*

Rusie Susie Bessie Dawson has a block in the quilt and was born in 1905 in Yazoo, Mississippi. Her father is William King Dawson.

His first wife was Sophronia Mary Irwin, born in 1867 and died in 1894. They had five sons and one daughter. They lost one son before he was two. Sophronia's sister, Epsie Birdell Irwin, married Virgil Homer Hamberlin, a great uncle to my husband, Jim. Her sister Effie Lavinia Irwin married Homer's nephew, Victor Carl Hamberlin, and all three sisters are the nieces of Jim's great-grandmother, Julia Helen Irwin.

Are you confused yet? I know I am, but the blood is very intermixed with the Hamberlins and Irwins. Both families lived in Mississippi in the late 1800s. It reminds me of the song we used to sing when I was a kid. "I'm My Own Grandpa."

Rusie's father remarried, and her mother was Docie Elizabeth Lewis. Docie died when Rusie was only fourteen. Docie had seven children that all grew to adulthood. Four sons and three daughters.

Rusie had a six-year-old sister at the time and a four-year-old brother that she most likely had to look after.

In 1927, Rusie married John Whitaker Futrell and signed her quilt block "Rusie Futrell." John Futrell's parents were James E and Ida Adela Irwin Futrell. Her mother-in-law had an orphan block signed "Ida

Futrell." She was cousin to the Hamberlins. Ida's father is a half brother to Julia Helen Irwin.

They lived in Yazoo City, Mississippi, when they joined the Church of Jesus Christ of Latter-day Saints. Their family and friends were very disappointed. Because of the persecution, the family decided to leave Mississippi. Carl Hamberlin told them about Kelsey. He said it was a place where Mormons could live in peace. Futrells found Kelsey to be a wonderful place—just the place to bring up their children. John Whitaker served as a stake president for several years.

Ida's oldest son, James, married Mamie Wade, the daughter of Berta Wade. The youngest son, Travis, married Hazel Davis, the daughter of Ethel Davis. Looks like Rusie, Ethel, and Berta's kids were all cousins.

Rusie wasn't baptized into the Church until 1928, only one year before she made he block in the quilt.

William King Dawson is also the great-grandfather of a member of my ward, Shane Dawson. He was our Gospel doctrine teacher and bought the home in my neighborhood where my daughter-in-law, Christine Frost Hamberlin, lived when she married my son, Jim.

Shane's wife is a Kelsey girl too. She is Jamie Ann Pritchett, whose great-grandfather came from Alabama to Kelsey in about 1910. Shane's grandfather, Luther King Dawson, and my husband's great-uncle, Victor Carl Hamberlin, were very close friends and worked together in their Kelsey ward.

The following is a family history written by Rusie's sister Larcie Laura Dawson Dixon. Larcie was a quilter but didn't have a block in my quilt. She was the one who captured how their life was in the early years before the Church was in their lives.

My father and mother moved to Texas from Mississippi sometime around 1916, bringing a family of seven children. We moved to a farm called Carter Place north of Kelsey. The second or third year we lived there, Mother was taken from us on December 31, 1918, and was buried in the Kelsey Cemetery on January 2, 1919, on Carl Hamberlin's lot just northeast of the gate.

In the next few weeks, we moved to the Marsh place, which is now the Roy Means Farm. My first year of school was while we lived there, and we went to the Kelsey Church school with Sister Myrtle Jones as my teacher. We lived there one year, then moved to the Elletts' place about four miles south of Kelsey. We walked to school and came by Sister Cummins's place each day.

The following year was 1920. We lived there one year, and in the fall of 1921, Brother Posey asked my father to go to West Texas with his family, so we loaded two wagons and moved to West Texas in covered wagons.

It was lots of fun for all of us but a great burden on my father with just two small girls to help with the smaller children. This took about three weeks traveling in the daytime and resting at night. Brother and Sister Posey were such wonderful people. Without them, I don't know what my father would have done. They were always there with a word of encouragement and a smile and were always helping him with his problems and family. Sister Posey mothered each of us, and her a mother of a large family and small children of her own. This was a large responsibility. There were Brother Posey, Sister Posey and six children, my father and seven children.

Regardless of the problems and the responsibility, there was always time for blessings on the food and prayers. Brother Posey was more or less a missionary. He always reminded my father the Lord would provide if he had enough faith. Without it, the Lord only knows what would've happened to a man with a family of seven small children, from two years the youngest to nineteen years the oldest.

We went to the farm of Mr. Brewer between Quanah and Childress. Both families camped there and helped gather the fall crops. When we finished, Papa rented a farm from Mr. Leonard. We all went to a small country school named Elba. There were several things I remember so well while living there.

Once, when a bad storm came up, all the older children had gone to a play at the schoolhouse. Papa, my baby brother, and I were home. We didn't have a cellar, and it was much too far to take us to the closest one, so he wrapped my brother and me in a heavy quilt and got in a large hole close to the house.

Once again, the Lord helped him protect his family. There was a lot of damage around us, but we were all fine. I was too small to realize the danger, but I've heard my father talk of his fear—not so much for himself but for his family.

Another thing was once when my brothers and I went to give the horses water; we didn't have creeks or springs. While we were returning, the horse my youngest brother was riding got scared by a rabbit and ran away. The horse ran into a barbed wire fence. When Papa got there, they had to cut the fence to get the horse out, and my brother didn't have a scratch. No one ever figured out why he wasn't cut to pieces.

We had a wonderful year, but it wasn't home, so in the fall of 1922, we moved back to Kelsey on the J. C. Humphrey place, now owned by Myron Bryant, in the house with my brother, Luther Dawson. We all had a wonderful year. My brother and his family were members of the Church of Jesus Christ of Latter-day Saints.

On the trip to West Texas, as I said before, Brother Posey wasn't only a wonderful friend but more or less a missionary. He had talked to my father about the Church, and the older children were all interested, so in the summer of 1923, we all decided to be baptized except a sister who hadn't at that time made up her mind (Rusie) and my baby brother who wasn't old enough. My half brother, Luther Dawson, and Carl Hamberlin were the elders who baptized and confirmed the five children that were ready in a creek close to where we lived.

We lived there one year, and that fall, we moved to the J. D. Bailey place, now owned by Milton Bailey, which we all called the brown house. We all liked to live there. It was a pretty place. While we lived here, my older sister married her husband, a young man she met while we lived in West Texas. There is where he carried her to live. It was really sad for the family. I sure missed her, and we were all together up to that when she married.

Soon after Sis left, my half sister, Myrtle Walters, and her two small girls moved into the house with us. This made us so happy; it was wonderful having a baby around. My sister owned a cow she brought with her.

Where Papa kept the cow, we always played. So one day, we decided to milk her and play with the milk. We did this for several weeks. They had decided to sell her and get another since she had failed so in her milk, so we told Papa what we had been doing, and of course, this followed with a large dose of a hickory tree, which we all deserved.

In the early summer, my sister's oldest child, Annie, took suddenly ill and lived just a few days. This was a terrible shock to the whole family and the first loss of a loved one since my mother's death.

We lived there and made a crop. That fall in 1924, we moved to Pritchett again on J. C. Humphry's farm.

We didn't like to live here much because everything was so strange. But with a large family, Papa needed a larger place.

In the spring after we moved here, my sister, who lived in West Texas, lost her baby. That summer, she and her husband visited us and wanted me to go home with her. I was so happy, but this didn't last long. I was awful homesick for my father and family.

My sister and her husband lived on a large farm in Clarendon, Texas, with lots of cotton. I helped pick cotton until school started. In late fall, we received a letter telling us Aunt Effie Hamberlin had died. This was a shock, and we were all grieved, for we loved her very much, and she was a dear friend of my father's. When the crops were all gathered in the fall of 1926, my sister Rena and her husband, Lewis Melton, and I moved to Elba, where we lived in 1922. They rented a farm from a Mr. Flint. Lewis's mother already lived there, so we had someone close that wasn't a stranger.

I liked the place fine there we had lots of trees and a beautiful yard. This we didn't have at Clarendon. The only trees there were several more miles on Red River; however, we could see for miles with nothing to hinder the view, so this new place was really pretty.

We lived just a short distance from school. Mrs. Melton, my brother-in-law's mother, had a large family. There were three girls and three boys, one girl just a few months older than I was. This was so nice for both she and I started to school, and everything was wonderful. My teacher and the children were nice and friendly. I liked school fine. It was while I lived there that I told I was a member of the Church of Jesus Christ of Latter-day Saints. I had lived here much too long not to be accepted. Things were as usual, except Mrs. Drake became a visitor in my sister's home after she learned we were Mormons. The Ellett family was related to her.

In the fall of 1926, I came home to live with my father. Soon after coming home, I started to school.

At the end of 1927, my brother and his wife sold out and went to West Texas. Papa broke up housekeeping, and I came to Kelsey and started school with my sister Rusie and Johnny Futrell, who had one child, David Childress. "DC" is what I called him.

I started school at Kelsey in the fall of 1928. One of the best schools I ever went to. Most of the boys and girls I already knew since I had lived in and out of Kelsey most of my life. Some of the happiest years of my life were while I was in school here. We had a wonderful teacher. The best year of 1929 was when our Bennion Hall was completed. We LDS boys and girls had one of the best schools in the county and the only gym of its kind anywhere in East Texas. Some of the finest dances and floor shows, and people came from near and far. We had a fine team of ball players, both boys and girls. One's life when young goes by quickly with something to go to each night. Church, choir practice, MIA, Relief Society, club nights, dances, and parties. The only time we ever left the community was Saturday when we went to town with the Heber Jones family to the show. They were great people.

I loved her story because I could relate to it as many of you can. My mother's brother and wife lived close to us in 1957—my uncle Jay and aunt Mary Whitlock. I loved to play with their baby. The first was a baby boy named after my dad and his dad, Marvin Jacob Whitlock. We all loved him so much, and I got to feed him and change his diapers.

Just getting to hold him was fun. He died of crib death at twenty-one days. I remember the night I heard a knock at the door in the middle of the night. It was my uncle Jay coming to tell my mother he had lost his baby. Uncle Jay and my mother just cried and talked for a long time, and my heart was broken. I did the work for my uncle years ago, but his wife, Mary, was born in 1929, so she was still alive, and I couldn't seal them all together.

The second baby was born in 1958, Enola Marie, and she was such a joy. After losing Marvin, we all spoiled her. She entertained us all with her smile and tricks. She had been walking and was so cute. They were at our house often, and I often spent nights with them to help my Aunt Mary.

In 1960 Enola got sick and had a fever, throwing up, and diarrhea. The doctor told her mother to give her fluids and aspirin. After a few days, she was too weak to hold her head up. Aunt Mary took her to the hospital emergency, and they admitted her and started an IV, but in about three hours, she died of influenza just before her second birthday. I remember how hard that was on me and the whole family. I remember the music at the funeral. It was so sad. I was twelve and didn't know families could be sealed together for eternity.

This week, I got an email from FamilySearch telling me I was cleared to seal the two babies to their parents.

The quilt and Larcie's story reminded me to make that happen. Today, my granddaughter, Marlee, and her husband, Aaron, had a baby girl named Charlotte Marie Rodriguez. My baby sister's name was Charlett. Spelled differently but pronounced the same. It was such a sweet day I decided to seal the babies to the parents even though I had to go by myself.

I couldn't help the tears that fell, but I shared the story with a sweet young couple I had never met before, and the sister cried with me. She said she felt the spirit so strong, and they thanked me for letting them be a part of the sealing. I was the one who was thankful for them and their willingness to be there to help me.

Abbie Buckley Lindsey, 1956, Kelsey.

Mary Medomosille "Med" Ault Buckley, 1917, Kelsey

CHAPTER 20

Behind Every Great Man

The spirits of the just are not far from us and know and understand our thoughts, feelings, and motions and are often pained therewith.

—Joseph Smith

Abbie Buckley was born in Tallahatchie, Mississippi, in 1887 to William Thomas Buckley and Mary Elizabeth Kendall. Abby made her block in the quilt when she was forty-two years old.

Abbie's husband, Joseph Milan Lindsey, joined the Church in 1900, and she joined in 1904 in Mississippi with her parents. They were married in 1907 in Kelsey. They were sealed in the Salt Lake temple in 1919. That was the same year Percy Hamberlin and his family were sealed in the Salt Lake temple. Her quilt block reads "Abby Lindsey."

Most Mormon communities have a few priesthood holders who are chiefly relied upon when circumstances of illness and injury are of a very serious nature. The elder is called to pronounce a blessing of healing upon the ailing person. The personal righteousness of the elder is the underlying basis for this special position of honor. Joe Lindsay was such a person. His life was a blessing to so many beyond his immediate family. As it is said, "Behind every great man is a great woman." I am sure Abby was that great woman. I don't know when their families came to Kelsey, but in 1910, they were all there on the census.

Abbie's first baby was a son she named Huey Madalyn Lindsey. Huey lived only two days and died on November 3, 1908. So many of these sisters lost babies. Especially their first ones. It always reminds me that we all make sacrifices that sometimes we are unaware of. Sometimes we choose to make them; sometimes the Lord just gives us what we need to become stronger. The fact is we need him in our lives, and we must trust him in his wisdom to make the best decisions for us. He will never steer us wrong. We do that ourselves. We need to have faith that the sun will come up in the morning to a new day.

In 1910, they had a son, Horace. Horace said in his history he was born in a three-room house between Kelsey and Enoch. His parents moved often from one rented farm to another, and in about 1915, they bought a small farm and house in Kelsey.

Horace left Texas in 1929 after graduating from Gilmer High School and married Mae Myrtle Busk in Utah. Horace lived to be 101 and had two sons and a daughter. Abbie buried her daughter Edna Laurene Monaghan in 1966, who died from a heart condition, but she had her for fifty-three years, and she gained two beautiful granddaughters.

The youngest daughter, Mary Faye Lindsey, died in Scottsdale, Arizona, in 2011. Abby died in 1972 at eighty-five, her husband Joe died in 1973, and yes, they are buried side-by-side in the Kelsey Cemetery.

Abby's nephew, Arthur Morris Buckley, married Mary Medomosille Ault. Med was the oldest of thirteen children born to Joshua Steven Ault and Mary Magdalene Wilson. She was born in 1899 in Cedar Glades, Arkansas.

When I found this story submitted by Ruth Buckley, I realized I had known Ruth from the beauty shop where I worked in the seventies and eighties. I never realized she was related to Ron Compton.

Her father and all of the children were working in the fields when two missionaries came by, and they asked if they could talk to the family. Father said yes if the missionaries would follow along with them as they worked in the fields. This the missionaries did, and at the end of the discussion, they asked if they could leave a Book of Mormon. Their father accepted one, and Med saw him up late into the night reading it. The next week, when the missionaries came, their father invited all to go into the house and listen to the lessons.

I have also heard that Father Ault built a small church for them to meet in. The anti-Mormons burned this down. This prompted them to move to Kelsey, Texas, where a small colony of Latter-day Saints lived.

I will now include some things written about Med by her younger sister, Lola, in her journal.

My oldest sister, Med, was a born leader and didn't have a lazy bone in her body. She would lead us out, and we followed her like chicks after a mother hen.

My father depended on her to see we kept busy in the fields during cotton chopping time. We were in the fields early, and she kept us working until late. However, I remember one time when Pa went to see how much we had accomplished after a week's work, and he came back home and said it wasn't enough and would go with us the next day and show us what could be done if we worked harder.

The next morning, my sister, Mildred, stayed in the store that father owned and worked in, and we headed to the field behind Pa. We had took our dinner. I remember it was salmon and sausage patties in split biscuits, boiled eggs, tomatoes, and blackberry cobbler. All in syrup buckets covered in cloth.

The ground was rocky, and our hoes clanked hard and fast as we worked. The sun beat down and sweat poured off our faces. The food was covered with ants when we uncovered the buckets at dinner. We had failed to hang the buckets on a tree limb. Word was sent to Ma, and she brought us more dinner.

The day was long and hot, and when quitting time came, all of us were exhausted, especially Pa. The next morning, Pa couldn't get out of bed. He was too sore. He could hardly walk for two or three days. Never again did he criticize the amount of work we did.

My sister Med could sew and make anything by looking at a picture. I remember she liked a boy living close by, and she had a date to go to the dance. She decided to make a new dress to wear, so that day, she whipped up that dress and was ready when he came that night. She was cute and pretty blonde.

Grandpa Ault worshiped her, and she asked him to come for supper once, and she cooked herself. She made chocolate pies, and the filling was runny so no one else would eat any but Grandpa and me, and we used our spoons.

After she went to Tyler to study secretarial schoolwork, we missed her, so one time, Ruby and I went by train to see her, and we were allowed to stay all night. She took us to a drugstore, and I tasted my first banana split.

Later she taught school and served an LDS mission as a secretary to President Samuel O. Bennion. President O. Bennion urged her to enter a national typewriting contest, and she won.

We had a beautiful mahogany organ. Med could play it very well, and I could play some hymns fairly well. We had a radio, and I remember the first one required the use of headphones.

Pa bought one of the first cars in Kelsey, maybe even the first, and I remember the new smell it had about it.

These few short stories give you an idea of what Grandmother Buckley was like. I know it was because of her that her children were brought up in the Church and taught to work.

She married Arthur on July 25, 1925. They lived in Freeport, Gilmer, and Kilgore, Texas. Their oldest child, a girl, died at birth. Then with the other seven, they left their successful dairy business and moved to Mesa, Arizona, in 1941 to be closer to the church. They had come to Arizona in 1932 and have been sealed in the temple. Her grandfather Ault and grandmother had moved to Mesa earlier, and they're both buried in the Mesa Cemetery. Every spring, the whole family would go to California to work in the fields harvesting crops, beginning with potatoes. This lasted all summer and into the fall. They would return late, but their mother made sure that they all started back in school. This was hard on all of them. She also made sure that they attended all of their church meetings.

Med got cancer, which she fought for several years, but after several surgeries, she died in Mesa on September 8, 1956, and is buried in Mesa Cemetery.

Today, I am a breast cancer survivor. When I found out that I had cancer, I was fortunate because I detected it early. I still had to go through surgery, chemo, and radiation. It was a long eight months in 1997.

It was an opportunity to get closer to my Savior. Med's grandson Ron once came to my house when my husband, Jim, was out of town and helped my son administer a blessing to me when I was not feeling well. I did not know then that his grandma had gone through the same thing. Ron's wife, Lisa has gone through breast cancer for the past year and is now being treated for a type of blood cancer. I am thankful for the priesthood and improved technology.

Robert Franklin and Mary Josephine
Martin Smith, 1910 Kelsey.

Lacoleon Smith and Alma Leroy Means on their
wedding day, January 25, 1933, Kelsey

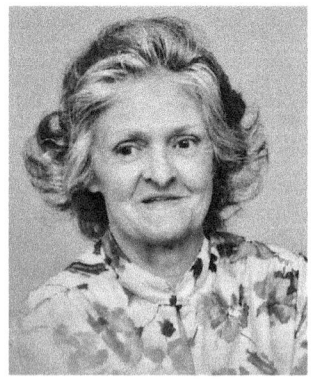

Velda Maleese Smith Bowers.

CHAPTER 21

The Rose in the Forest

Mary Josephine Martin was born in January 1858 in Yazoo County, Mississippi. She had seven brothers and five sisters. She was always honest in her dealings with others. She was a good worker and did anything that needed to be done.

She married Robert Franklin Smith in 1880. She signed her orphan block "Joe Smith."

Robert Franklin was first married to Mary Catherine Jones in 1874, and they had three children when his first wife died in 1879.

The 1880 census says Frank was twenty-nine, Joe was twenty- two, Amanda five, and Jack three. The baby Maude had just died.

She started married life with an instant family of three, and then they had six children: five girls and one boy. All were born in Yazoo County.

The Smiths sold their home in December 1904 and moved to Kelsey, where they could worship without persecution.

Grandma Smith, through her early training, became a very compassionate person. This was a great help during the Church's early years when there was much persecution. When she came to Kelsey and joined the Relief Society, it strengthened her even more in compassionate service.

Grandma Smith gave a lifetime of service. She often sat with the sick or helped care and dress the dead.

When the tornado of 1908 hit Kelsey and tore up seventeen homes, Grandpa, who is quite sickly and feeble, was home alone. Grandma was gone to sit with the sick.

When Grandma Smith's mother died in 1891, she left a quilt that she started for her youngest son. Mary Josephine promised to finish it for her brother, and she did. It's a beautiful quilt called "The Rose in the Forest." I marvel at the artistry. Such delicate stitches! She didn't give it to her brother however. He joined the mob to persecute the "Mormons" in Mississippi. She gave it to her only son, my father. He passed it on to his first daughter, Lacoleon, and she passed it on to her first daughter, Patricia. It is still on display in Kelsey It is old and began over one hundred years ago. It took several years to complete. It was never used. When I was a child. We were only allowed to look at the beauty of it. The colors have faded, but it's still very beautiful to me.

In 1894, Grandma Smith inherited eighty acres and money to build a house from her father. She moved into their new home in 1895.

In February 1898, the Mormon missionaries came to their home. The missionaries were welcomed, and they taught many people in the area. The Smiths were taught and touched by the spirit.

They were baptized in 1898, along with many others; Grandma Smith's family disowned her when she was baptized. Some people in the area were prejudiced against the missionaries and those who accepted the Gospel. As the missionaries continued to teach and baptize, mobs were formed, and the missionaries were threatened.

When the missionaries were forced to move out of the area, the destruction of homes and families began, but the missionaries did not forget the Saints they had left behind. When they heard of the Mormon settlement in Kelsey, they passed the word along to the members.

Contributed by Sherri Smith 2020

I am unsure whether she has the quilt or if someone else in the family has it. I hope to see it someday. Quilting was an everyday thing for the sisters in Kelsey. They taught quilting to the girls at a very young age. A lot of the Kelsey kids remembered playing under the quilting frames. Some frames were placed on stands on the floor, but some sisters had them attached to the ceiling to be raised when they needed the room to be cleared.

My aunt Ethel taught me to quilt. I often had a quilt going. Olive helped me when I made them for my babies. It is a great place to bond with friends and family. It's kind of like hunting is for men and boys. Quilting is *the rose in my forest*. My son Forrest loves quilts more than any of my kids. I sent Mary Josephine's and her I I granddaughter Velda Meleese Smith's block to her daughter Patrice Denkers in Oregon.

Velda was born in 1913 and has four brothers and four sisters. She was born just a few days before Halloween so that probably was a holiday she enjoyed. When I looked at her birth record, I noticed Belle Cummins was the midwife. Belle filled out the paperwork. I recognized Belle's handwriting. So I looked at all her siblings; sure I enough, Belle was there for most of them. But then I noticed Moroni Hamberlin signed several of them as the medical witness.

When I couldn't find much written on Velda, I felt terrible. It reminded me that we all must write down what we know about our I loved ones, so they are not forgotten. It also reminded me of the movie Coco. I never want them to be forgotten.

Velda's father, John Bunion Taylor Smith, did write the following! history, which helped me to understand where Carrie Lamarchand Dilley got her name.

A great many of the Saints moved to Kelsey, a Mormon colony in the Piney woods of Upshur County in East Texas. These included the Hamberlins, Slaters, Futrells, Dawsons, Cargils, Dillys, Isonhoods, my father's family, and others. My parents got the spirit of gathering and moved to Kelsey on January 25, 1905, but before they moved, my baby sister, Bonnie, passed away. When my parents left Yazoo County, I would not go with them. I was going with a girl named Lemarchand

Dilly, and we were planning on getting married, but she passed away on August 19, 1905, and was laid to rest in the Phoenix Cemetery. And then, on the first day of September 1905, my beloved sister, Carrie Bell, passed away and was buried in the Kelsey Cemetery.

That was indeed a bitter stroke to me. Two that I dearly loved taken away at the same time. When my father left Yazoo County, I kissed my dear sister, Carrie, goodbye. Now she always called me Bud. She said, "Bud, I will never see you again in this life." I laughed at that but later lamented that I didn't take her prophecy seriously. But I want to say that she will see me in the presence of the Lord in the next life.

It was during these lonely days that I reflected upon the teachings of my very dear friend, Frank Jardine, to always, in times of trouble, remember your best friend, our Redeemer, and seek him in humble prayer. He will give you aid and comfort, and this is the thing that I did and found great comfort in so doing. Frank's teachings have gone with me through my life, and he will ever be a shining light for this poor mortal body of mine and has held me from sin many times.

After the death of Lemarchand and Carrie, I was so broken up that I was almost mad, so I decided to go to Kelsey. My sister, Willy Dilley, her children, and I left Yazoo on November 24, 1905, and arrived in Kelsey on the twenty-fifth, ten months after my parents left Yazoo County.

Lacoleon doesn't have a block in the quilt, but she wrote her family's history.

My Memories of Grandma Smith By Lacoleon Smith Means

There could be a history book written about Grandma Smith if I were only familiar with the facts. She was reared in a large family of twelve children in and around Yazoo, Mississippi. One thing is for sure: she wasn't afraid of work. I never heard her ever mention anything about going to school. Cousin Rae Cargel recently told me that before Grandma was married, she never had to be told to do anything. Rae said, "She would take hold and do anything there was to be done, regardless of where or what it was. Shingling a house or anything else." Ray also said, "Grandma was always truthful and honest in all that she did."

After Grandpa died in 1914, Grandma lived alone at their homeplace in Kelsey. She had about an acre of land, which she would plant nearly half of it in cotton, the rest in corn—enough for her meals and grain for her chickens. The chickens furnished her with plenty of eggs and meat. She had a few fruit trees, peaches, apples, plums, two medlars, and two fig bushes. This was enough to furnish her in fruit and have some to sell.

She also had some grapevines and a blackberry row all the way across her patch. Each year, she would make blackberry wine for medical purposes (diarrhea and upset stomach).

Many people came to her for wine in case of emergency. There is an herb that she called senna. She always had a row of that to be used as a purgative. It was a small plant with beautiful yellow flowers. When the leaves were ready, we would strip the leaves from the stems and dry them in the shade, then pulverize the leaves and package them to sell for twenty-five cents per package. Most everyone around used it. We would help her work her patch then she would help us. When Dad killed hogs, she was always there to help us. It always fell my lot to help her cut the fat and cook out the lard, make the souse meat, and grind the sausage. We always cut and hauled her wood for her cookstove as well as for her heater.

Each spring and summer, she would hoe cemetery lots for people who had moved away to help out on her budget.

One day, she went out to trade a setting of eggs with one of her neighbors so she could set her hen. She put her eggs in her big apron pocket, and on the way, she fell and broke her arm and all of her eggs. I had to stay with her until she was able to do for herself again.

In her spare time, Grandma pieced and sometimes quilted quilts for the public. Many times, she would piece quilts on the half for people.

In about the middle of Grandma's garden patch, she had a storm cellar where she stored part of her canned goods. But what it was used most was for protection against storms. When the weather was so unsettled many times, we would spend a big part of the night out there. How glad I was when we could go to the house and go to bed! Brother and Sister Ellett were always at the cellar with Grandma almost every time it lightninged.

Grandma was a perfect housekeeper. She had a feather bed, which she kept all fluffed up all the time. We didn't dare get against it. In the wintertime, we liked to go to Grandma's house and bog up in her feather bed on cold nights.

It was a thrill to us to think Grandma would spend the night with us. We would get after her to go home with us, and she would say, "Oh, I don't sleep good on someone else's bed." We thought that was so strange because we always liked to go to Grandma's and sleep.

We always liked to go to Grandma's and eat her good cooking. How good those big hot biscuits and butter were. They would almost melt in your mouth. And her cakes were delicious. When she made a cake, it was always a jelly cake or a coconut cake. If she didn't have coconut, she would put the egg white frosting on it anyway.

Grandma did drink her coffee and dipped her stuff, for which she will pay the penalty; despite all that, she did lots of good in her community. When she was needed with the sick or anything, she was always there. She and Sister Belle Cummins spent lots of time together. They would spend the night with each other, and they spent lots of time reading until bedtime. Another thing Grandma Smith did to pass the time was crochet, and she did some of the most beautiful work a person ever saw.

She would wear two or three petticoats when she went out places, and she always had crochet on them and little tucks. She crocheted lace to go around the bottom of them. She kept two to be buried in and kept them done up spick-and-span, ready for use. She kept them in her trunk, showed us where they were, and told us what to do when she died. She kept them all freshly starched and ironed. She wore skirts gathered full and blouses. For everyday wear, she wore an apron with a big pocket on it for her box of snuff and snuff brush.

She always wore her hair balled upon the top of her head until the last few years of her life when she had it cut short. I was in my teens before she had it cut.

She taught me how to chop cotton, but it is funny; she did not teach me how to like it.

Grandma Smith had always told us that she hoped she'd never be sick a long time for folks to wait on, and she wasn't sick only about fifteen days before she died.

We (Roy and I) had moved from Shady Grove, Texas, into the house with her on the last of December 1932 before she died on February 10, 1933. After she got sick, Mother and Dad came down and stayed with us through her illness. The weather was so bad then. Everything was frozen over, and the roads to town were impassible at this time. There was not a family in the community without sick folks.

The Relief Society presidency were the only ones, Blanche Bell and Daisy Jones, free to help anyone. Old Sister Creel was buried the day Grandma died. There was a double funeral held for Grandma and Brother J. S. Prather. They had to break the ice to dig the graves.

There was no funeral home or cars at that time, so Heber Jones went to town in his big flatbed truck, brought the caskets out, and took them to the cemetery for burial. We nearly froze before the funeral was over.

Each time I read a story, it brings all my childhood memories back. Funny, the things you remember. My grandma Whitlock (Martha Baker) was tall and thin with black hair until the day she died. I spent many nights with her at her house when I was little, but she lived with us from when I was ten until I was fourteen, and she died at our house. She wore an apron with pockets that she kept her handkerchief in. She liked to dip snuff; in her later years, she would have snuff in the corners of her mouth she wiped with her handkerchief. I still have six of her handkerchiefs in my drawer.

She made cornbread on a skillet on top of the stove. I loved to spend the night with her. She always made me feel special even though I had forty-eight cousins. I can still see her smile and the little twinkle in her eyes. One was brown, and one was blue-gray from the cataract that covered it and probably made her almost blind. She never complained about anything.

Back: Andrew, Myrtle, Hester. Front: Willian H.,
Chauncey, Margaret, and Horace Jones, 1961 in Kelsey,
the year before Emil, their last child was, born

Back row: Chauncey, Andrew, Horace, and Emil Jones.
Front row: Chauncey's wife, Elsie Stark, Hester Jones Means,
Myrtle Jones Woodward, and Emil's wife, Melba Brown.

CHAPTER 22

The Real Myrtle Jones

Myrtle Jones was tough to find because she didn't marry until October 1929. Because I had Jones already, I was looking for someone married to Jones. I was so happy when I found one in Upshur County. She was married to Chester Jones. He was twenty-six, and she was twenty-one. They came from Arkansas and had a new baby girl named Marian Ruth. She sounded perfect.

I made her a family tree with all her ancestors, but her maiden name was Roark, and I couldn't connect her to the Kelsey Jones in my tree. I couldn't connect her with anyone, but I found a descendant who was happy to have the quilt block.

She lived in California and owned an antique shop. We talked on the phone and sent emails back and forth. She was so excited to learn about her family, but she said they had no Church of Jesus Christ of Latter-day Saints members in her family. At first, I thought the sisters in the quilt had just been her friend and invited her to quilt. I sent her the orphan block that Myrtle Jones had made. She was so excited and told me how this had taken her back to remember her grandmother and how much she had loved her, and I sent her all the old photos of Myrtle Roark Jones that I had found. She loved them.

It was weeks later that I came across a picture of the Kelsey band, and there was a picture of the real Myrtle Jones. My heart dropped.

I knew I had sent the block to the wrong person. What was I going to do? Ask for it back? I felt terrible at first.

I felt much better when I started the tree for the real Myrtle Jones. I knew it was sent to the right person. I sent the person an email and told her I was sorry, but I had found the real one I had been looking for. I told her that her grandmother didn't make it but that I hoped that every time she looked at it in the frame where she had put it, she would think of Myrtle Roark Jones, and she could remember the 1929 quilters.

I had told her what I knew about them at the time. She offered to return it. I knew Myrtle would want her to keep it. I knew she would think of her grandmother when she looked at it.

The real Myrtle Jones was Lenora Myrtle Jones, and she wrote her own life story, so I will let her tell you all about herself.

Th Story of My Life By Myrtle Jones Woodard Gray

I was born on August 15, 1900, to William Harrison and Margaret Motes Jones in Horner, Perry County, Tennessee. I was blessed by elders of the Church of Jesus Christ of Latter-day Saints and given the name of Lenora Myrtle Jones.

I had a sister ten years older than me. Her name was Samantha Evalena Jones. She was born on December 16, 1889. We called her Lena. She was very good to me, and I liked her very much.

My other brothers and sisters, except John, were younger than me. John was born in 1899 and died a few hours after birth. Andrew Jackson Jones was born in 1902.

My father didn't talk much about his relatives. His father and his mother both died when he was quite young. I never did hear him mention his father's name.

All I remember is that his father was a hooper, a maker of barrels and kegs. His mother's name was Mary Minerva Morgan Jones. He said that when he was a young boy, he had only one suit of clothes a year.

His mother spun the thread on a spinning wheel, wove the cloth on a loom, and then cut out and sewed up the cloth by hand. They had no machines. My father said he had sat up many nights and held a candle for his mother to see to do all of these things.

He had a sister named Mary and a brother named Andrew Jackson; when his mother died, he lived a while with his uncle. The uncle's wife was mean to him, so he ran away. He never heard from any of his family after that.

He worked for other people at whatever he could get to do, which mainly was farming. But somehow, in his travels, he learned to fix watches, clocks, and sewing machines. He then made his living at that trade.

We have never found much genealogy about my father's ancestors or kindred. My brother Andrew spent a lot of time and money trying to find more genealogy but was unable to find anything he could be sure of.

When we lived in Tennessee, we had services at the home of a member of the Latter-day Saints Church every Sunday. I can remember that we crossed over a small mountain to get there. It seemed like a giant mountain to me, but it was small compared to the mountains in the west. My brother, Andrew, and I walked, and my father pulled Hester and Heber in a little wagon to the place where the services were held. We enjoyed the trip and services.

One Sunday, an old man appeared in the congregation. He preached to the people. No one saw him when he came or left; some people looked for him to invite him to dinner, but he couldn't be found. He appeared several times and preached to the people. He preached the same doctrine that the people of the Church of Jesus Christ of Latter-day Saints believed. Some people ask him to baptize them. He said he couldn't because he didn't have the power, but soon, two men would come who would have the authority to baptize them.

Soon two elders of the Mormon Church came, and a good many of the people were baptized by them. The strange old man quit coming, and no one knew where he went or where he came from. The people there who were Mormons or Latter-day Saints thought he might be one of the three Nephites or John the Beloved.

My father never joined the Mormon Church. I don't know why because he believed the doctrine. My mother, my older sister, my mother's father and mother, and one of my other sisters joined the Church.

At the time they joined, there was much prejudice against the Mormons in Tennessee, where they lived, so I think they were brave to join. There was so much prejudice that year where they lived, a mob came one night and shot and killed two elders who were holding a cottage meeting at the home of one of the members. One of the family's sons was also killed. The elders' names were Elder Berry and Elder Gibbs. They were buried secretly by the members of the Church. Their families wanted their bodies brought back to Utah for burial. Brother Brigham H. Roberts was sent to Tennessee to get their bodies. He was dressed in disguise as an old farmer. One of the members drove to the train station in a wagon to meet Brother Roberts. The elders' bodies were sent back to Utah for a proper burial. The member who met Brother Roberts was Church, and he also took Brother Roberts and the elders' bodies back to meet the train.

After my father and mother heard through the missionaries of a place in Texas where there was a Mormon colony, they had thought of moving to Utah but decided it would be too cold there. They then moved to Kelsey, Texas. I was seven years old at that time. It was the first time I had seen or ridden on a train.

We came as far as Gilmer, Texas, on the train, then hired a carriage to take us out to Kelsey, which was about six miles from Gilmer.

Arrangements had been made by the branch president for a place for us to stay. We stayed with some people by the name of Lee for a few days until we found a house to rent. We didn't stay there long before my father and mother found a house with a few acres of land, which they bought. The first people who lived in Kelsey were two converts from Alabama, John and Jim Edgar. They came there in the late 1890s, and soon after, a few other families, mainly from the South, were attracted to the area.

They held their first meetings under an old oak tree and later studied the Book of Mormon in their homes. I heard a log chapel was built first, but when we moved there in December 1907, they had a three-room lumber building, which was used both as a church and schoolhouse.

I didn't go to school the first year we were there. I cried when Mother started to get me dressed to go, so she didn't make me go as I didn't know any of the other children. By the following year, I had got acquainted with some of the children and wanted to go. I made two grades that year.

They came from Salt Lake and laid out the townsite. Families from the Southern states who had been converted continued to be attracted to the locality. In 1907, there were seventy families, but by 1910, 103 families were there.

A nice wood chapel was built in 1910, beautifully located on a hill in the center of Kelsey. Most of the lumber was sawed by a sawmill, which was owned by a member of the church who had moved into Kelsey. By 1912, a two-story brick school building was finished, and our first school was held. We were all very proud of both the chapel and the school.

The Kelsey Saints were enthusiastic boosters of their little gathering place. A pamphlet published in 1911 proclaimed, "All the good things grow in Upshur County; a man can live better with less work in Upshur County than any other place in the world."

The people at Kelsey had started from scratch. Now they had houses, a church, a school, and stores and had planted trees and shrubs. At one time, there were three stores, the sawmill, a cotton gin, the church, and a school, so the people of Kelsey had a reason for pride.

Nonmembers in the surrounding areas were not always so enthusiastic about the Mormon colony. There were occasional flare-ups of hostility. One time, there was a threat that a group of nonmember men were coming to Kelsey to burn all the houses. We were asked by our branch president to pray for our safety. This we did.

On the night the men were to come, a big rain came, and they backed out of coming. A nonmember who lived near Kelsey told my father that it was true. They met at his place with their kerosene, matches, and other things needed, but the rain came and they didn't come to Kelsey. They never talked of burning the colony again.

But even the non-Mormons had to admire what the hard work and cooperation of the Latter-day Saints accomplished. They didn't have much to do with us except in business ways, but we enjoyed each other. The non-Mormons liked to come to our July 24, picnics. Every year on July 24, we had a picnic in celebration of the day the pioneers arrived in the Salt Lake Valley. A free dinner furnished by the Kelsey people was always served. Everybody went all out to prepare good food to take to the dinner. Everybody enjoyed it. I think a lot of people came just for the good free dinners that were served.

In the morning, a program was usually put on, and then in the afternoon, they had races and other games for the children. Stands were put up where homemade ice cream and lemonade were sold. That night, they usually had a dance. The money raised from these projects was used to pay the expenses of the church.

My school days seem to pass pretty quickly. When I finished all that was taught in our school, I decided I wanted to teach. At that time, we didn't have to go to college before we taught. We took a teacher's examination at the county seat. If we passed it, we got a teacher's certificate. I started teaching when I was nineteen years old. I taught the first and second grades at Kelsey. I enjoyed teaching very much.

Our first schools had no desks in them. We sat on a long bench and laid our books on the bench by the side of us. We recited our lessons on other long benches facing the teacher's desk. We didn't have many books. One reader lasted us all year. The lower grades had reading, spelling, and arithmetic. The upper grades had these subjects and geography and history. The parents had to buy the books then, so some children had no books at all. My parents managed to get books for us. It was hard to learn much without books.

We didn't have much playground equipment. The fathers made a few seesaws and swings. We made balls from twine. We played singing games like "Marching round the Levy" and others.

There were a lot of young people in Kelsey when I was a teenager and a little older. We had a lot of good times together. A group of us would meet almost every Sunday afternoon at someone's house and sit and chat. We all liked to sing. We had choir practice every Saturday night. Our good mission, President Samuel O. Bennion, sent missionaries to help us with our singing, lead the choir, and teach us music. We had a band for a while. President Bennion sent a band leader to help us get started.

We played for the fair, jamborees, and a few other things in Gilmer and put on programs at Kelsey. By this time, there was another little colony near us. It was called Enoch. We had a dance hall at both Kelsey and Enoch. Sometimes we would go to dances at Enoch. We went in a wagon pulled by horses or mules. There were very few cars at that time.

We put chairs in the wagon to sit on. We would all sing going and coming. We sang both popular and religious songs. After a while, both dance halls were burned down the same night. No one knew who burned them, but new ones never were built in their place.

Our home life was good. We weren't rich, but we had plenty to eat and plenty of good clothes to wear. We always had a vegetable garden that furnished a lot of our food. We raised hogs and chickens for meat and eggs. Mother helped other people can fruit. They repaid her by giving her fruit for our family. She could sew well and made most of our clothes, even our winter coats and the boys' suits.

Father worked as a jeweler. He fixed watches, clocks, and sewing machines for a living. There wasn't enough work in Kelsey, so he traveled on foot over the county to get more work. Sometimes he would be gone a week or two at a time. By doing this, he made a pretty good living. There were six of us children at home at one time in our life.

My sister Lena married before we left Tennessee, so she didn't come to Texas with us. Lena had four children, and she died during the pregnancy with the last one. Only one of them lived to be grown.

We were all musically inclined. My father was a very good all-time fiddler. I have never seen anyone better. I learned to count on the organ to his music. My brother Heber picked the guitar and sometimes the mandolin. We all could sing and enjoyed it. We sang together quite a bit. I sang a lot of solos. My sister and I sang duets together at home. We sang quartets; two brothers could sing bass, and another tenor.

I joined the choir when I was quite young. We were taught music along with our choir practice, the notes time, the different keys, and so forth. In a few years, I was made director of the choir. I held that position for seven years. I also held other positions in the church.

I met Etheridge at one of our conferences in Kelsey. It was the only branch in the South at that time, so all of the conferences were held there. We enjoyed them very much.

Etheridge and I married at the beginning of the Depression, so we had some hard times. Neither of us had any money. I helped my father and mother and the children at home with most of mine. One winter of the Depression was really hard. We lived mostly on milk and bread. I remember for Christmas dinner. We had milk and bread with egg custard. After that, I got to teach school, and Etheridge worked part–time in the oil fields. Later he got permanent work.

Myrtle married Emerson Etheridge Woodard in October 1929 in Miller, Arkansas. It was just a few miles from where they lived in Cass, Texas, on the 1930 census.

He was a farmer, but they did move back to Kelsey by the July 24 big celebration in 1930 because her first son was born on that day in Kelsey.

She was teaching school, and Emerson was still farming on the 1940 census of Kelsey, Texas. They had two sons: William Pressler, ten, and Lawrence Ebberson, five.

She taught school for forty-one years. She lost her husband in 1964 and her oldest son, William, in 1977. He had married Carma Rae Hatch of Vernal, Utah, and they had three daughters.

Her second son, Dr. Lawrence Ebberson Woodard, married Marilyn Messeldine. They had one son and two daughters.

His obituary says Dr. Woodard dedicated his life to serving others twice as a full-time missionary and for forty-six years as a teacher. First, as a high school debate coach, he groomed his students at Excelsior High School to win the California State Championship of the National Forensic League. After earning his doctorate at Brigham Young University, he coached debate and taught speech and theater at Brigham Young University, James Madison University, Bridgewater College, and Eastern Arizona University. He finally retired as a professor at Southeastern Louisiana University. He was a dedicated leader in the Church of Jesus Christ of Latter-day Saints, serving as bishop in Hammond, Louisiana. She didn't have a lot of posterity at the time of her death, but they are still growing, and I know she is proud of them. She is the real Myrtle Jones.

Audrey and Laura Bryant. High school
days in Kelsey. 1928, Kelsey.

Laura Bryant became a nurse.

Back: Myron, Early, Carl, and Lelia Irene.
Front: Audrey, Nomie Church, Emmons,
Robert, and Pauline Bryant, 1920, Kelsey.

Carl and Julia Hamberlin Bryant's barn. 2023, Kelsey

CHAPTER 23

The Bryants

Laura, Pauline, and Audrey Bryant are the daughters of Robert Emmons Bryant and Margaret Nomie Church. They each have a block in the quilt and were born in Kelsey.

To understand the Bryants, we must start with the parents, and Nomie Church helped by writing an autobiography.

Margaret Nomie Church Bryant

I was born in 1879. My parents are William Leonidas Lorenzo Church and Callie Dona Letsinger. We lived at Duck River in Tennessee, and Pa fished. He always wanted me to paddle the boat for him.

When I was five, my two younger brothers, William and John, and I were blessed by Elders John H. Gibbs and William S. Berry. Both of these elders were killed by a mob the very next day.

I was baptized when I was fourteen in 1895. I went to school until the fourth grade. I was the only Mormon girl, and the others shunned Mormons.

I have known Bob, my husband, all my life. He used to take me to school on his horse. One time, he went to Idaho to visit his sister, and while there, he went to a carnival. He decided to give a man a dime to find out what his future wife would look like. When he got the dime out, he saw my face. He came back to Tennessee and started going with me and other girls. One day, Bob told me that if I would marry him, he would buy me lots of pretty dresses.

A few days later, when all the family was gone, I put on Ma's best dress, put her saddle on my horse, and went to meet Bob. Mom saw me leave, and when I crossed the bridge on Duck River, she guessed where I was going. Bob and I got the license, went back to his house, and got married. He already had a house built to live in. We went home the next day and told my mother and father, but they didn't say much. (They were married on February 17, 1897. I was born fifty years to the day later.)

My father and mother moved to Texas about 1901, then to Oklahoma. Then we came to Oklahoma when Earley Belle was three in about 1903. It was a wild place with fine land and lots of cattle. We lived in an Indian man's place, and he was good to us. We could just drive us a cow and milk all we wanted, and wild hogs were plentiful in the pecan bottoms, but there were no good houses to live in and no church or school close to go to.

Our few neighbors didn't go anywhere, only visiting on Sunday. We had a father, mother, brothers, and sisters but were not satisfied to not have a church.

(Leila Irene was born in 1903 in Oklahoma.)

One day when I was going to get a bucket of water, I looked down and picked up a little gold dollar. I had never seen a gold dollar before. On a little farther, I picked up a little gold ring, so I ran back to the house. Bob was fixing to go to the little store and post office, so I wrapped up the little dollar and sent for the Deseret News. One came to us soon, and there was a piece in the paper about Kelsey, a Mormon community in

Texas, in 1904. It wasn't long before we came to Kelsey and bought this place. We have left, but we have always come back. We went to Oklahoma just before Carl was born. It took us three weeks to get there. We got there, and Carl was born the next night.

(In September 1905, Carl married Julia Hamberlin.) Back in Kelsey, they had four more children. Myron Bryant was born in 1909, Laura Pauline in 1911, and Audrey in 1913. And the last, Emmons Church Bryant, was born in 1916.

We went to the temple when Audrey was four months old and stayed in Salt Lake for a while. We went back to Tennessee, but it was so far for Earley and Lelia to walk to school that they wanted to come back to Kelsey, where they could go to school, as they knew we had a good one here. The missionaries used to teach here and were teaching then. We always had lots of missionaries. They always liked to stay with us. When Emmons was a little boy, some elders were here, and he told them he was always glad to have elders come because he knew we were going to have a good dinner, but that ended as time went on. The elders would come and stay with us for weeks at a time in Tennessee.

My grandfather, Isaac Emmons Church, had a brother, Hayden Wells, Church, who joined the Mormon Church and went to Nauvoo. He crossed the plains and settled in St. George. I have heard they lived in St. George, and some are still there.

One of his great-grandsons was here at Kelsey on a mission years ago when we first came here.

When President Bennion was mission president, we sure had a good time with so many conferences. He always came here and stayed with us and would stay here and visit all the saints and have conference with lots of missionaries and good speaking for two or three days.

I was sick for a long time with gallstones. We sold out and went to Arizona. Brother and Sister McGinty and family went with us on the train. Earley took care of Emmons since he was small.

We got to Arizona and lived in Brother Ault's place, close to Oscar Ray and Brother Ault's father and mother. We went to church in Gilbert, Arizona, and the children went there to school. There was a nice church there, but I had to go to the doctor at Mesa very often and got better. Brother Posey and family came to our place. They had the flu, and most of us took the flu, and after that, the children had measles. All were really sick except Myron. He went to bed and covered his head and was soon well.

We were there two years, and we lived next to the railroad. One day, Emmons was playing out close to the railroad and came dragging up a snake. It was dead, but that didn't keep it from scaring us all. He was just two years old, and all the children picked cotton. There was a lot of it. Laura and Audrey decided they wouldn't pick, so Bob told them if they didn't pick, just quit eating. They did just one time but soon fell in line. We were there two years and went to Utah in 1919. I did love to go to church in Gilbert. The church leaders were from Mexico and were good leaders.

I am so thankful that so many of the quilters left their histories and shared how they felt about things. I loved reading about their lives, but the more I read, I found they had so many of the same life experiences that I did. It was scary. Laura Bryant wrote her life history also.

My Life: Birth to High School Graduation

I, Laura Pauline Bryant Strasburg, was born October 4, 1911, in Kelsey, Upshur County, Texas. I was the fifth child of seven children born to this union. I was born about sundown in a two-story, six-room home attended by Dr. SW Craddock of Latch, Texas, and Belle Cummins, a midwife. I weighed five and a half pounds at birth. I was blessed by Oscar Ray at the Kelsey Church of Jesus Christ of Latter-day Saints, on November 5, 1911, but I was just a few months old. I took quite sick with the intestinal flu and wasn't expected to live, so they say. But my mother was a good nurse; at that time, she was also nursing a baby boy, a neighbor the same age. In those days, bottle-fed babies were unheard of, and a lot of babies died from starvation or else had to live on what they called sugar teats.

I started school at the age of six years to a man by the name of Landy Foster. I thought at that time he was an old man, but he must've been only about twenty-five years of age. He was really strict, and I was scared to death of him. I had to sit in a broken- down desk, and when my only book would fall out on the floor, he would have me bring it up to him at the front of the room. He would hit the book with a ruler and tell it to stay in place, which would scare me as I must've been timid and shook up from the experience. I only went to him for a short time.

At about this time, my mother was sick a lot of the time, and my father sold the farm we were living at and moved to Gilbert, Arizona. This was about 1917. I went to school in Gilbert a short time. All I remember about the school is I took every disease that came along, and whereas I wasn't very sick from the diseases, the older brothers and sisters really suffered.

I learned to swim in the irrigation ditch. I remember my brother Myron being a sleepwalker and nearly getting kicked by a horse at night. Oh, how Carl could ride horses so fast. At about this time, the brothers tried to smoke, how Papa whipped him, and how scared we all were.

My sister Lelia made such good cookies in the home economics class. The bread was so terrible at this time due to the war. Also, the water in Arizona was worse to drink than taking medicine like Epsom salt.

In 1918, Audrey and I hated to work so bad, especially picking cotton. It was tall and sometimes had worms on it so we decided to quit. My dad had a rule. "If one didn't work, one didn't eat." We didn't go without eating long. We soon started to pick cotton and work.

It was about this time I had a sick spell. It must've been rheumatic fever, for I was really sick and would beg an old neighbor man to come and minister to me, but he wasn't even a Church member. We lived next to the railroad track, and how we loved to watch the trains go by.

There was a large hay barn about two blocks away from the house we lived in, and one night late, the barn filled with hay caught fire and burned to the ground, which almost took our house as the sparks, and real big ones, fell on the roof.

In 1919, we left Arizona to go to Utah as my mother wasn't getting any better and was referred to the Salt Lake clinic doctors. Mother had been ill for years with gallbladder trouble. My older sister, Earley, kept a diary of the trip. My father went to Salt Lake with my mother to see the doctors and have her operated on.

He then came back to Price and chartered a railroad car to bring the horses and wagons back to Texas. With Earley and Lily in charge, the other brothers and sisters came by train back to Texas to my grandparents' home. What a trip, what a bunch, and what a site we were.

Emmons would cry and scream that he didn't want to get on an old train. They were so crowded, and we would have to lay over at several places on the way for hours. Also, Audrey and I would be put on the floor so others could have the seats. I remember getting to Grandma's, and they even had a telephone on the wall.

What a good cook Grandma was, and her biscuits! No one could make better on the whole earth.

Papa arrived several days later than we did. When we got back to Texas, my father rented a place in Eden until we could get back to the old place He bought the same place back, paying $1,000 more than when we left, and the place was nearly wrecked in the two years we were away.

My mother was operated on for gallstones and had over one hundred removed. She was in the LDS hospital for forty days and nights. Her doctor was Dr. Ralph Richards, who I later came to know and helped with operations at the LDS hospital while I was in the nurse's training. I cared for his mother several times when she lived at the Covey Apartments in Salt Lake City.

I started school at Gilmer but only went a few days, I think, then we moved to Kelsey. When I started going to school at Kelsey, Myrtle Jensen was my teacher, then Susie Wade.

I was baptized on June 5, 1920, by O'Dell Ellett in Kelsey, Texas, in what is now called Virgil's Pond, confirmed by Charles F. Bell on June 6, 1920, at the Kelsey church.

The family always said when I was little that I was a tomboy and loved to climb trees, run, and play ball. One day, I broke my arm at the wrist. How it hurt! Dr. SW Craddock of Latch, Texas, came to set up for me. No, nothing for the pain. He put a tight splint on my arm, and that night, I was suffering so bad that my mother loosened the bandage as my fingers were so swollen and had turned black pretty soon. Everything got all right, but it about cured my tree climbing, except for persimmons. I learned early to help my mother milk the cows, something my dad would never do. Although he did love good milk. One thing we always had plenty of was good milk to drink. Also, we had good meat, bread, syrup, and vegetables. I learned to help with the housework. I helped do many jobs in the field, such as chopping and hoeing cotton and planting, hoeing peanuts, and planting and stripping cane.

When Taylor Smith was making our cane into the syrup, he was the best syrup maker in the county. Once a bunch of kids were playing too close, and I ran by just as he was skimming the foam from the cooking juice of the cane being made into syrup. A big ladle of hot foam struck the side of my face. It didn't burn too bad, but oh the excitement. It sure wasn't a place for kids to play, and I should've had a licking but didn't. It was my own fault.

I also thinned corn and helped gather it in the fall. I helped to saw and cut wood. It took a lot during the winter and to cook with. I would grumble at Aubrey because she wouldn't pull the saw like I thought she ought to.

I loved to drive and ride horses while they baled the hay and took water to the hired hands. I was a good cotton picker. I could keep up with anyone. The most I ever picked in one day was 222 pounds, and that is a lot of cotton.

In the fall each year, at hog-killing time, Audrey and I would run and cover our eyes and ears so we wouldn't hear or see the hogs killed. We couldn't stand to hear the loud squealing, but after, we enjoyed the good meat.

Mama could make the best sausage and soap, and we would stir it in the big black kettle outside.

One day while we were playing close by, Papa and my brothers were cutting wood. An axe flew off the handle and struck Audrey in the leg. It was terrible, but it healed up good and had no aftereffects; Audrey seemed to have lots of accidents.

My brother Myron had his eye put out by a friend who wanted to show him he could throw a piece of glass. It struck Myron and put out his eye. How bad the folks all felt at the time. Myron had his head bandaged up, and they brought him a little hatchet. As he was cutting wood on a block one day, Audrey, who was learning to walk, came and put her hand on the block just as he chopped. It got her left hand, almost cutting off two fingers. My mother is a good nurse. She hurriedly stuck the fingers back together, put a sugar and turpentine poultice, bandaged them up, fasted, and prayed. Then in due time, they healed with not much stiffness and only scars around the fingers where they were injured so severely. To me, this was indeed a miracle, for the tendons and nerves were all cut and crushed.

Myron was quite a teaser one Sunday while the folks were to church. He and Audrey wanted to see me walk with my feet tied together. I tried, jumping for a while. I finally fell in the kitchen, striking my chin as my hands were tied. Later on, from the bruises on my chin, it started to swell and hurt. It had to be opened and drained by Dr. Craddock again. That was another misery to me. I have two large scars under my chin today.

We loved to go fishing and swimming. My brothers built a big swimming hole close to home. We had the spring that was really so good. It was a good place, and lots of people came each day to swim. I went to school each year at Kelsey. It was a mile to walk and one big hill to climb. On the way home at 3:30, we would have to hurry home to work.

My schoolteachers were Landy Foster, Myrtle Jones, Susie Wade, Cornelia Hamberlin, Earley Bryant (my sister), Carrie Tolan, Thurza Boyle, Reva Dalton, Bertha Topham, and others I can't remember. Many Mutual teachers, Primary teachers, and Sunday school teachers. I was a Sunday school secretary for years. I enjoyed it very much. Some of the things I remember during the school years were the good times we had. The parties, the May days, and the opossum hunts.

The Halloweens, the candy-making parties, the dances at Kelsey Dance Hall before it was burned down, the watermelons. How Mr. Jones, our neighbor, taught a lesson to the boys who had stolen some of his choice melons.

For a while, about this time, my uncle Gerber came to live with us as his wife got burned to death on Christmas morning. They were always so good to send us presents at Christmastime. Also, after my grandmother Church died, Grandpa Church came and stayed for a while. He could play the violin. We called it a fiddle.

My playmates and best friends were Bertrell and Bonsall Havens, Alice Bender, Virgie Chevalier, Loretta Alexander, Beatrice Bell, Mary Winnie and Mildred Jones, Vera Wade then Lacoleon Smith, Alma Ellsey, Goldie Edgar, and Erma McKnight, my best friend, and many more like Wilma Dotson, and Sarah Ashford.

I remembee one Halloween night Lelia scared us, so Bertrell fell and broke her arm. Earley would love to tease me about the boys. I remember when she and Myrtle Jones went away to Commerce to school or college and some of their experiences where they stayed.

Once each year, the folks' good friends would come and bring a load of melons. That was the W. R. Henderson family, and what a time we would all have.

Earley bought a new car about this time, and how we thought it was super also. Myron got him a little one-seated car with a rumble seat. On Saturdays, I would go to Gilmer with the neighbors. They had a new car, and how great I thought that was. I was really thrilled for Saturdays to come. That was a big day then.

Earley got married to William Harvey Hooper; Lelia went away to work in Missouri for President S. O. Bennion at the mission home. She sent us lots of new dresses. Earley bought me a ring for Christmas, and I lost it.

Some of the boys I dated during high school were Leroy Lindsey, Irvin Henry, Rawleigh Alexander, Joe Corbett, Bob Simmons, and Andrew Bender, and I went steady with Foy Thomas Chevalier until I left home to go to Salt Lake City for training.

I graduated from Kelsey High School in 1929.

I found this story recently and was shocked at the details of her life as it was so much like mine. I was born with an enlarged thymus gland that made it hard for me to breathe. My dad said he used to sit up at night and rock me to ensure I was still breathing.

They gave me large doses of radiation in 1947 to shrink it, and the doctor said if I lived to be three months, I would probably outgrow it. And I did.

I was born in Mesa, but we moved to a farm in Blythe, California, when I was five and starting school. I learned to swim in irrigation canals, chopped and hoed cotton, and hated the times I watched them kill the hogs and ring the chicken's necks. I loved shelling the blackeyed peas and picking watermelon in the fields. I was a tomboy too and loved climbing trees.

When I was four, I fell off the fence where I was watching my dad load the sheep and broke my left wrist. Then when I was five, I accidentally chopped off my brother's pointer finger on his right hand. I cried more than he did. He was three, and the doctor stitched it back on. I thought my brother was the accident- prone one.

My parents smoked, and my brother always tried to smoke. When we played house, we pretended to smoke like they did.

That was not all we had in common. On March 16, 1947, she had a daughter, Laura Pauline Strasburg, who only lived a few hours. They took the baby by C-section because the mom was hemorrhaging.

I was thirty days old when that happened, but it was almost precisely what happened to me twenty years later. The doctor told me they could not hear a heartbeat, so they decided not to do a C-section and let me go through the labor and delivery.

I know what Laura went through, and somehow, it seems so sad to me now, even though I know they are all together again. I know that the hard thing in life make us stronger. I feel such a bond with all the sisters in the quilt—some much more than others.

Laura had married a return missionary who served in the Central States Mission and came from a long history of members. They had one son in 1937, so she had grandkids. She became a nurse and worked in the LDS hospital in Salt Lake City for a while. She was a widow for the last eight years of her life and died at the age of eighty. Reva was one of her teachers and often talks about her and her sister Audrey in the journal.

Audrey Bryant married a young man from Pickett, Tennessee. His name is Leo Virgil Means, and his family joined the Church in 1903 but didn't come to Kelsey until about 1910. His mother, Flora Mae Amonette, came with her mother, Louverna Katherine Boring, when she came to Kelsey.

This is a story by Jennings D. Means that was submitted to FamilySearch by Naomi Jill Means.

In 1910, my great-grandmother, Louverna Katherine, came to Upshur County with her children. Her story was one of sorrow and joy. In 1894, she and her husband John became the first persons in Pickett County, Tennessee, baptized into the Church of Jesus Christ of Latter-day Saints. Even though they had joined such an unpopular cause and faced much prejudice, they were well respected in their community. Even fifteen years later, as I visited Pickett County, I found several old-timers who remembered them with respect. John's friends and neighbors remembered him as a great preacher of righteousness. They said he could quote much of the Bible verbatim.

In those days, the Cumberland plateau was a timberman's paradise with a tremendous virgin forest of substantial tulip poplar trees, some five to ten feet in diameter and nearly two hundred feet tall. Like many of his generation and locality, John was a saw-logger and a timberman. Unfortunately, he suffered an accident when a tree hit him in the head. After that, he had moments of lucidity, but then he would lapse into insanity. Soon, he had to be institutionalized. He died later in a Knoxville, Tennessee, institution, and at his death, one of John's many brothers said of him, "He was the best of us."

With reports from Knoxville evermore discouraging Great-Grandmother, Kate faced a dilemma. She had a large family to support, and even worse, she had marriageable-age children with no prospect of finding other Mormons to marry.

Then some Mormon missionaries came visiting and told her of a Mormon colony in Kelsey, Upshur, Texas. It was not a difficult decision for her to make. She wrote to the presiding elder in Kelsey about the prospect of moving. He returned an answer that she should not come unless she had means of support, for times were very hard with no work available. Fortunately, as the presiding elder later proclaimed, she never received his answer.

Against severe opposition from the Amonette family, who said she was taking John's little children to Texas to starve, she sold their belongings in Tennessee and moved to Kelsey.

Indeed, times were hard, and they suffered much, but the charity of their neighbors was boundless. She and her children found employment working for her neighbors. She was an accomplished seamstress, and they worked on local farms. They prospered, and soon, she owned a small farm of her own and could support her family.

She and her family found the joy and peace in those piney woods they had forsaken all to find. They could worship with others of their faith; her children could marry others of their faith.

In later years, her children blessed her and told her how great a blessing it was to be a part of this community. Kate served her church and community well. Having been a recipient of the charity of her neighbors, she soon became the dispenser of charity to her community. She served several years as president of the women's Relief Society, and her community revered and respected her highly.

In September 1922, after spending her last bit of energy seeing her youngest child firmly situated in a teaching position in Utah, she returned to her beloved Kelsey, very ill.

Her son-in-law, Joe Means, picked her up at the railroad station in Gilmer in a horse-drawn wagon and drove her home. She sang the hymn all the way home, and the remainder of that day, "I Know My Heavenly Father Knows" by S. M. I. Henry. Louverna Catherine Amonette died that evening with that hymn still on her lips. In her last breath, Grandma Kate reaffirmed her faith in God, for whom she had forsaken all.

She was laid to rest in the northwest corner of the Kelsey Cemetery. Her adjoining farm lies about three feet west of her burial site.

This story is of the conversion of John Amonette written by the oldest daughter, Susie Esther Amonette Wade, in Mesa, Arizona, in 1977. It was submitted to FamilySearch by Gene and Joy Wade.

Well, he joined the Mormon Church when I was a baby. Before that, he was a Campbellite. Two elders knocked on the door one day and asked for a place to stay all night. And we just had a small home and a big family. And Mother sent'em to his mother's home because she never turned anybody away and they had more room. But he left a pamphlet. And she was busy fixing dinner. When Dad came in, he saw the pamphlet lying on the table, picked it up, and read it. And he said, "Where did this come from?" She told him about the men coming and leaving it, and he said, "Where they go?" She said, "Up to your mother's," so he went up, got'em, and brought'em back home, and they stayed there and talked about it all night. And they baptized him.

Before they came through, he had decided that the church was not right that he belonged to and told Mother that the church that was right had apostles and prophets, and there wasn't one of that kind on earth. He had ever heard of Mormons.

The neighbors in their story that helped so much were all the sisters in the quilt. Their children grew up, and two of their daughters married sons of Berta Wade. And of course, her daughter, Floy, who married Joe Means, and grandson, Virgil Means, married Audrey Bryant, who has her block in the quilt along with her sister Laura Bryant. Audrey died in 1972 of Alzheimer's disease. She was fiftyeight and had two daughters.

It is truly a blessing to have been on both sides of charity, even though sometimes it is hard to have others help us.

The death certificate of John says the doctor who was with him when he died in the institution in 1915 had been treating him since 1905. He was in the institution for five more years when Kate left Tennessee. That would have been so hard to leave him, but she was blessed to have found Kelsey. She has a great posterity in the Church today.

Laverne Miller Lindsey (Yellow Rose) 1935, Gilmer, Texas.

Hubert and Laverne Miller Lindsey. 1944, California

CHAPTER 24

Blessed

Even amid unique trials and challenges We are truly blessed!

—*Dallin H. Oaks*

I couldn't end these stories without sharing one more that Myrtle often told. I recently found it again written by Steven Lindsey, but he said he had also heard it from his aunt Myrtle many times.

Myrtle's youngest brother, Hubert Hefley Lindsey, was born in 1912. They said he barely survived infancy when he had pneumonia. Thanks to a devoted mother, adoring siblings, the Gilmer doctor who made several carriage trips to the Lindsey home, and the faith of the Kelsey Latter-day Saints community, he survived.

As a young man in the Kelsey LDS branch, Hubert became aware of the Miller girls, as were so many of the young men in the area. There were six of them, and they were all said to be stunningly beautiful.

(They are the daughters of Wade Hampton Miller and Wilhelmina Gertrude Arrington. Ironically, they are the granddaughters of Martha Crouch Morris, the sister of Belle Cummins. That makes Belle their great-aunt. Now Belle Cummins fits into the Lindsey tree. The treads of the quilt and life are never-ending).

Hubert had his eye on one in particular, who had beautiful blonde hair and blue eyes that he often referred to as his "Yellow Rose of Texas." When the older two girls became promised to men, he probably decided he had better make his move on the apple of his eye, Dorothy Laverne Miller, before someone else did.

One day after church services, he asked her to attend a barn dance with him, which was to be held the following weekend in Kelsey. This was in the summer of 1935. He arranged to travel on horseback to Gilmer, where the Millers were living at the time. He had asked his father if he could use the horse to pick up his date for the dance.

They danced, talked, laughed, and overcame their awkwardness with each other during the evening. Laverne was only sixteen, and Huber was twenty-three, soon to be twenty-four years old. The young couple had several dates during the following week.

Apparently, her mother thought Huber was frequenting their home a bit too often. One night, after promising to have Laverne home by 9 p.m., he returned her home a few minutes before the clock struck nine. Laverne invited Huber to sit on the front porch with her and visit while the nine o'clock hour approached.

Right at the stroke of nine, his future mother-in-law came around the corner of the house from the back of the place with a three-foot length of two-by-four in her hands. Hubert did not see her approaching from his rear, so by the time Laverne's horrified expression registered with him, he got clubbed over the head. Dazed, maybe even unconscious, he regained his senses as her mother, Gertie, was ushering LaVerne into the front door, stopping only long enough to hurl the length of lumber in Huber's direction.

Undaunted, Hubert advanced in his efforts to court LaVerne. Within a few weeks after saving up his dollars from hauling hay, cutting sugarcane, and harvesting watermelons through the season, Huber purchased a "friendship ring" for his new love.

Together, they placed it on the ring finger of her right hand. Hubert indicated he wanted to save her left ring finger for an engagement or wedding ring. Laverne was ecstatic and carried away in romantic notions of her Prince Charming, knight in shining armor, and Sir Galahad— all stories she had read in her ten years of school.

She was taken with his good looks, and he was smitten by her personality and beauty. "The very best of all the Miller girls," Hubert often said later in life.

He also, along with several of the other sons-in-law, long declared his mother-in-law to be the meanest biddy ever to walk the face of the earth. He and his brothers-in-law declared that she was just plain too ornery and mean ever to die and that she would probably outlive everyone in the family.

(I imagine she would seem that way if you couldn't see her side of the situation. She was raising six beautiful daughters without the support of a husband, and I am sure she wanted the best for them. Maybe she thought he was too old.)

The very first day, after accepting the friendship ring, Laverne was eager and excited to show it to her future sisters-in-law while they worked in the Gilmer laundry. Laverne stood at her workstation in the center of the rolling iron with two of Huber's sisters, one on each end. It took three workers to feed the sheets through the ironing machine. (The laundry did all the hospital and doctor's office linens in the area.) Myrtle and either Sadie or possibly Blanche, who both worked there, already knew about the ring from their baby brother. Still, they were excited and happily enthused to hear Laverne's version of the previous evening and to see her ring. Laverne first showed the ring on her right hand's ring finger to her future sister-in-law on her right. After doing so and having some happy and giddy conversation, she turned to her left to show her ring to Myrtle. As she swept her right hand around her, a loop of heavy ribbon that was tied in a bow securing the cover of the large roller of the iron fell over the small stone of her new ring, snagged it, and pulled young Laverne's hand into the large roller of the ironing machine. In those days, there was no emergency quick release on that type of machine.

Since it was powered by steam, it could not be stopped suddenly. They couldn't get it to release her hand. A young boy on his way to school was hailed down by the laundry supervisor on duty and told to run two blocks to a machine shop and bring back a machinist in a hurry. These ironing presses later earned the appropriate and deserving name of "Mangler."

Meanwhile, poor Laverne's hand was crushed and badly burned in the ironing machine. The pain, horror, and tragedy are hard enough to imagine. But trying to relate to those circumstances and their effect upon the soul, mind, and heart of a sixteen-year-old girl who had happily fallen in love and just lived through a whirlwind courtship can only leave one heartbroken when you consider the magnitude of the painful torture rendered by the hot and consuming Mangler ironer and the subsequent amputation and loss of Laverne's right hand.

Aside from being gravely injured and having suffered a horrible shock, she fell into deep depression for months following the accident. Her faithful and devoted companion, frequent caretaker, constant suitor, and sometimes nursemaid following the horrible accident was her new beau, immediate fiancé, because he proposed marriage immediately after promising to take care of her for the rest of her life.

They were married on June 6, 1936, in Pittsburg, Texas, but like my Hamberlin family in 1940, they are nowhere to be found. They must have stayed close to home and family for a while because LaVerne had to adjust to not having a right hand. She would have had to retrain her brain to a new way of life. And she did just that.

WWII began in September 1939, and the family histories say they moved to California during the war, taking their adopted son, David Michael Lindsey, with them. David was born in February 1942 in El Paso, Texas. The birth index says his parents are Hubert and Laverne, so they must have gotten him at birth. How they got him is probably a great story by itself, but I couldn't find it for the life of me, although I looked for days.

Hubert worked for the US Army Corp of Engineers, building defensive gun and antiaircraft artillery bunkers up and down the coast of Northern California. By the time the couple began having children, he was working long, hard, and hot days at the Bacon American Brass and Iron Foundry near the family's home in Oakland, California.

When Bacon American moved to Indiana years later, his family didn't want to make that move so Hubert went to work for the Mare Island Naval Shipyard, where he served many years with distinction and gratitude from the US Navy, having earned federal "top-secret" security clearance. He contributed significant "practical" and "common sense" information to navy investigation review boards and helped determine the reasons that caused the sinking of the Polaris class nuclear submarine USS Thresher.

Hubert and Laverne had been married for six years and must have wanted to have their own family when they adopted David. It was almost nine more years before their first child was born in November 1950.

Steven Edward, John Wayne, Marilyn Elaine, Harold Hubert, and Paul Jeffery gave them five boys and one girl. Their family was complete.

Laverne raised six children, who all learned to be left-handed because she taught them to do things the only way she knew how. They often chuckled later about everything they did that mimicked her, though the doctors said they were all right-hand dominant.

They played cards with wax paper or tinfoil empty boxes to hold their cards. They all insisted on using the cardholder even though they didn't need them. They grew up thinking that the way she did things was how you were supposed to do it, and so did many cousins. They never thought of her as being handicapped.

I thought that was the end of the story and that I had learned so much about the Lord preparing a way for us to do things if we ask for help, and she did.

Today, I found another piece of the puzzle in a posting from Bill Grubbs, Joye Hamberlin's son and Myrtle's grandson. I will give you some of the highlights.

The Days Following My Father's Death
By Steven Edward Lindsey

Outside family and old friends from Gilmer, Texas, my mother had only a few good friends. The friends that she had were all active church members. Chief among her friends was a dear woman named Faye Gadd. Faye is close to my mom's age but is a few years younger.

Faye was a good Mormon girl from the country in Utah, and my mom was a good Mormon girl from the country in Texas. Faye knew my mother for over thirty years; she was, I think, my mom's best friend. They were young mothers together, having babies at the same time, and became friends over the years.

I was in the last month of my mission serving in western Canada when my parents were in a car crash that killed my dad and also caused the death of the three teenage boys who were in the other car that crossed over the middle of the highway to hit my dad's side of the vehicle.

I had not even felt like I had finished my mission when, just a couple of days later, I was arranging for a mortician and making mortuary arrangements for a funeral in California and one in Kelsey.

(Both parents are now buried in the Kelsey Cemetery. Joye Hamberlin's husband, Bill Grubbs, officiated Hubert's services in Kelsey.)

The weeks after my return and my very rushed head-spinning release were filled with doing the business necessary to settle in. Arranging my parents' finances, doctors, lawyers, insurance claims, house payments, funeral arrangements, etc.

Thankfully, Faye Gadd and so many other loving sisters in the Relief Society were paying attention to basic housekeeping, laundry, and feeding of a family of now six at home. A nurse was home with Mother, Harry, and Jeffery as we were to go to a doctor's appointment later that day. One of the many things I had to do during that grievous and crazy time was apply as a proxy, as my mom was in critical condition for months. She later attended my dad's funeral on a gurney with an IV in place. I had to apply for my mother's and siblings' survivor benefits with the Social Security Administration. A visit there entailed sitting and waiting for several hours. I filled out the paperwork and waited for my call to the window.

The nice lady at the window was empathetic. She stamped the forms and asked a few questions. One was "Is your mother disabled?" "No," I said. As so many others had not done, I never thought of my mother as disabled, even though I always knew she did everything with only one hand. The clerk finished the paperwork and told me we'd get a check in a few days.

I ran out, started the car, and began to pull away, realizing I had a tight schedule to keep. Then it dawned on me what had just happened. I had just applied for my mother's Social Security benefits and claimed she was not disabled. I was horrified at my stupidity, or it felt like stupidity to me. I parked the car, stopped the engine, fed the parking meter, and ran back in, hoping I would not have to start all over in line again.

Within moments, the very nice lady who helped me saw that I was waiting and called me over to the window, asking another applicant to step aside for a moment. I said, "Excuse me, ma'am. Does it matter if my mom is disabled? I mean, does it matter how much money she'll get? Because if it does, well, she is disabled." You can see how that sounds. I stepped all over myself trying to explain and then told the basic story of my mom losing her hand as a teenage girl. She made the corrections that greatly impacted the money she received each month.

After all my errands, I dropped by the Gadd home to pick up a casserole Faye had made for our family's dinner. I sat in the living room with Faye and her husband, Bob, waiting for the dish to finish cooking. During the conversation, I shared the story of the mistake I had almost made on the application at the Social Security office.

They both look surprised. Actually, shocked is a better choice of words. Faye jumped up and ran to the kitchen. I heard the oven door slam shut and the baking dish clatter on the kitchen counter. Suddenly, Faye appeared at the kitchen door and, while wagging her finger at me just like a stern and reprimanding parent, told me in no uncertain terms that she was going to drive me back to the Social Security office the very next morning and see to it that I corrected that fabricated tail I had told. And see that the false report I had filed was brought into line with the actual truth. Had I not learned anything about character while on my mission?

I could feel a little ire arise when I suddenly realized that my mother had been so good at masking her disability throughout her entire life that these two people, my parents' closest church friends, did not have a clue either about her disability.

I had to take Faye to my mother's bedside that evening to convince her that I had only been telling the truth while revealing my awkwardness about learning to navigate in the "grown-up world."

Of course, I never thought about other people's perceptions because my mother was so often in the company of immediate and extended family that she never concealed her amputation from any family member. We all knew her sisters, brothers, in-laws, nieces, nephews, and cousins, yet she hid it from the world outside our family.

I know my mom was deeply disabled by the psychological effects of that loss, especially in a modern Western world that was mesmerized by the likes of beautiful starlets marching by her television window in the world that she seldom ventured out of anymore since that accident. She was always staying at home or visiting other family homes, except to take her children to church.

I think on her deathbed, she was still "frozen in time," somehow in the time of her life when she was whole. Much of her faith in the Gospel was rooted in her high hopes, and sincere expectations taught us in church about the glories of the morning of the First Resurrection, coming forth from the grave restored, complete with a perfect body. She was only fifty-two when she was widowed. Daily, she yearned to be with my father again. I think, just as much as anything else, she also yearned to have her body back again.

Another important thing I have learned from these women is that no matter what is going on in our lives, we are not the first ones who have ever gone through that before, and we won't be the last. All things really are for our good. We just have to trust in his plan and his timing and know that we are his children, and he will always be there for us if we follow him and keep his commandments.

Reva Virginia Dalton Topham, 1904-1938.

Ruth, Lewis, Thurza Ellsworth, and
Lewis Boyle Jr. 1929, Kelsey.

Apostle David O. McKay and President Charles E. Rowen, 1932, in front of Bennion Hall. The new Gymnasium that was built in 1929 in Kelsey, Texas. President Rowen was married to Irene Noble of Mesa, Arizona. She is connected to Paul Noble, one of my favorite neighbors.

The oil well that was close to Kelsey with cars from several towns that came to see it. The biggest oil will ever to hit at the time was in the southern part of Upshur county on March 29, 1929.

CHAPTER 25

Reva Dalton's Journal 1927-1929

To get the feel of what life was like then, Reva's journal helps us to know how they lived and worshipped.

The mission president was Samuel Otis Bennion. In 1933 he was called to be a general authority of the Church and continued to preside over the Central States Mission until 1935.

Louis F. Boyle was called to be the superintendent of the Church-sponsored school, Kelsey Academy, in Kelsey, Texas.

Thurza Ellsworth Boyle was called to teach personal hygiene and nursing. She was in charge of the health and well-being of the Relief Society sisters.

They arrived in the field on September 2, 1928, and were released on December 4, 1933.

Thurza is related to some of my favorite people: Sylvia Farnsworth Ricks, half of my book club, and my former bishop and stake president, Cory Paul Ellsworth. President Ellsworth is an author, songwriter, playwright, and all-around great man. He blessed us all with his production of 1856: The Musical.

While serving her mission in Kelsey, Sister Dalton lived with the Alexanders but sometimes spent the night with other members and investigators.

The elders when she first arrived in Dallas in 1927 were Willcox and Moon, then Kearns and Wrigley came up from Waco for the conference. Her companion was Sister Stark. Later she went to Kelsey to replace Sisters Morgan, Brinkerhoff, and Campbell. Sister Stewart was with her when she taught school.

Reva Dalton's Journal: Written in Her Words

Friday, November 18, 1927

Conference is this morning, the first one I have ever gone to in the mission field. We had priesthood meeting this morning with all the elder and lady missionaries. President Bennion and David O. McKay were the visitors. Each missionary had to talk from a certain form David O. McKay gave us; first was the age, but President Bennion said we four girls did not need to tell our age because he knew we were each just seventeen and it would save us the bother. Both the North and the East Texas Districts had conference here in Dallas.

For lunch, all the missionaries, about twenty of us, went to a cafeteria. After we all went through and got our food, one of the waiters asked what church we belonged to. When we told her, she said, "I was just sure you are Mormons, for down here, everybody but Mormons drink coffee."

In a meeting that afternoon, Elder Woolly from North Texas, Elder Kearns, then Sister Stark, and next I talked. We others were the only missionaries called on during the conference. Elder Woolley was the only one from the North Texas district who talked; we were from East Texas. I talked for twelve minutes, and the others talked for only five. They said President Bennion told them as they came up to talk for only five minutes and nothing but the Gospel. Well, I wonder why he didn't say anything to me. I talked on "obedience to law."

While I was up, I wasn't at all frightened, but when I sat down, I could think of a million other things I could've said. I really felt very discouraged, but after the meeting, Apostle McKay came to me and said, "Sister Dalton, your talk was excellent. You held well to your subject, and your illustrations and applications were very fitting. I felt much consoled." He did not say anything to the rest. Maybe he thought I needed it worse than they did.

After the meeting, we all went down to Harper's to have our picture taken. They wanted to send it to the Improvement Era and the Liahona. President Bennion told me he wanted to talk to me and for me to come down to the Jefferson Hotel. Sisters Summer and Denison, President Funk, and President Jeffrey wanted to see him, so they went too. We wrote letters until he came, then he told me to go with him. He told me he had arranged for Mr. Boyle to teach in Kelsey next year and that I was to be the principal in Enoch. I told him I would rather not, and he said if I needed to go to Austin again to see about it, he would pay my way. He told me all about his business. When he finished talking to me, it was time to go back up to dinner at the meeting house, so the other kids did not get to talk to him. When we got back to church, I helped serve the Relief Society dinner then we had a meeting and a spiritual feast. It was too that the house was filled to overflowing. The most people that have ever been in there were in attendance. Sisters Summers and Denison came over this morning at seven and went to meeting.

David O. McKay is an orator. I just set spellbound every minute he was talking. Mrs. Booth, an investigator, talked to him, and she said he looked just like she thought an angel would. President Bennion asked me if we didn't want to go to Kelsey with them to conference. I told him I would like to, but I didn't have the money. Sister Stark is the captain of the ship, and she says we are going, so I guess we are. We can come back with the elders and lady schoolteachers when they come here for Thanksgiving, so we will have to pay only our way down.

Saturday, November 19, 1927

This morning at seven o'clock, Elder Bennion came to see if we were ready to go to Kelsey. We were, so we walked down to meet President Funk. Then we went down to get some stockings for Sister Stark. We tried to get some thread at Woolworths, but it was too early. The doors were unlocked, but I couldn't find anyone except the janitor and one clerk who said she didn't work in that department.

We went on down to the train and were all waiting when here came Apostle McKay and President Bennion.

We waved to them, and they came in and spoke to us but went into the other car because they had some writing to do. President Funk sat and talked to us for a long time. Then we went in the other car. We were both so tired we fell asleep.

Soon President Bennion came in. He laid a candy bar on my lap, and I woke up. I looked right up into his face. I said, "Oh, I was nearly asleep." "Nearly," he echoed. "You were asleep. I tried to put this in your purse, but I couldn't. I was going to surprise you. You were both asleep, and I passed right by you once and did not see you. When I came back, I saw two little girls dressed almost alike sitting so close together, and here you are."

The other train was an hour late into Gilmer, but Elder Campbell was there in the teachers' Ford for us. He sat with Apostle McKay and me in the front while

President Funk, President Bennion, and Sister Stark sat in the back. All the way over, I felt so sick to my stomach. I was afraid I'd have to stop, but I did pray so earnestly for the Lord to help me.

When we got there, the teachers had a really nice hot dinner for us. We ate and ate. When we had finished, Apostle McKay said, "Well, I wouldn't exactly say that this dinner has saved my life, but I would say this: it surely made it a lot more comfortable."

President Bennion called me in and had me tell Apostle McKay about my teaching certificate and ask him to see about it when he got back home. President Bennion surely bragged me up to Apostle McKay. That

night, we all went to the school play. After the show, we all went over to the teachers' place made and ate marguerites.[1] Then we went to bed. Sister Smith and I slept in the middle, and the other girls were on the outside. It is still chilly. Yes, cold.

Sunday, November 20, 1927

This morning, we were late to the teacher training class. I felt bad, but that didn't help much. We were waiting for Elder Campbell to come for us. During Sunday school, Apostle McKay had four lady missionaries get up and sing "In Our Lovely Deseret." He told the story of Damon and Pythias, the two great friends. (It's a beautiful story of the worth of a man's word.) Sister Smith and Huff were invited out to dinner, so Sister Stark and I went over to Sister Whitehead's.

Oh dear, of all the dinners, but then it was like the elders tell us about in the country districts. We

---

1   A marguerite is a Ritz cracker with peanut butter topped with a large marshmallow. Broil until brown.

had a good meeting. President Bennion, Apostle McKay, Elder Campbell, Sister Huff, and Sister Smith were the speakers.

We came home with Brother and Sister Bradshaw and had a huge dinner, and it was surely good. Sister Bradshaw was sick, so we went to meeting with Brother Bradshaw. Sister Stark and I sat in the audience, but President Bennion sent down for us to come up to the stand. We thought that we would have to preach, but we didn't. We are staying here at Brother Pritchett's tonight; we are to sleep in the room all the schoolteachers have stayed in for years—some honor, ah? They kept us talking until I felt that I could not endure it any longer.

Monday, November 21, 1927

We slept fine in spite of the fact that we were on a feather tick. We had a good breakfast, even tenderloins. We took our shoes and stockings off and went out to pick peanuts off the vine to send home. While the Pritchetts went into town, and Sister Stark went with them to mail the nuts, I stayed home and wrote letters. They came back, we pieced and talked, then they were going to town to see Ben-Hur, so they took us over to Sister Bradshaw's. There, we popped corn, sang songs, and had prayer, and after I took my exercises, we went to bed.

Tuesday, November 22, 1927

Again, this morning, I took exercises, but not being used to it is, I am sure stiff and sore. As Brother Tom Bradshaw took the children to school, he took us over to visit Silas, his son's school, and some poor excuse of a school it was too. We were just visiting the principal's room when Brother Bradshaw came for us. After we got back, we ate dinner, wrote receipts, and again, picked peanuts to send home. President Funk came while I was out picking peanuts, and because I wouldn't come out until I was cleaned up, he called me vain. It surely made me angry.

We went over to Wade's to stay all night. Had a good supper, but I didn't eat much except for figs, for I had eaten such a big dinner at Bradshaw's'. Again, they balled me out, saying I was too high toned. Elder Campbell took us to choir practice. President Funk had a little trouble with a kid who wouldn't take his hat off. He surely said some mean things right in the church. He came up and wanted President Funk to fight him. He said, "I'm not going to let an old Yankee come down here and tell me what to do." He waited on the outside for a while with his knife, then decided not to spill any blood. He let the oil out of the teacher's car, cut the lights, and fussed with the spark plugs. The kids (President Funk and Elders Campbell, Huff, and Smith) were sure mad; they wanted to go over to Gilmer to see Ben-Hur. When we got back to Wade's, Brother Wade kept us up, asking the same questions that he has asked every new missionary for twenty years. Finally, we did manage to get in bed. Sister Stark got disgusted as it was so hot. I felt that I couldn't sleep without air, but I did—in the usual way.

Wednesday, November 23, 1927

This morning, I was awakened by the smell of frying tenderloin. I hurried and got ready for breakfast, for when there is anything edible, I'm always there. Elder Campbell was late to breakfast, and we had to wait for him. I wrote letters. Then President Funk came about ten o'clock, and we both sat and wrote letters.

Then Sister Wade took her girls over to see Emma's new house. Oh pshaw! It makes me want more than ever a dear "little house" by the side of the road.

President Funk took us down to get the teachers' laundry. That was the first time I have ever seen anyone iron by heating irons the good old-fashioned way in the fireplace. I sat right between two windows and just nearly melted.

We then went and took the teachers their mail. They had some Thanksgiving parcels come from home, so we helped them eat their cakes, cookies, apples, etc. They wouldn't let us visit school, so we went in the car with President Funk. We went over to President Lindsey's for a while, then we went out and helped President Funk with the car, and again, we climbed up in the loft and ate peanuts. These were real large.

When we went into Bradshaws' to say goodbye, Sister Bradshaw wept, so we know she did not censure us for eating too much. We all ate at "the Little White House."

President Funk picked and picked and, yes, picked on a duck he had bought for Thanksgiving since all the elders would be in; finally, he became disgusted and skinned it. He had bought two, but the other one he gave away; he had had all he wanted.

We went up to the school to the teacher's program. It was really good; came home and immediately started for Dallas. Yes, even forgot our prayer but were brought to a remembrance of it. Sister Huff was driving. We were going at a good speed, and off came a wheel and down we went. Oh, we had been having so much fun.

It was a delightfully warm day, and we were singing. Sister Smith and I walked back to Hamberlins' for a hammer.

Elder Campbell went to Lindsey's place for the Kelsey teachers' car. While we were gone, President

Funk put a nail in the wheel to hold it on, and he and Sister Huff went to Gilmer. Elder Campbell came and took Smitty, Stark, and me to Gilmer, and when the car was fixed, we all came to Dallas. The first half of the way, Sister Huff, President Funk, and I sat in the back, then the girls changed, and we all ate hamburgers and fruitcakes. They got so cold by the time we got to Dallas they were all three sitting on only half of the seat. When I came in, there was a letter waiting for me from Austin telling me that they would issue me a certificate. Sister Stark's package from home was there when we came in, and I just decided my folks didn't care about me. But my lamentations didn't last for long for just as we four girls—Sister Stark, Smith, Huff, and I—were ready to climb in bed, in fact, half of us were in bed, here came a special delivery package from Ruby and Elva (Reva's sisters) for me. It contained a very delicious cake. Sister Stark said it was the best one of all. It came just in time; it was ten minutes to midnight. I was so happy.

You can read her journal on her FamilySearch page. I am only giving you the times she spent in Kelsey with the sisters in the quilt. It was ten months before she returned to Kelsey, and she spent so much time with the sisters who made blocks. I have omitted some things, but everything in this is her words. Some were misspelled, but I knew who they were because I had group sheets on all the sisters. She never forgot her time with Apostle McKay, and he remembered her too because he was the sealer when she married Silas Topham on May 16, 1933, in the Salt Lake temple.

She loved her time in Dallas and found it was hard to leave and go back to the small community of Kelsey. Her new companions were Sister Stewart, Sister Brinkerhoff, and Sister Morgan. The elder was Campbell.

Wednesday, September 26, 1928

Last night, Sister Morgan played hide-and-seek with the rats while Sister Stewart lay here, trembling in fear. But Brink and I slept peacefully through it all. The Bradshaws are some of the most wonderful people I have ever met. Ethel Bradshaw offered to make me a linen dress, so I am going to let her. We went to Gilmer and filed our certificates. Mrs. Palmer said I could teach in the high school. We met the superintendent, Mr. Walker. We went to hear a murder trial. It surely did affect me. Sister Morgan and I stayed with Bradshaws again tonight, and the other three went to Berta Wade's (Ethel's mother). Sister Morgan felt so lonely she cried and cried. We hunted for a place to stay and finally decided to stay at Alexander's—with a few reservations.

Thursday, September 27, 1928

I tried to drive the car. It rained and rained, and oh how I did skid and skid. Yeah, boy, right off the road. Sisters Brinkerhoff and Morgan said they would not stand and let me drive between them. Anyway, we laughed ourselves sick; it meant "sink or swim," and I made'em swim. The girls have nearly died laughing. They say Barnum and Bailey would hold no attraction for them now—anyway, we all have permanent waves in our backbones. I tried to blame it on the roads. Last night, Sister Morgan didn't feel so good, so I stayed with her at Bradshaw's, and Brink, Stewart, and Campbell slept at Wade's. Tonight, we had a wonderful meeting at Wood's. I enjoyed talking tonight, and we had a splendid crowd. The Jenkins came ten miles without any lights on their Ford, and Moses Wood told me the greatest happiness he had was being with the missionaries and listening to them talk. I know he spoke from his heart, for as he said it, tears rolled down his cheeks. We are here at Friddles' tonight. Sister Friddle said the LDS girls are the prettiest in the world. On the way to the meeting, we climbed out of the car, went up a path, stood in a circle in the grove of trees, and had prayer. I am to sleep with "Brink" tonight.

Friday, September 28, 1928

I awoke with a sudden start this morning when Sisters Morgan and Stewart came rushing in. They had just heard Sister Friddle say she didn't see how she could get breakfast for such a bunch unless they got up and helped her, and it was only 5:30 a.m. Some greeting, ah not? We wrote a few letters, then we went to Bryant's, then to Tom McKnight's, and then to President Green's, after which we all went out to Talino's. They immediately fell in love with me, and they wanted to give me all they had. We had a nice dinner and a very splendid meeting. We held it on the porch. A fine crowd was in attendance. Sister Stewart and I went home with the Hawkins not by choice but because they asked us to, and "we must get acquainted with our investigators." I am feeling quite punk tonight. Oh, how I did wish they would let us go to bed.

Saturday, September 29, 1928

Sister Stewart slept very little last night. She chased bats and dogs all night. I felt worn out so slept soundly all night. Had biscuits and pear preserves with water for breakfast. How some people can live the way they do is beyond my conception. We went to Talino's for the other three kids who slept there. I guess my medicine had the desired effect. Anyway, I am much better today. Had a faculty meeting today. Oh dear, my schedule is filled. I know I'll have to have the blessings of my Father in heaven if I am to do half justice to my schoolwork and my missionary work.

After meeting, we came home, pressed our clothes, and straightened our trunks. At night, President Campbell took Sister Stewart and me down to Bryant's to dinner. Sisters Morgan and Brink were at Bradshaw's. We went to choir practice then the president brought us home. We are to sleep in our new home tonight. We bathed in a thimble just to make ourselves think we were clean.

Sunday, September 30, 1928

Had breakfast at 7:30, wrote letters, and went to meeting at 9:00. Sister Brink and I went to the parents' class and did enjoy it. We all four (Sister Morgan was still sick at Bradshaw's) had dinner at Wade's, then went for Sister Morgan, and Sister Ethel Bradshaw gave us some more ice cream. We all came to a special meeting at two o'clock. Sister Brink and Elder Campbell talked, and during the afternoon, we came to our place and visited. At night, we went to Enoch and held services. Elders Boyle and Campbell and Sister Brink talked. After the meeting, Sister Morgan and I stayed with Elder Campbell at Bradshaw's, and Brink and Stewart stayed at Lindsey's. We went to bed at ten o'clock. First Sunday I haven't had a headache for a long time.

Monday, October 1, 1928

We awoke just before the alarm went off at 2:30 a.m., and we were on our way to Big Sandy to take the kids to the station. I've been up many times in my life at 2:30, but never before have I gotten up at that time.

We left Big Sandy and started home at four o'clock. Elder Campbell told us to call at the station and get some gas, but it was closed so we just exercised our faith and prayers, and the Lord blessed us exceedingly. We did not run out of gas, and the car went just fine all the way. When we got home and had been here about ten minutes, I looked out, and the tire was flat.

It had just gone down after we stopped. On our way down, Elder Campbell stopped, and we all climbed out and had prayer; I was impressed too. I laughed at Sister Stewart as we started home. She said, "I go like a lamb to the slaughter." We laughed. I thought she meant because she was riding back with me driving, but she met coming back here—just the two of us.

Tuesday, October 2, 1928

Today in school, they had me give a sample of elocution before I gave it. There were three of them who wanted it, and afterward, there were eleven. It surely did rain here; in fact, it rained off and, on each hour, or so. Tonight, we went to Mutual, and they gave me the junior girls and Sister Stewart, the Gleaner girls, to teach. We went with Sister Alice Alexander and the lantern.

Wednesday, October 3, 1928

We have worked and worked on our program, and each day, we make a little change in it. I wonder if it's settled now. We are both trying to get caught up on our correspondence, but I still have plenty more to do. Sister Stewart and I went to town with Elder Boyle.

Thursday, October 4, 1928

Teacher's Institute. Oh me, oh my. Sister Boyle was sick, and that made us late this morning because we rode in Elder Boyle's car. Just for fun, we ate dinner in the school cafeteria; we just wanted to try it. I thought I would have plenty of good naps during Dr. Brock's lecture in both the morning and afternoon sessions, but I thoroughly enjoyed it. He has been through the mill too. He is now president of the Baylor University at Waco. I am surely disappointed at not getting to go to Dallas this weekend for the fair. All the kids will be there. Brother Tom Bradshaw is going to take us next weekend. We went to Relief Society meeting with Rawleigh (the fifteen-year-old son of Alice Alexander) and the lantern. (They walked.)

Friday, October 5, 1928

Hebrews. The Institute here is so different than it is at home. They are yet fifty years behind the times, but then Utah is about third in school education and Texas about thirty-eighth. I quite enjoyed part of it, but oh my. It was so hot at noon that Sister Stewart and I left in our Ford. We took it to the garage to change the batteries, and while we were in there, it rained and rained. We were almost afraid to come home. We stopped at Tom and Ethel Bradshaw's and had cake and pie. Then she started to sew on my green linen dress, and I began to take my old blue one that Aunt Amy made for me eight years ago to pieces. We surely had a good supper, after which Sister Bradshaw and I sewed until 10:30 then we went to bed.

Saturday, October 6, 1928

Well, sir, I either dreamed a rat ran over my face or it did. Anyway, it was so plain I sat up in bed and gave a little scream. I also dreamed I owed the Colcord Beauty Shop fifty cents, which is too painfully true, and I had completely forgotten all about it. We sewed until 2:30, then we came home, and on the way home, I killed the engine. A man came out of nowhere, a fine-looking fella too, and he cranked it for us. When we got home, we had to read our mail, and I had a nice letter from Aunt Lola containing a dollar and one from Sister Morgan. It was a cute one too. We didn't get our washing out until nearly dark. Then we had to hurry to choir practice. We went with Loretta Alexander and the lantern. On the way home, Elder Boyle carried the lantern. He asked us to have hot loaf bread, butter, and onions with them, so of course, after a "great deal of persuasion," we consented. While we were eating, Sister Alexander sent Loretta Alexander up with a freezer two-thirds full of ice cream, and the Boyles, Sister Stewart, and I ate it. I can't remember ever eating so much ice cream. It is a good thing for us that in the morning is Fast Sunday. Oh me for fat!

Sunday, October 7, 1928

Our darn clock was slow, and as per usual, we were late for nine o'clock teacher training class; Tom McKnight talks altogether too much. After Sunday school, we—Elder Boyle, Virgil Means (later Audrey Bryant's husband), Hester Jones (Myrtle Jones's sister who married James Oscar Means), and I—practiced "I Know My Father Knows." We sang that in meeting this afternoon, then Sister Stewart and I rushed home for a wonderful chicken dinner and reached meeting in good time. It was a funny meeting. Bishop Green said, "Brother Bell (Charlie, Blanche Lindsey's husband) has something to say." My heart ached for him. I had to offer the closing prayer, and it was no easy task. President Green wanted to meet the missionaries after the meeting. Then we went out to Victor Carl Hamberlin's for another dinner and spent the afternoon, came home, and rushed to meeting, after which we called a meeting to arrange for an entertainment to get funds to paper the four classrooms at church.

Monday, October 8, 1928

We had school the entire day today. I rather enjoyed it, and I hoped the boys and girls did. I had to go to a director meeting up to Boyle's. We have decided to call our club the "Hill and Dale Booster Club," which was my suggestion. We are to meet once each week. I do hope we can accomplish half of what we have planned. I nearly fainted when they elected me the head of a committee to promote an educational agricultural two-day "Round-Up." When I came home, everyone was sleeping soundly. Stewart stood on the porch tonight until I got to Boyle's.

Tuesday, October 9, 1928

Had faculty meeting at eight o'clock this morning. This is quite a lot of fun to teach high school, first graders, second graders, and primers. I went to Boyle's after school to write a letter to President Bennion to see if he could be here for our Round-Up. When I came home, I hurriedly took a bath but had to eat supper before I was hardly ready. Sister Stewart wanted to know who was senior here and who was boss. Some

of the girls, Sister Stewart, and I went to Sister Dixon's[2]
to cheer her up with our singing. Instead of cheering her
up, I'm afraid it had the reverse effect. I drove the Ford
and had to drive in low all the way so we could have
some lights. Came back from her place, went to officers'
meeting and then to Mutual, and I taught the junior
girls, then had a meeting after to ar ange for a program
for our entertainment. Sister Stewart and I have charge
of the games; I have to give a reading too, and so do two
of the girls in my elocution class. When we went out to
the car, Flave Henderson cranked and cranked. Finally,
we found the boys had turned the gas off, and then we
reached home all whole and glad to be that way. Sister
Alice Alexander (Loretta's sister) came with us.

Wednesday, October 10, 1928

Yesterday, I got a letter from one of my investigators
in Waco. She sent me a dime she owed me. Today, I had
a letter from Farley's. We had "missionary class" this
morning and a faculty meeting tonight after school. In
our domestic science today, we had eleven girls trying to
make one pan of noodles. Well, I was worn out. Thank
heavens, it doesn't come every day.

I corrected the theme papers until I couldn't see
any longer, then I rushed home, ate my supper, and we
went to meeting at Ida Dotson's without even changing
our dresses. I preached on "misfortunes are only
opportunities in disguise." Elder Boyle was following
the way of all absent-minded professors; he called on
Brother Hamberlin to open and close the meeting, and

---

[2] Sister Loretta Dixon was due to have a baby at that time. She must have thought
a lot of Reva Dalton to name the baby girl Reva Eldeen Dixon, born November 13,
1928.

he wouldn't believe us when we told him. His wife almost pulled his coat off, trying to keep him from singing all the verses of "Who's on the Lord's Side, Who?" They are so good to us—yes, the Boyles.

Friday, October 12, 1928

After school today, Elder Boyle and I went to Bradshaw's to get the tire on our Ford fixed. While he went to town after it, Sister Boyle and I had Sister Bradshaw cut our hair. It was after dark when we started home. I drove alone in our car behind the Boyle's. When I got home, Sister Stewart was all ready to go back to Bradshaw's. We went to stay all night so we could get an early start to Dallas to the fair. The car stopped so many times on our way there, and we could not imagine what was the matter with it. Bradshaws were in bed when we got there.

Saturday, October 13, 1928

Got up at 2:15 a.m. and left for Dallas at about 2:50 a.m. Enjoyed the ride over and did not have a bit of car trouble. Ate our breakfast on the way. It consisted of rolls and chicken, and don't forget the cookies. Reached there at about 8:30 then we went shopping.

Sister Stewart let me go to the girls alone, and I reached there OK. We surely did enjoy seeing them again, and Elder Kearns was so cute. We had our baths. Velma let me wear her dress and shoes. I felt quite smart. The rest had been to the fair, so Sister Stewart and I met Elder Kearns down to the fairgrounds, and we looked around and ate until that had grown monotonous. Then we met the kids, and we were going to hold a street meeting, but it began to rain so we took the car and came home.

Sunday, October 14, 1928

We went to Sunday school, and I had to give a talk on "home." Oh me! Oh my! It surely did seem good to see all the people again. I just couldn't find enough time. Sister Kennison tells me Sister Stark is to be married. The Bradshaws were ready to go right then, but we got them to wait until we went down to the Wayside Inn and ate with the girls. We didn't even get to say goodbye to the elders then we started home. For supper, we ate hotdogs and came home and stayed at Bradshaws' all night.

Monday, October 15, 1928

Started home from Bradshaws', but the car wouldn't go. Brother Lamar Hamberlin started it for us a number of times, but it wasn't getting any gas and wouldn't go. We had to come home with a drummer, who was nice enough to bring us, and so we got to school tired, hungry, and dusty, with not even time to wash up. Sent Heber Jones, Myrtle's brother, for our car. Those who dance must pay for the music.

Tuesday, October 16, 1928

Oh, so tired, stiff, and sore today, but went to Mutual anyway. They gave Sister Stewart the position of teacher in the Gleaner girls. I'm teacher of the juniors. We are studying "The Great Women." Interesting too.

Wednesday, October 17, 1928

Tonight, we had a party here in the church to get funds to paper the church. Elder Boyle made the penny auction sale a huge success. They contained everything from safety pins to lemons. The Relief Society sold ice cream and cake and did very well. The Mutual sold marguerites and red lemonade. It was a huge success, but Sister Boyle and I have been asked to take charge of the games. We had a lot planned, but they didn't even ask us to lead them.

Thursday, October 18, 1928

School, as per usual, went to Relief Society tonight.

Friday, October 19, 1928

As I came home from the schoolhouse, I saw Elders Campbell and Moon; they had just got in. We had dinner at the Boyle's, and then we all went to Talino's for a cottage meeting. On the way there, we ran out of gas, and Elder Boyle had to send us a service car.

We had a good evening. President Campbell and I had a good visit. We went out to Med Buckley's and had ice cream, and a "norther" (cold, strong wind) had just come up, and we nearly froze while eating it. Danced a Virginia reel to keep warm. On the whirl, Sister Stewart and I had a terrific bump, and that ended the fun. The elders brought us home and went back and stayed all night. I missed Chauncey's (Myrtle Jones's brother) wedding dance. (Willie Alexander and Zelma Lindsey were married that day.)

Saturday, October 20, 1928

Stewart washed today, and I cleaned the rooms. The elders came before we were ready, but they sat in the yard and chewed sugarcane until we were ready to go with them to the Joneses'. They took us to Stanley's, and there they made us stay. Oh, what next? Now I know what the Bible means when it speaks of the four corners of the Earth. We are now in corner number four. We had a good meeting that night because I talked on prayer for three-fourths of an hour. We were almost afraid to go to bed for fear of bedbugs, but to our great surprise, we were not carried off by morning.

Sunday, October 21, 1928

Stewart ate breakfast, but not me; there were too many flies. Mr. Stanley is very bitter toward the North over the Civil War days. He kept saying, "No, sir. You'uns all don't know nothing'bout hard times," and I believe he is right. Which is telling the truth: the Northern or the Southern history?

The elders came and took us to Barker's, where we spent an enjoyable hour, then we went to Thompson's for dinner. After dinner, we had another meeting. Two of the Barker girls were just on the verge of being baptized but backed out. They promised Elder Moon that he could baptize them. We ate supper at Barker's and went back to Stanley's for a meeting. The house was filled with people, mostly new; one woman laughed most of the time Elder Moon was talking. After the meeting, Mrs. Stanley gave Elder Moon and me each a bottle of fruit and Elder Moon an old fiddle, which he brought home. We came home that night after meeting and how thankful we were, for it got fearfully cold just after we reached home.

Monday, October 2, 1928

The elder visited our school this morning, and tonight, the Boosters Club met in Enoch; two Rotarians were here from Gilmer, and they gave wonderful talks. All the officers sat on the stand, and to my consternation, Elder Boyle called on me. I told the story of Helen Keller and Caruso. Lemonade and the cake were served to at least one hundred people. Flave Henderson, Wilma Dotson, Sister Alice Alexander, Alma Elzey, Sister Stewart, and I went in our car.

(The story of Helen Keller and Enrico Caruso is about her putting her fingers on his mouth and throat, listening to him sing and how she felt. He did a private performance for her. It is a beautiful story).

Tuesday, October 23, 1928

I helped Loretta make marguerites for her party tonight. We all went to Mutual, and when it was over, Mr. Ellett, Kitty's husband began to campaign, so we'uns got up and came home to party. I acted my foolish part. We played games in the house, but the boys would not come in so we went outside and played games. Then I came in and served the refreshments, and they went home.

Wednesday, October 24, 1928

Tonight, Stewart went to Gilmore with the Boyles. I had no idea where she had gone. She came home, and we went to Relief Society.

Thursday, October 25, 1928

We held cottage meetings at Sister Grantham's. I had to talk, and I gave mine on service. We had a good meeting—lots there. Leroy Perry brought his English work to me.

Friday, October 26, 1928

Had our parent-teacher meeting. The superintendent and Mrs. Walker were out. They are always so nice. Elder Boyle gave me a flowery introduction. I felt very much elated. I had to talk for a few minutes.

Saturday, October 27, 1928

Washed, looked for play, went to town to get things for banquet, came home, and was going to correct papers but decided to go to song practice with Sister Alice Alexander. Came home alone, sat up, and corrected papers. It was awfully sultry when suddenly it started to rain, and then it cooled off immediately. Can't imagine snow at home. Everything is so pretty and green here. Elder Boyle sent a telegram to President Bennion to ask him to put conference off until the Round-Up and the play can be arranged. Oh, that play does worry me. Why it doesn't come is more than I can tell. I'm nervous, so nervous.

Sunday, October 28, 1928

At breakfast, Sister Alice Alexander said she was going to see that they let me stay here for two years. We went riding with the Boyles but didn't go far. We were late for Mutual. Sister Stewart and I were in pure agony for fear we would have to preach, but they called on Elder Boyle again, to our surprise.

Monday, October 29, 1928

We had school as usual tonight. Loretta and I went in our car and gathered up donations for the Boosters

Banquet. I had to dress the chicken at night, and Sister Stewart was mighty sweet. She helped me. Oh my, it was cold. I helped Rawleigh Alexander with his English.

Tuesday, October 30, 1928

We, our domestic science class, gave a banquet for the Hill and Dale Boosters Club. Mr. Adams of the state university was to be here, and the banquet was to be held at 5:30. Elder Boyle met him at the train, or rather, he was supposed to, but at 7:00, Elder Boyle came and said Mr. Adams did not come. Several days ago, I went in and ordered our rolls, and tonight, they had forgotten the order, so Elder Boyle went all over town and bought out the strangest-looking rolls. I just couldn't help shedding a few tears after waiting so long, but the girls were so sweet to help. We even had to make the ice cream after he came. Much to my surprise, they had me come into the banquet room, and they gave me three cheers. They expressed their appreciation. We had more ice cream than we could eat so we brought it to Donnie Burnett and Loretta Alexander. It was nearly ten o'clock before we finished our dishes.

Wednesday, October 31, 1928

Mr. Adams came out today in a service car. I stayed home and took a bath. Sister Stewart went with Sister Boyle in their car to Relief Society, but it rained so hard that no one came. Then we were all going over to Enoch to a party for that ward, but it rained until we were all afraid of slipping off the road. Lucy Farley (Manie's daughter) waited until the rain was over. We wanted her to stay all night, but she refused.

Thursday, November 1, 1928

Gee! I came home tonight with a headache that nearly sent me wild. We were invited out to Victor Carl Hamberlin's for dinner, but I was unable to go.

I just took an aspirin and lay on the bed. The Boyles and Sister Stewart said they had a wonderful dinner. Oh, I wonder why I have those terrible headaches. I never did have one until I came into the mission field.

Friday, November 2, 1928

We had a party at the church given by the Boosters Club. They sold red lemonade and marguerites. I made them. Sister Stewart and I played or led the games. They were so noisy. I gave a prized doll, broke my beads, and found only half of them. Went to a booster meeting upstairs during the party. A member of the officers wanted me to take full charge of the banquet for conference and the Round-Up, but Elder Boyle felt that it was too much; besides the four programs, I had charge of the play too. Brother Lindsey said, "President Bennion said he was sending another teacher down here who was as good as Sister Boyle, and I see he was right for Sister Dalton is."

Saturday, November 3, 1928

Regular Saturday routine, Sister Stewart wasn't very well, but she went to Gilmer with the Boyles. I watched and waited for them, but by 8:00, they had not come, and Loretta and Donnie asked me to go to the dance with them, so I quit my serving, loaned Loretta a pair of socks, and away we went in the Hoppy. (Donnie's car was a Hupmobile, very fast in the day.) Loretta and

Donnie sat in the front. Rawleigh and I were in the back. Oh, we got mud splashed all over us, but they treated me royally. Donnie said I was the best dancer he had danced with.

Sunday, November 4, 1928
We preached at Enoch at night.

Blue Monday, November 5, 1928
We had a glass of bread and milk in a hurry and went with Boyles to town to see about banquet things.

Tuesday, November 6, 1928
Election, but we are so far removed from civilization that we don't know anything exciting is happening. I went to Boyle's to a booster meeting. Sister Stewart took my class. They gave me eleven jobs to do and see that they were done for the banquet. Oh me! Oh my!

Wednesday, November 7, 1928
We are still wondering how the election came out. Oh yes, we have a radio, but not here. We are in Texas...

Thursday, November 8, 1928
Went with Brother and Sister Alexander out to the syrup mill. Went to Hamberlin's. Cornelia played the piano to practice all the musical numbers for the roundup. Decided for Flave Henderson, Wilma Dotson, Byron Wade, and me to sing "Oh, Happy Home among the Hills." It is hard to get people to do things. Laurene came for her musical reading; I helped her make it smoother.

Friday, November 9, 1928

It rained, yes. We are both home, and I am worrying about the play. Why doesn't it come?

Saturday, November 10, 1928

I washed, Elder Carlson sent us a picture, and the play came. I got Goldie Edger to typewrite some of the parts, and Loretta helped her. I bought them some candy from town. We took Sister Boyle into town, and she did some more Round-Up business.

I cranked and cranked the Ford, and oh the hills we pushed it on to get it started. It is the bunk. I went to choir practice alone. Sister Stewart said she couldn't sing, and she didn't want to go.

Sunday, November 11, 1928

We went to Sunday school at Enoch to see about the girls serving. Vera Wade went with us. Then we went on over in their car. Sister Bradshaw suggested we draw names of where to place the girls so no feelings would be hurt. The Boyles came here and had dinner with us. We spent the afternoon at home. I went out in the yard and studied for fear I would be called to preach and would be unable. I went up to the choir, and they called on Sister Stewart. I think I'll sit in the choir most of the time; the presidency haven't any eyes in the back of their heads.

Monday, November 12, 1928

Armistice Day. Today I went to church, and we practiced our play. Sister Stewart brought the mail up to me—a letter from Bullock and Sister Smith. I didn't have time to read my letters until I was crossing the branch. I sat on the bridge and read my letter, but one of them was a proposal so unexpected it nearly knocked me off the bridge. I know my answer already. Stewart went to town with the Boyles.

Tuesday, November 13, 1928

Back to school, I went alone to Mutual so I would be there to practice the play. I went to ask J. C. Wade if he and Effie Friddle had their duet for the program, and Byron Wade gave me "Hail Columbia" because I didn't put Vera Wade in the play.

He also said I said his sister was slouchy; that is a lie, and I told him it was. He talked very disrespectfully to me before he even knew that I was guilty. After he left, I couldn't help but cry. I could hardly practice the play that night. There is no royal road to the mission field. There are so many hills and so many unexpected lost lands.

Wednesday, November 14, 1928

It rained like the deuce all day. I took a load of boys over to pick turkeys at Sister Bradshaw's. Got Vera as we went over. I wanted to prove to her that I hadn't said what they said I did. I went to Sister Ethel Bradshaw's and found she had simply misunderstood. We both cried and cried. The boys picked the turkeys, and we tried to get the car started so we could come home. We all pushed it halfway to Lindsey's. Then Brother Joe Lindsey (Abby's husband) came along and pulled us girls in the car to his house. We left the car there and came home in Lindsey's car. The boys had to walk all the way home. I ran in the house, ate a bowl of bread and milk, changed my wet clothes, and went to practice. Everyone was chewing sugarcane. Horace Lindsey, Abby's son, brought me home in their car.

Thursday, November 15, 1928

We had school just half the day, and then we went to the church and practiced the play all afternoon and at night too. They cooked turkeys at Boyle's for the banquet.

Friday, November 16, 1928

Tonight was the famous banquet, and today was the first day of the Round-Up staged by the Hill and Dale Boosters Club.

I had to get all the names written on the place cards for 250 people, set tables for them, make the salad, and do numerous other jobs. Just as I was cutting cabbage, fast and furious, I cut my thumb. It seemed that it never would stop bleeding, so I came home, put adhesive tape on it, and went back. Couldn't get the cream we should have had for the salad but thought we would do the next best thing. I was just mixing the salad with my hands when in came Elders Moon, Bingham, and Widdison with President Williams from West Texas and President Hopkins from Oklahoma. It was very much of a surprise. Then when President Bennion came in and spoke to me, I was just rushing around. Sister Stewart and I ran home to change our dresses, and when we got back, nearly everyone was there—yes, and a new elder was there from Louisiana, Elder Nichols. I introduced myself to him. He was very nice, I thought, but I couldn't talk long because I had to help serve. Then Sister Boyle and I went up to the head of the table, and they introduced us. I talked to the elders for a few minutes after the banquet, and then

I went to wash dishes. Oh my, how it did rain all that night. Elders Moon and Campbell slept in the church so nothing would be gone.

Saturday, November 17, 1928

At 7:00, we went to the church and started to mop, wash dishes, dust, and sweep so the church would be in order for the meeting at 10:00. The elders came up long before we were through, and oh, how it did embarrass me. I was just finishing the backstops when President Bennion came out there. I did not go to that meeting. I came home, put my hair up, and put caustic acid on my toe, and was in the kitchen when in walked Elders Hopkins and Campbell. I could've shriveled up and blown away from embarrassment. We went to meeting in the afternoon and heard a clever lecture on "whether to kill a potato beetle with a red brick or a green one."

We had a matinee in the afternoon for the kiddies, and then our play called "A Perplexing Situation" with a program at night I had to take charge. Most of it was impromptu. When we sang our quartet, I nearly died. I got stage fright but lived after all; when it was over, we cleared the stage and went home.

Sunday, November 18, 1928

We all went to Enoch in our car. We came home and went to meeting, fearing we wouldn't escape talking, but we did. After meeting on the way home, Donnie told me Loretta was going to stay out of school and asked me if I would excuse her the next day. I said "NO", but when I got home, they told me they were going to get married, so I had to.

Monday, November 19, 1928

The song is ended, but the melody lingers on. We must settle down now to the regular routine. We went to town with the Boyles to return the barrel dishes and met Elders Campbell and Session. They had just posted a card telling us about our car they had just taken to the garage. Now we know we will get some mail tomorrow. Loretta Alexander was married. Now she is Loretta Burnett.

Tuesday, November 20, 1928

Eventful day? Went to Mutual.

Wednesday, November 21, 1928

Elder Boyle was sick, and oh my! I had both his class and mine. Joy? Yeah, boy! Went to town and got dishes for Loretta's present. Sister Boyle took us in her car.

Thursday, November 22, 1928

Donnie got our car, and boy, that set us back $74. President Bennion said if it did not run to go into the garage and give them "hell," and after we had paid out so much money, we will do it if it isn't right.

Friday, November 23, 1928

My domestic science class gave Loretta Burnett a dinner at the schoolhouse. Sisters Stewart, Boyle, Alexander, and Loretta were the honored guests. We gave her cooking utensils. All went off fine, and she was real thrilled.

Saturday, November 24, 1928

Sister Stewart did two week's wash. I cleaned. We went to Gilmer and then came home and went to choir practice. We met Myrtle Jones's beau, Emerson Ethridge Woodward. She was very nervous; she must have been thrilled. Got ice in town. Loretta made ice cream, and oh, how we did eat.

Sunday, November 25, 1928

Nothing unusual happened. We went to Boyle's to see how Elder Boyle was getting along and had ice cream. Found we were a half hour late to the meeting; they had changed the time from 6:30 to 6:00 and we didn't know about it. Myrtle Jones wanted us to preach so her fella could hear the Gospel, but we felt bad because we weren't there, and Brother Shirley was called upon.

Monday, November 26, 1928

Went to Moroni Hamberlin's for sweet potatoes to send to Stewart's people. He had just been building a new road, and we got stuck. Had to hurry back to Gilmer with Brother and Sister Alexander to see Wings. It made me smiley around the lips and teary around the eyes.

Tuesday, November 27, 1928

Went to Mutual, but no one came. It was too cold and rainy. Brother Shirley told us some of his experiences in the war and why he dedicated so much of his time to the church, a promise to the Lord.

Wednesday, November 28, 1928

School today, but holiday tomorrow. Elder Boyle came back to school and received a lovely box of candy for Thanksgiving.

Thursday, November 29, 1928

Thanksgiving now! I told Stewart she must sit down and write out a formal blessing for dinner, for I knew she would have to say the blessing, but she kept putting it off until we got to the table. They called on me, and she laughed, and then what should I do but stop right in the middle and laugh too? It was awful, but we couldn't help it. They kept playing, "Hallelujah, I'm a Bum." I asked for a Hawaiian tune; they wanted to know which one. I told them just any one would do. We had sweet potatoes, beans, and pie, went up to Boyle's, ate fruitcake, and planned to go to Gilmer to the show. When we got on the hill by the Friddles, the drama of married life was enacted. "You won't go unless you go over my dead body." Too muddy to go to the show, so we came back and spent the evening at Bradshaw's.

Friday, November 30, 1928

Had school today of our own choice so we could have a longer vacation for Christmas. The kids in Dallas had planned a real Thanksgiving, but we taught school. They had dinner at Lukin's and my favorite bean salad too. We went possum hunting and some wild chase. It was quite the fun. Dewey McKnight was our Romeo. He carried the lantern so the schoolmarms could see the way. We built a lot of fires and ate enough persimmons to last a possum for years. Some wild hunt too.

Saturday. December 1, 1928

We hurried this morning and cleaned the real estate off our shoes so we would not get a tax notice for last night's jollity. Boyles asked us to go to Pittsburg with them, so we hurried with our washing. It was a beautiful day, and we enjoyed it immensely but had to do a detour all the way. We got our Christmas cards, and I got some shoes. Not sure I like them. We came back about eight o'clock.

Sunday, December 2, 1928

Stewart was sick this afternoon, so I went with the Boyles to Enoch to their fast service meeting, but they had it immediately after Sunday school. It was a beautiful day, so we drove on out to Talino's to see about a meeting. Saw a wrecked freight train. Came back and went to Mutual. They had me on the program for a retold story. I did not know one, so I simply told him I had been asked to tell a story but would have to tell the truth. I didn't know anything about it, so I'll simply give a reading that illustrates what Elder Boyle had said about yelling for things we want. I read The Tree Toad.

Monday, December 3, 1928

Sister Boyle gave a dinner tonight for the faculty board members and their wives. We all thoroughly enjoyed ourselves very much. Elder Boyle told me about Sister Boyle's sister being so very ill. He didn't know whether to give her the telegram or not. The decision was negative.

Tuesday, December 4, 1928

Went to town to mail the sweet potatoes. Sister Boyle had found out about the telegram and went into town to see about it. We got back and were late for MIA, and I had the characters go in a room and practice Go Slow Mary. It is a play of two hours and fifteen minutes we are putting on for the Relief Society. I like it very much, but it will take a lot of practice.

Wednesday, December 5, 1928

I took the lantern and went alone to practice our play at the church. We didn't get home until late.

Thursday, December 6, 1928

The commercial club at Gilmer is staging an agricultural short course. We took a load of students, and I took Beatrice Bell, Jessie Lindsey, Alma Miller, Laura Bryant, Mildred Jones, and Letha Hamberlin. After we came home, I went to the church to practice. Brother Arthur Emmett Lindsey came up and listened to our practice. Then they walked home with me.

Friday, December 7, 1928

Today, I took the other group of domestic science girls to the short course. It was very cold, and we had no curtains on the car. I had to separate Vera Wade and Goldie Edgar. They had a regular free-for-all fight, and it was all over the itch. We practiced the play again tonight. Leroy Means knew all of the first act lines of his part. Sister Stewart's birthday. Moroni Hamberlin's house burned to the ground.

Sunday, December 8, 1928

We went pecan hunting today: Donnie and Loretta Burnett, Virgil (Viola Perry's son), Sister Stewart, and me. First, we went to Pittsburg and thought we could go to the pecan orchard and pick up pecans on shares but found the orchard all underwater. We came back and went to Winona to the biggest pecan orchard in the world at 10,000 acres. Even they wouldn't let us pick them up on shares, so we had to buy some. Oh, I have never seen such large ones in my life. We ate our lunch on the way there and ran out of gas on the way home. We got home OK. I went to practice the play again tonight. That is quite a strenuous business.

Sunday, December 9, 1928

Invited to a birthday dinner, came home, and wanted a bite of chicken but got fooled. For the birthday dinner, we had corn and meat, cake and pie, and pie and cake. There were Nancy Aaron, Flave Henderson, Wilma Dotson, Leroy Means, Lacoleon Smith, Sister Stewart, and me. We spent the afternoon at the Hendersons', took Nancy home, and then went to church, where I had to talk. I took too much time. I talked on "the influence of good and evil in the world." So many people came up and told me how much they enjoyed it.

Monday, December 10, 1928

Elder Boyle is sick. I have his classes and my own. It is no easy task either. I went to church to practice the play with my pal, the lantern. Had to send Clarence Lindsey home today, and he didn't come to practice tonight.

Tuesday, December 11, 1928

Sent Maurice Dixon and Syril Hamberlin home for throwing in the school room. I told them to tell their mother what they came home for. We went to Mutual but did not have practice tonight. A change of high school teachers was suggested so the work would be more evenly distributed.

Wednesday, December 12, 1928

Elder Boyle is still sick. I went as usual to practice.

Thursday, December 13, 1928

Clarence forgot the playbook, so he and Beatrice could not practice, and neither could the rest of us. We had to go down to his place for it. More practice, especially on "calm." He asked me to be calm—the big calf. Oh, such demonstrations of feeling.

Friday, December 14, 1928.

We went to Sister Bea Shore's birthday party and had a very nice time and a lot of delicious things to eat. Then I took Sister Lindsey home, and one wheel ran off the bridge. Nothing serious. Soon back on, then I got Sister Stewart and Horace Perry, and we all went holly hunting. Got the back of the car filled. It is beautiful too. I went to practice again. Laura Bryant and Horace Perry weren't to practice.

Saturday, December 15, 1928

We told Laura Bryant, Erma McKnight, and Sister Alice Alexander we were going to Gilmer and would be ready at 2:00. They were here promptly, but we had so many boxes to get and so much holly to wrap that we weren't ready until four o'clock, then Sister Alexander thought it was too late and she didn't go with us. When we came home, it was raining so I drove the car up to practice. As soon as choir practice was over, we started our show. When I was ready to come home, the car wouldn't go. I don't know what the matter was. I was the last one at the church. I called "Chauncey" as loud as I could, and he and Leroy Means and Shelton Mitchell came and fixed it and got it to go. We had a hard time finding Erma McKnight and Laura Bryant in town tonight.

Sunday, December 16, 1928

Sister Stewart went up to help Sister Boyle. I started to walk to Sunday school, but the branch was so high. I took Brother Henderson, and we went to church in our car. Brother Shirley and I were appointed to make up a Christmas program. President Green asked if I didn't have a nice young man at home waiting for me, and I had to tell him no. It was so funny there were very few people there. Sister Emma McKnight brought me some exquisite rosebuds. I took two loads of people home after Sunday school. At 2:00, we practiced our show again. It rained, oh my yes, it rained; only Texans know how it can rain here. It rained so hard that Lindseys went home by way of Henderson's, and no meeting was held at the church. We had not practiced on Sunday before, but we told President Green if he would let us, we would never ask again.

Monday, December 17, 1928

Tonight, we went into town. Laura Bryant, Erma McKnight, Sister Alice Alexander, Stewart, and me to buy our Christmas candy. Took Sister Boyle and came home in time for a hurried supper and to rush to church—Stewart to a meeting and me to practice. After practice, they wanted me to come into the meeting. George Henderson has so much dry wit we all nearly laughed ourselves sick, but we all would have frozen stiff. If he hadn't. Uh oh, it was some norther. I sent my aunt Amy some rosebuds for her birthday. She surely was surprised.

Tuesday, December 18, 1928

After Mutual, we practiced, and I came home frozen stiff and with no fire. I was mighty glad I had a warm bed. Some of those kids just won't do their kissing parts.

Wednesday, December 19, 1928

School as per usual and practice in the usual way. Oh, it is so hard to get these people out to practice. Gave exams to my classes and Elder Boyle's.

Thursday, December 20, 1928

Elder Boyle came up for his history class and then went home again, but we didn't dismiss school. Oh no. After practice tonight, we arranged our Christmas

candy. Just after we got in bed, Sister Stewart heard a noise (all imagination). She was afraid to get up, so I did and lighted the lamp and put it on the table. If they wanted to eat it, they would have service "Deluxe," a box of homemade candy for a Christmas present from Mrs. Elliot in Dallas.

Friday, December 21, 1928

I held school only half the day today, and then we went to the church and practiced all afternoon and at night too, for tomorrow night is the play. Virgil Means and Chauncey Jones wanted to go to town; they bet me a bar of candy they could be back in half an hour. I knew they couldn't because the roads were all washed out from the big rain. I got the candy! Oh, it is awfully cold. We heard of a man in Lackawanna, Texas, being drowned in the rain last Monday, and I received a hand-painted portrait.

Saturday December 22, 1928

I received a huge box of candy. Yeah, boy, a five-pounder and a book for Christmas. Boyles wanted us to go with them to Marshall, but I was afraid I wouldn't get back in time for our practice, and I had to fix the stage. I went all over the town for dishes, chairs, and furniture for the stage. We had our practice and then our show at night. The Relief Society sold popcorn and peanuts. Our show Go Slow Mary went off fine, but the people nearly froze. It was so cold.

Sunday, December 23, 1928

The Christmas program was given this morning in Sunday school. Since it had all been previously arranged, we had no idea we would have anything to do, but they asked me to tell what Christ's life has meant to the world. I did my best. They asked Sister Stewart to tell a story, and she said she couldn't. At night, she went into a committee meeting, and again, I was called on to talk. This afternoon, I read Where Love Is There God Is Also, a book given to me by Sister Smith for Christmas, so I told that story. Laura Bryant and Erma McKnight spent the afternoon with us.

Monday, December 24, 1928

"'Twas the day before Christmas when all through the house not a creature was stirring, not even a mouse." I stayed home this afternoon and wrote letters while Sister Stewart decorated the Christmas tree. Today, a car was given away, and Brother Wade won it. We knew there would be a jam, so we went into town early this morning and got our trading over to avoid the rush. When we came home, we found a lot of mail for us. Oh, so many Christmas cards, one of them especially beautiful. We went to see the tree. It was lovely. The first all-holly Christmas trees I have ever seen. Sister Stewart gave me a box of lovely stationery. The Relief Society gave me a box of handkerchiefs for the part I took in putting on that play. I received a lot of other handkerchiefs and cushions from Maurice Dixon.

Tuesday, December 25, 1928

Last night, I forgot to say that the mother of Maurice, Ava Dixon, came and introduced herself to me and wanted to know all about Maurice.

This morning, before we were up, Ruth and Lewis (the Boyles' young children) came in calling "Christmas gifts," and it reminded me of my childhood days—twenty years ago—when I couldn't wait for five o'clock to come. Our screen was locked so Santa left a stocking of candy, nuts, bananas, oranges, and apples for us up at Boyles'. As soon as we were dressed, we ran up to Boyles', and while there, we received the surprise of our lives: a Christmas present. Elder Boyle came home, and Brother Alexander gave us a Utah apple. Then at noon, we went back to Boyles' and had Christmas dinner with them, and what a dinner it was. We took pictures, but there they were, the bunk. Sister Stewart came home and went to bed. I went for a car ride with the Boyles and found out all the radishes were pledged. It was a beautiful day, and we enjoyed the ride. Loretta and Donnie went to the dance with Sister Stewart and me over to Bailey's. We had a good time, and I had some especially good dances.

Wednesday, December 26, 1928

This morning, we left for Dallas. On our way through Gilmer, we got our mail. Floss sent me a very dainty, pretty apron and oh so many Christmas cards. Boyles got a box of candy, and we ate candy on the way over. We stopped at the filling station in Terrell. When we got to Dallas, we were afraid the kids would be gone to meeting, but they were waiting for us. The elders were there too. They went to meeting, and the girls stayed home and talked to us. I felt rotten though. I had such a sick headache.

Thursday, December 27, 1928

We went to town about noon and shopped until 1:00. Then we went to the show at the Majestic. It was Blindfold. Quite an eye-opener to me. After the show, we shopped some more, went home, had supper, and went out to Lukin's.

When we got there, we found that they had cooked dinner for us, especially, and told Elder Kearns to tell us, but I guess he forgot. The elders all went to the sticks today. They wanted us to stay all night, but we couldn't. Came home and talked until midnight.

Friday, December 28, 1928

We wen to Fort Worth with the Boyles. Saw the sister missionaries, but the elders had the flu. Boyles took us through the Swift packing plant. Oh, I shudder when I think of it. I know now I'll never be the same. The cozier (Shochet is what he is called) was there preparing all the meat for the Jewish people. We ate lunch on the way home. It consisted of cheese and bread, apples, grapes, and cookies. As we got back at night, Sister Morgan went to meeting. I wrote a letter until she came back. There, we all sat on the floor and ate candy nuts and talked until 12:30 a.m.

December 29, 1928

Boyles called for us. We bade the girls goodbye and started on our way, stopped at Sears, and then hunted coats in town. Stewart looked for a dress, but while she was trying one on, the clerk said she had one on sale that would just fit her. I liked it so much I bought it and then went back to Green's and got some beads to match it. I had just looked at them a few minutes before but felt I couldn't afford them. Finally, we all got together and started on our way home. Our car went on the blink at Terrell, and we were in a garage there for an hour and a half. Came home and reached here about ten o'clock had so much mail. We didn't get to bed until 11:30. I had another box of chocolates.

Sunday, December 30, 1928

After Sunday school, Eva Dixon came and talked to me about Maurice for two hours, and I guess I wouldn't have gotten home if it hadn't been that Donnie Burnett came along and called, "Come on, Peewee. Let's go home." When we got there, everyone had eaten, but they saved dinner for us. Donnie and Loretta then went with us over to Enoch to see Pearl Arrington. She wasn't there, so we went to Rosewood but met her on the way to the meeting. Elder Boyle went to Gilmer but got back to Kelsey in time to talk on radishes. We went into meeting to learn the care of smallpox. Sister Boyle said to open the blisters with a sterilized needle, cover sore with carbolize salve, cover this with bismuth powder, and then with talcum powder to exclude air.

Elder Boyle gave out that there would not be any school, but Bender said there would.

Monday, December 31, 1928

We had school today, but there was only about a third of the students there. Elder Boyle was with the radish growers all day, so I had his class.

Tuesday, January 1, 1929

New Year's Day. A holiday. Everyone is afraid of smallpox. I wrote letters all day, and at night, as we were getting ready for Mutual, Leroy Means and Lacoleon Smith came and wanted us to go to Enoch to see The Country Kid. We went up to Mutual to take her books, and Virgil Means got in with us. It surely was cold as we left. Virgil and Leroy let the water out of our radiator, but it took them nearly half an hour.

Wednesday, January 2, 1929

Just as we were eating breakfast, Elder Boyle came and told us there wouldn't be any school on account of eight new cases of smallpox. He wanted us to take him to town, we did, and on our way home, we stopped at the Bradshaws' and visited. They wanted us to come over and spend the evening, so we told them we would tomorrow night. I worked on my diary when we came home. I had to get it caught up. The Primary sent me $2.50 for Christmas. I surely was surprised.

Thursday, January 3, 1929

Wrote letters and sewed on LD's (I have no idea what this was) until time to go to Bradshaws'. We had guinea (fowl) for super and other good things. I crocheted and talked until time to go to bed. We put our shoes and everything up on the chair. (Mice maybe?)

Friday, January 4, 1929

When we got up, it was raining so we decided to wait until it quit to come home, but it didn't quit so we went out to start the car, but it wouldn't start. We cranked, pushed, heated water, and dried out the coils and spark plugs, but it was all in vain. Vera Wade and I wanted to come so Sister Stewart came with us. Oh, we waded in mud up over our shoes, and as we walked, I couldn't help feeling sorry for the elders. My dress had come when we got here. I tried it on and went up to Boyles' to an Athenian meeting—talked, crocheted, and ate, then brought Sister Boyle some lunch and read Kenilworth the rest of the evening.

Saturday, January 5, 1929

Everything we own is dirty. It is two weeks since we washed and I was going to wash today, but there was such a cold "norther," and the well was full of muddy water so I will have to wash it some other time.

We have read, studied, eaten chocolates, talked, and put wood in the stove today. I must study my Sunday school lesson. Hooray! I'm now caught up on my diary!

Sunday, January 6, 1929

We went into the parents' class this morning for Sunday school because Sister Stewart lost the lesson. We went to Testimony meeting this afternoon and bore our testimony. I was told that I would have to give a reading tonight, so home I came and studied and studied to give Franz. Well, I gave it, but how? Had to make some of it up. Oh yes, I am the elocution teacher. Ha! Ha!

Monday, January 7, 1929

Nothing extraordinary happened. We just stayed home tonight, and I wrote letters and tried to catch up on my letters. I can't help but wonder why I don't get an answer from my pictures. (They sent them off to be developed.)

Tuesday, January 8, 1929

We went to MIA with Elder Boyle, but as usual, we were late. I had to go up to Sister Stewart's class for my girls. We studied Ernestine Schumann Heink (a famous opera singer of the day) and read Around the Corner to Gay Street.

Wednesday, January 9, 1929

We went to town in the Ford to see if Elder Boyle's car was fixed, but it wasn't. We had our lights fixed, and I had a haircut—glory, hallelujah! We were to have a treat, but it did not come. Andrew Jones, Myrtle's brother, came in and sat on my desk and talked to me for a long while today.

Thursday, January 10, 1929

I was going up to Boyle's to make out reports, but just as I was leaving, Elder and Sister Boyle and the children came. They wanted to go to Jones's in our Ford to administer to Andrew's mother—her fifth stroke of paralysis—my such vitality. I told him I would sit up with her tomorrow night, but they don't think she will live through the night. They came to school for Andrew and Emil Jones this morning, so I dismissed them just after the number work.

Friday, January 11, 1929

Brother Alexander and several others have been fasting since early this morning for Sister Jones. They are too fast twenty-four hours. We are going to stay to Jones's tonight, but since they expect her to die any minute, they think they had better send someone who can lay her out. Elder Boyle took us as far out as Sister Futrell's, and from there we met Bob Simmons and Heber Walton, and they went with us. We ate popcorn balls and helped them with the sick folks. Oh, the snuff dipping! I stayed awake and read Kenilworth part of the time until about three o'clock, and then I got sleepy, so I stood up but went to sleep standing up so. Stewart pulled me down, and I went to sleep on her lap.

Saturday, January 12, 1929

Seven o'clock came, and we started to walk home or to meet Brother Alexander. Met him nearly at Jones's.

She didn't last the night. We came home, helped with breakfast, cleaned up our room, and went to bed.

We got ready and went to Sister Jones's funeral, held at three o'clock. Rather strange, they never gave the family a moment alone at the funeral. They played "Home Sweet Home" for the march. We went to the cemetery, and I sang in the choir then went and helped them clean up the house. I intended to leave, but they begged me to stay, and I did until I felt that I must go. I said I wasn't afraid, but Andrew insisted on walking with me anyway. We did sleep hard tonight because we slept so little today.

Sunday, January 13, 1929

Elder Boyle gave the lesson, and I have to give it next Sunday. After Sunday school, I went to Boyle's to make out reports, but they had company, so I came home. Beatrice Bell and Jessie Lindsey were here all afternoon, so I showed them my clothes and pictures, and they nearly went into ecstasies over them.

At night, we called at Lindsey's, and Sister Lindsey went with us. We went into town, and Elder Boyle bought us an ice cream pie. On the way out to church, we had a flat tire but could not change it because our spare tire key was home. And we had no pump. I had to talk in meeting. Brother Arthur Lindsey said I could have his time, and I took it. I don't know how long I talked. My text was titled "Satan Is Ever Looking for Our Weaknesses." Elder Boyle said I gave the best talk he ever heard me give, and before we left, Sister Lindsey and so many others gave me compliments. As the Lindseys climbed out of the car, Brother Lindsey said, "Well, Sister Dalton, after listening to your sermon, I think I can be a better man than I have been, and it will give me a great deal of food for thought. I learned to know Sister Flossie Lindsey better too. Oh, I have had such a headache all day."

Monday, January 14, 1929

I still have the headache, and I've hardly been able to go all day. I went up to Boyle's to make out report cards. Oh, it's all nonsense. Elva's Christmas present came today.

Tuesday, January 15, 192

Went to MIA and had not only my own class but the women came in too. We are taking up the Ten

Commandments now. The Gleaner girls came down, and I read them a funny story. I did not get to finish it, so I read some of it in general assembly, and I could hardly keep from laughing. They called on me to dismiss, and I wanted to laugh so badly I didn't know whether I prayed for radishes or sick folks. I could hear Stewart snicker every once in a while. I almost told them, "I begged to be excused. I prayed last Tuesday."

Wednesday, January 16, 1929

I feel better today. Went up to Boyle's to "learn to rear children" and to hear the discussions of the "literary digest." I crocheted. They gave me a topic for next time: "Are Sing Sing Men Happy?" We expected Sister Stewart, but she didn't come.

Friday, January 18, 1929

My second-year students debated today and resolved "that whispering should be abolished in the study room." Laurine Lindsey and Emma affirmative—won. John and Leatha had the negative. Sister Alexander entertained the Athenian Club. I helped her fix and serve the lunch and wash the dishes. They chose Cornelia Hamberlin, Eva Dixon, and me to entertain the Athenians and their husbands next Friday night. Oh dear, and President Green will not let us have the church house. How will we ever do it? We got a letter from Elder Hopkins, a nice one too. Father said on his card today he would leave California next Monday.

Saturday, January 19, 1929

Today is Loretta's birthday. Just while we were in the middle of our work this morning, Elder Boyle sent down and asked if we didn't want to go to Leesburg to see their new gymnasium. We hurried as fast as possible. I washed my hair, and we each had a bath. Expected him every minute, but he did not come. He wanted to leave as soon as possible, but he did not come until nearly two. As per usual, it was a beautiful day so didn't wear our coats. Flave went with us. One of the teachers there had been to Utah and was very impressed with Salt Lake City. Stayed a week and loved running water. We looked so terrible. I was embarrassed. She was impressed with the missionary system.

Sunday, January 20, 1929

I hurried this morning and went to teacher training. Had to give the lesson, lead the singing in Sunday school, and give the lesson in our class. Sister Dixon and I met afterward to arrange an entertainment for the Athenians to entertain their husbands next Friday night. Sister Stewart and I both studied this afternoon for fear we would have to preach tonight, but Elder Boyle took up all the time rehashing just what he had Thursday in PTA. Oh, I'm so tired of it. I was late for Mutual doctoring my sore, sore toe. Sister Dixon talked to me about Maurice—ancient history.

Monday, January 21, 1929

Had Velda Smith get a pasteboard and tack it up and write, "Please park your gum here." The students thought it was quite a joke. Went to town tonight to arrange for refreshments for Friday night. Wilma Dotson went too, to see about the French pronunciation of our play. Mrs. Walker helped us. Sisters Bennion, Perry, and Dixon went with us. Today has been a beautiful, warm day. Sister Ida Dotson volunteered her son, Carl, to me, and it came right out of the clear blue sky. She came and spent an hour with us tonight.

Tuesday, January 22, 1929

School all day. Nothing unusual; I went to Mutual and had a fun class. After we studied our lesson,

we talked about patriarchal blessings and tried to impress upon the girls the necessity of prayer. When I suggested that we hadn't read their stories, they said they didn't care; they would rather hear me talk, so I did.

Wednesday, January 23, 1929

Always two sides to a story; today, Beatrice Bell read a theme about how I walked with my head up and my shoulders back. Then Sister Alexander said a woman told her she just wished she could walk like I did. In domestic science today, we made some very good oatmeal cookies. Erma McKnight wasn't there, so Dewey McKnight went home and got some sugar and eggs, for which we gave him a plate of the cookies.

Here is a true-to-life theme Homer Knight handed in this morning.

Our teacher, Miss Dalton, was always looking for someone chewing gum. One day, she was grading English papers at her desk and did not pay much attention to anyone. I kept my eye on her for a long time, and then finally, I began to study and did not notice her. When I looked up again, she was not to be seen. I thought she had stepped out of the room, so I yelled, "Chew your gum, men! She's gone!" Everyone began to chew and pop their gum very loudly. Dewey McKnight, Aubrey Means, and I popped ours the loudest. Those who didn't have gum in their mouth were just putting it in. When I chanced to look behind me, there was Sister Dalton watching the whole room with great interest. She gave out a sharp command: "Homer, Dewey, and Aubrey, park your gun, and the charges will be five cents for parking space."

Tonight, we had current events in the school room. I gave "The Good in Sing Sing's Bad Men." It was a very interesting topic. We had turnips and greens out of the garden today. A "norther" is blowing tonight, and it's real drafty.

Thursday, January 24, 1929

11:05 p.m. But I want to tell you, diary, what I have done today. Early this morning, Elder Boyle said he wanted to thank me for the splendid preparation I gave my topic last night. I let the students chew their gum. Didn't ask a soul to take it out. Sister Bradshaw helped me fix my new black dress. She was at Wade's. Oh, what a tale of woe I heard. It has rained nearly the entire day. Erma McKnight has been sick, so we went to see her tonight. We had popcorn, both sugared and salted. Wrote to Millie.

Friday, January 25, 1929

Tonight, the Athenian club entertains their husbands. Sisters Dixon, Hamberlin, and I were the committee. Everyone seemed to have a wonderful time. We had them draw for partners, and some of the combinations were positively laughable. For refreshments, we served cookies and punch. I sang with Hester Jones and Sister Myrtle Hamberlin. Everyone seemed to thoroughly enjoy themselves.

Wednesday, January 30, 1929

Got my days mixed up. We went to a literary digest class. My topic was "The Refueling of Aeroplanes." (British proper spelling of airplanes.) Then we went to a dance down to Paul Wade's. Both of the musicians were there. Sister Stewart danced with Tommy—a waltz.

Friday, February 1, 1929

We had a Relief Society party. It was called a "Pie Supper." I made a pie, and Loretta put her name on it, and Sister Stewart and I put our names on one of Sister Alexander's. Sheldon Mitchell and Opal Lane got my pie. But poor Sister Stewart. Chester got hers. After school today, we went and got Sister Perry and took her down to Addie Mae Ault's for the Athenian Club meeting. Then we came back, and it was raining, but we went to church.

Saturday, February 2, 1929

Raining today, couldn't wash. Oh, it was cold. Went to Gilmer in the afternoon. Rawleigh wanted to go to Gilmer with us, but he got impatient before we were ready, so he walked. But we caught up with him, and he rode with us, so did Sister Perry, Brother Lindsey, and Beatrice. I went to choir practice and practiced the play afterward. When I came home in the car, Sister Stewart came out to meet me. On the way in, I was stargazing and fell over the wood pile. Sister Stewart tried to move me, and I asked her to leave me. I said, "Oh, don't move me. Don't move me." She bathed my arm in hot water for hours before I could get any relief, but finally, I felt better, and we went to bed.

Sunday, February 3, 1929

I didn't go anyplace today. Sister Stewart got Sister Boyle to come and rub my arm, and she bandaged it up for me. I sat here all day by the fire with my arm on a pillow. Sister Henderson came to see me while the rest were all gone to a meeting. I got Norma Alexander to write and tell Father about it. My arm hurts so bad wish I could have a doctor see if it's broken.

Monday, February 4, 1929

I went to school today, but it wasn't because I wanted to or at least because I felt like it. I can move my fingers a little today. Sister Boyle says the ligaments in my arm are torn loose and that it is badly bruised. I will have to learn to write and eat with my left hand. Oh my. Yesterday, Sister Stewart had to help give me a bath.

Tuesday, February 5, 1929

Went to Mutual. The girls were telling me about Amanda McKnight asking in Sunday school to have me prayed for that I would soon be all right.

Wednesday, February 6, 1929

Well, we, us, and company gave me a bath. I had to write on some of the themes today, and Maurice Dixon said, "Miss Dalton, are we supposed to read this Chinese writing at the top of the page?" Just lefthanded. This left-handed eating is some business. For my birthday, Sister Stewart gave me a nice box of Coly's bath powder.

Tuesday, February 12, 1929

Mutual tonight, but oh so much noise upstairs. They were trying to sing, and nothing would do but what we sang too—yes, Boy Scouts, Chester, and all.

Thursday, February 14, 1929

I have been practicing for so many nights on the play called June Time. It is clever but oh so hard to keep people taking their parts. Tonight, the Athenian Club gave their party in the schoolhouse. Sister Stewart, Bea Bell, and Loretta Burnett were on the committee to entertain. We had a wonderful time. I got Ben Dixon's pretty valentine. Sister Perry came with Buncas Farley (Manie's son). I read Baked Beans and Culture. Stuttered on some of it but started over. Donnie and Loretta went with me to get ice and salt for the party. I can't drive because of my arm. The invitations were heart-shaped; other hearts were all colors, hidden in different places. They had each group hunt; the one who got the most hearts won.

Friday, February 15, 1929

All met in assembly upstairs while I helped clean the room for Myrtle Jones's students and clean the domestic science room. I went to practice our play June Time.

Saturday, February 16, 1929

Sister Stewart washed, and I cleaned the house. It was very warm. The Boyles took Aunt Mary to Tyler. I just have my arm out of the sling, but I can't begin to straighten it.

Sunday, February 17, 1929

I had the lesson in Sunday school today. Tonight, Brother Shirley came to Sister Stewart and me and told us he wanted us to preach. Sister Stewart asked him to let her lead the singing instead, so he did, and I preached on the word of wisdom.

Monday, February 18, 1929

Bad weather again, back to school.

Tuesday, February 19, 1929

Too rainy tonight to have Mutual; we just stayed home.

Wednesday, February 20, 1929

I went to practice the show June Time. Came home, and Carl Dotson, Ida's son had been there.

Thursday, February 21, 1929

Sister Stewart and I went to town for salt cookies for her Gleaner girls' night. They are entertaining the "M" men, and tomorrow is a holiday, and we were afraid the stores would be closed. Today is the first time I have driven the car since my arm was hurt. We stopped in to see Viola Bradshaw; she has been so sick.

Friday, February 22, 1929

Washington's Birthday holiday, we went into Gilmer for ice for the party. Norma and Imogene Alexander and Sister Viola Perry went with us. I went to practice in the afternoon and then helped Sister Stewart make the ice cream. The invitations were in the shape of shields. All over the room were hidden letters spelling Washington. They were cut from different colors of paper. They chose four different groups to hunt all these hidden letters. When they had found them all, they asked them to trade with the other groups until they had traded off all the letters they didn't need. The side who had the most complete "Washington" won the game. Fun, I'll say.

Saturday February 23, 1929

I washed this morning and then went to the bake sale given by the Athenian Club. I helped sell hot dogs, and then Letha Hamberlin, Sister Stewart, and I went to the jail to see Newie Bailey. Oh, such sadness; Mr. Wall joked to us about going down to the hatchery.

Sunday, February 24, 1929

Sister Stewart gave the lesson in Sunday school. We studied this afternoon, but no meeting was held. It was too rainy.

Monday, February 25, 1929

It was sure rainy and muddy all morning, but this afternoon, it came out bright and warm. They commenced work on the gym, and I went to practice our play.

Tuesday, February 26, 1929

Went to Mutual tonight. Letha Hamberlin (Victor Carl's sixteen-year-old daughter) has changed classes, but we are having both girls and boys.

Wednesday, February 27, 1929

We had a dance at Moroni Hamberlin's new house. Oh, how they teased me about Carl Dotson dancing with me so much. We took Johnny Futrell and his wife, Rusie, home.

Thursday, February 28, 1929

Sister Stewart went with me up to practice tonight. She was to find all the fault she could with our play, but they played it P-U-N-K, and I felt very much discouraged, so I went to practice on Friday night. Made banana pudding for Rawleigh Alexander.

Friday, March 1, 1929

Elder Boyle left early this morning to meet President Bennion in Gilmer and take him and Elder Bennion to the Rotarian luncheon. I have had the students all day and the worry of this play. I dismissed them at 2:30, and as I came down the hill, my hat in my hand, I met President Bennion along with Elders Bennion and Boyle.

I was horrified he gave me a box of candy for Sister Stewart and me. I went to the church to practice. Laura Bryant went with me to gather up chairs and everything. On the way up the long hill, we ran out of gas, and I had to back down to Ault's store and get some gas. Just while we were getting ready to practice, here came Elder Bennion. Well, I was horrified I couldn't do anything then. I barely had time to run home and change my dress before it was time to start the play. We had prayer before the play started, and oh my. That play went off like a whiz. They never had taken their parts as well as they did that night. The audience laughed and laughed. President Bennion complimented me on it. The Relief Society sold popcorn and peanuts with chances on a quilt, and Kyle Whitehead got it. (Kyle is the son of Sister Whitehead.)

Sunday, March 3, 1928

We were to meet President Bennion up at the church, so we went early, and he talked to us; we had to talk in Sunday school. Elder Bennion drove our car over to Enoch for us. We were to stay there to meeting that night, and we went to Pritchetts to supper. It rained so hard we thought the bottom had fallen out of everything. We didn't have meeting. Sister Stewart and I went to bed and left Elder Bennion writing letters. I had to offer family prayer. It almost embarrassed me.

Monday, March 4, 1928

Got up this morning, had breakfast, and started on our journey homeward. Water had been all over those Kelsey Creek bridges and for a long way had run over the road, but with Elder Bennion at the wheel, we arrived safe and sound. Came home changed my dress and went to school. After school Elders Bennion, Saurey, and Bingham came up there and wanted us to take Elder Bennion in our car to Nance's. We got stuck. Yes, stuck in the mud. Our Ford dragged on the old high centers. We met some oil trucks; they told us they would help us out of the mud, but they got stuck and we couldn't get down the road. We got a man to let us go through his cotton field or we may have been there all night. I went to the schoolhouse and had a Shakespeare class. Sister Stewart and the two elders talked, and soon Carl Dotson joined them. After he went, we four talked. They went to Hamberlin's to stay. We took them as far as Dotson's.

Tuesday, March 5, 1928

Elders were sitting on the south side of the schoolhouse. We wanted them to talk in assembly, but they wouldn't. Boy Scouts and junior girls met in my class; they seemed to like it. Conference was over once more. I feel like I had been to a sideshow and had tried to see them all.

Wednesday, March 6, 1929

Elder Boyle took the agricultural boys to Marshall, so I had the rest of the students all day. I had a Romeo and Juliet class here at home. The house was full.

Thursday, March 7, 1929

We had a faculty meeting to decide what our closing program should be and to arrange for the county meet. I have the declamation. Oh my! Homer Knight Emil Jones, Alva Lindsey, and Laurine Lindsey are entering. The first three are juniors, and Laurine is a senior.

Friday, March 8, 1929

The Athenians Club met at Sister Blanche Bell's. We went up and got Sister Viola Perry and took her down there and just got there in time for refreshments. It was raining so I took Sisters Perry, Dixon, and Boyle home then went back to Sister Bell's. Saw such pretty hawthorn blossoms. Talked and ate supper. Yes, imagine where we put it. Then came to the Busy Bee party given in honor of the Bumble Bees. We had a good time, but on my way up, it was so dark I couldn't see where I was going so, I stepped off the road, tore two buttons off my dress, and tore my stockings. We went back to Sister Bell's. It rained so hard Sister Bell came in to see if we were OK.

Saturday, March 9, 1929

Came home from Sister Bell's. I washed and then sisters Perry, Alexander, and Letha Hamberlin went down to town with us. We went to the "M" men's party for the Gleaner girls. We had banana ice cream, cake, and punch and were afraid it had too much to it. I couldn't drink mine, but I wouldn't let them know I didn't. I poured it out.

Sunday, March 10, 1929

We learned in Sunday school that Elder Bowman was coming over here to hold a meeting at five o'clock. Sister Stewart wouldn't even stay to Sunday school she went home immediately. I had to give the lesson on Samuel, but we didn't have a class to give it to until Sunday school was over. We studied until time to go to the meeting, but it was late when we got there so we didn't go in. We tried to get President Green to let us off from preaching. I said I couldn't preach, and I couldn't when I got up, so I have determined never to say that again. President Bennion says we must talk every Sunday night. Elder Bowman came home and had supper with us and spent the rest of the evening, then we took him to Hendersons' to spend the night.

Monday, March 11, 1929

Elder Bowman came up to school while I was having domestic science, after which we went to a faculty meeting, and he went with us. They wanted us to have a display for the domestic science department. I told them I would try. Elder Bowman and I went with the Boyles to Percy Hamberlin's and Muckleroy's. Oh my. I surely learned something. Sister Stewart had gone to practice. We came home, had supper, and went to Gilmer to the show. I drove the car; he surely did compliment me on my driving. He sat and talked to us a long time after we got to Hendersons'. He wrote a pretty sentiment in my autograph album.

Tuesday, March 12, 1929

We went to Mutual, met with Sister Stewart's class, and sang songs. We want to sing some of these songs at our junior Boy Scout party next Friday night.

Wednesday, March 13, 1929

School all day, same old story! Six months from now, we will be laughing about present tragedies. I told Maurice's mother how naughty he was, and she didn't believe it.

Thursday, March 14, 1929

It rained again as per usual. I have had the domestic science girls all this week but Tuesday.

Friday, March 15, 1929

The domestic science girls made chocolate pudding. Sister Ava Dixon visited our class. She went to town with me. I had to get ice for our party of juniors and Boy Scouts. I heard her life story all the way to town and back. But I enjoyed driving the car anyway. I made the ice cream then came home and got ready and went back. We had a lot of mothers there. Served ice cream, chocolate sauce, and cake. Rawleigh and I brought our freezer home and made some more ice cream, called Sister Alexander, and gave her some in bed.

Saturday, March 16, 1929

I hurried with my work this morning then I went up to the schoolhouse to clean. Rawleigh, Shelton, Audrey, and Velda helped me. I came home, had my bath, then Vera Wade came, and we practiced "Hail to the Brightness of Zion's Glad Morning." We sang that as a double quartet tonight with Laura Bryant and Goldie Edgar. This is the Relief Society celebration.

Sunday, March 17, 1929

Brother Shirley taught our class. We thought we were going to Enoch tonight, but Elder Boyle said they would go there so we were sent here. I talked for twenty-five minutes on prayer. There was no noise in the building. I enjoyed talking tonight.

Monday, March 18, 1929

I was writing letters when Carl Dotson came in to see about plays. We told him we were coming over to spend the evening. I crocheted and looked at old pictures. Sister Alexander went with us on Tuesday.

Tuesday, March 19, 1929

We went to Mutual and had a wonderful lesson on "Thou Shalt Not Bear False Witness against Thy Neighbor." Someone threw an egg in at the window. Oh my!

Wednesday, March 20, 1929

We were preparing for the county meet—practice, practice! I'll be glad when it's over. John Ault hurt his foot.

Thursday, March 21, 1929

We surely wish John could go to the county meet. Alva Lindsey won third place. At first, she tied for second place, but then it had to be taken back to the judges and she won third. Oh, Columbus! She has to try over again tomorrow night. We started out to Wood's but saw our boys playing ball with Big Sandy. I got so excited I nearly pounded Sister Stewart's arm off. After the game, we went to Wood's, came back, and called for Laurine, Alma, Laura, and Sister Perry. We surely did have a time getting my dress finished for the exhibit. I was up sewing this morning at six thirty. I forgot to say last night we went over to Lindsey's— enjoyed it.

Friday, March 22, 1929

We went to the county meet early today. Took Laurine Lindsey, Irma Blyn McKnight, Artie Slater, son of Lottie Lindsey, and Horace Perry. Laurine won second place out of twelve girls in declamations. She read The American Spirit Incarnate. Then we went out to Talino's, but they were all in the field, so we just stayed a few minutes. When a man was passing us on the way out, he ran into the gutter. We went into Gilmer again tonight to hear the tryouts, but the girls didn't change their place. Oh my! It has been so hot today, just like a July day. Oh, I'm glad we don't have to go to the meet tomorrow. Flave gave his boys a quarter for each "home run."

Saturday, March 23, 1929

We didn't go to town today. I washed, and this afternoon, we went over to Sister Ethel Bradshaw's to tell them we couldn't stay because Sister Stewart had a "boil on her nose," but they finally persuaded her to stay, so we came back after our dresses for Sunday school tomorrow. On the way back, we picked up some fellow going to the oil well, so we went too. Quite some well! I had no idea it was that large. We went back to Bradshaw's tonight, and Autie, Ethel's stepdaughter, played for us, and we went to bed. It has been as hot as it ever is in July at home. This afternoon, I simply had to lie down while I was shortening my georgette dress two inches. I felt I had lost every ounce of my vitality.

Sunday, March 24, 1929

Oh, I feel so punk today. I went to Sunday school in Enoch; we thought we would stay in the parents' class, but they asked us to go into the Old Testament class, and when we got there, they were simply running wild. They asked us to take the class; Stewart would not so I had to. I just had to appeal to them to be gentlemen. Jewel Wilburn Pritchett left the room, and I was happy. The class then went fine. After Sunday school, we came home and studied, then went over there to meeting again; I preached on prayer and Stewart on preexistence.

Monday, March 25, 1929

Tonight, we went over to Brother Shirley's to visit. I can't help but think, We live to learn in life's hard school. How few married people are really happy? His war experiences and all his souvenirs were very interesting. If ever I saw one really true LDS, he is surely it.

Tuesday, March 26, 1929

It rained all day. Tonight, Rawleigh said the water in the "branch" was up to our knees. Sister Alice Alexander would not go to the meeting, but we went and were prepared to wade, but the water had gone down. All kinds of flowers are in bloom: violets, lilies (on the table now), and hyacinths. We had radishes today for dinner, and it has been so hot that this morning's milk was sour by tonight. Elder Boyle said he had a "trade cast" for me. He said the people here were creating quite a sentiment to ask President Bennion to let me stay again next year. That surely thrilled me, even though it is impossible.

Wednesday, March 27, 1929

I had a letter from Sister Leinbach; she says her husband is doing better. Reading the Bible. Domestic science girls made cheese croquets—didn't get the cheese hot enough. They scrubbed the floor. I had a lot to do tonight, but Virgil Means sat and talked to me for an hour and a half or so. Mose Whitehead (son of Lucinda Tefteller) was going to throw Chester down the stairs to take his cap.

Thursday, March 28, 1929

We went to Sister Boyle's to the Athenian Club social. Just got there in time to eat as usual. Went down to Bryant's and visited them, then took Laura, Audrey Bryant, and Sister Alice Alexander to Enoch to see My Dixie Rose, a very pretty little play. Oh my! How it did rain while we were there, and the roads were so slick when we came home that J. C. Wade got stuck on Jones Hill, where the bridge was washed out. Heber Jones drove our car through, so we came sailing home.

Saturday March 30, 1929

The Athenian Club had their big sale today, which did quite well. We went to town and took Sister Emma McKnight, Erma McKnight, and Rawleigh Alexander. I took my dresses to the cleaners, had my hair cut, went to the bank, and wanted to finish my shopping. And had to go to Wood's home, but it was too late. We just had to hurry to the Hunt's and McKnight's and rush home because we had dinner at Brother Jasper Lindsey's. We enjoyed it too. They have a nice family. That Dodd fellow coaxed us to come to Enoch tomorrow night.

Sunday, March 31, 1929

We had a good Sunday school class. Brother Shirley was our teacher. We studied all afternoon and then went to Enoch to preach tonight, but a "terrible cloud" came up, and everyone was afraid so Sister Stewart just talked on the Resurrection, and then we left. I surely was disappointed because I didn't get to give my Easter sermon. I had spent all afternoon preparing, but the audience weren't. We took Loretta to Indian Rock, Brother Alexander went with us, and then we all stayed to meeting in Enoch. We went to Whitehead's to dinner, and it was some dinner too. We had eggs fixed in six different ways, and oh such pie and cake.

Monday, April 1, 1929

Today is the day we see ourselves as others see us the rest of the year. Elder Boyle promised the boys and girls if they would come to school this morning, we would take them on a trip this afternoon. Didn't expect everyone, but to our surprise, they were all there. The bell and the songbooks were missing; Elder Boyle was quite the angry man.

This afternoon, Flave and I took our students (Elder and Sister Boyle were too busy to go) over to Young's pasture, and oh how we played ball. When we came home, we went gathering sweet gum. Scyril Hamberlin whirled and threw a ball glove. It just glazed the side of my head. We went to Dotson's to an April Fools' Day party given by the Gleaners; things were clever. Just outside the door was written, "Private, no trespassing."

On the looking glass was written, "Watch the fool look." On the bed was a $5 fine for sitting here. There were several bottomless drawers. We served a buffet luncheon.

Tuesday, April 2, 1929

We went to Mutual—as usual, we were late. Just after we got there, the lights went out and we were left in the dark, so we just had to sing songs till the light came on. We practiced our pantomime, "And the Lights Went Out," after Mutual, I had to come home alone, and it surely was dark. I just had to feel my way down the hill.

Wednesday, April 3, 1929

Dewey McKnight talked quite disrespectfully to me because I had not asked him to be in the play. The Relief Society harvested their radishes, and Sister Stewart went with hem to Rosewood to take them. We stayed home tonight.

Thursday, April 4, 1929

We went to town and took Sisters Perry, Muckleroy, Alexander, and Erma McKnight. I got my dresses from the cleaners, and then we went out to Sister Wood's but had to rush home so Sister Stewart could go up to see. "M" men's play. I stayed here with Ruth and Louis Boyle, Norma and Imogene Alexander. I played the piano, and we all sang Sunday school songs. Then while I did some mending, we had a program; everyone but us had gone off.

Friday, April 5, 1929

Loretta came up home. We did not get home from
school till nearly dark. We had a lot of work at school.
We all went to the boys' play. It was good; it was called
Wooing under Difficulties. They surely took hold of it
in fine order.

Saturday, April 6, 1929

I washed today, and sun burned my neck and
nose— not because I did not have my big "tracking"
hat on but because there was such a terrible wind. It was
so hard it tore our clothes when we put them on the line.
We went to practice "And the Lights Went Out," but
Myrtle didn't come to song practice until eight o'clock,
so we were all there together wanting to practice, and
it was rather a mess. Then we all went to the oil well.
There was half of several towns there! I quite enjoyed it.

Sunday, April 7, 1929

Sister Stewart and I have felt quite lonely or
homesick today, and we can't figure out just why. It
may be because it is so near time to go home, or it
may be because they are having conference at home. I
went to teachers' training class, then to Sunday school,
then the fast meeting, and then to a supposed Mutual
program, but no program had been arranged so Elder
Boyle, Sister Stewart, and I did the talking and the
fighting of bugs. Oh me! Oh my! I think Elder Boyle
talked better than I have ever heard him. He compared
the Gospel veneer to the mahogany and oak veneer used
on furniture—a splendid illustration. Let us as Latter-
day Saints have a solid mahogany faith and not a faith of
veneer. Stewart talked on the Resurrection, and I talked
on obedience to law. We all hit the pulpit and stomped,

but that was to keep the bugs away. We rode home in Boyle's car. I stood by the car for a long time, and Elder Boyle told me how much he appreciated the attitude I had taken this year and the splendid work I had done. While I ate supper, Brother and Sister Alexander sat and talked to me. Brother Alexander said he hoped I would find someone for a companion who was worthy of me, but he feared I never would.

Monday, April 8, 1929

We went out tonight after school to see as many people as we could. We went to Victor Carl Hamberlin's, to Dotson's, to Percy Hamberlin's, and to Henderson's, then we had to rush home because I wanted to practice at seven o'clock. When I sat down to eat, I had fifteen minutes before I should be at the church, but I "swallowed" my supper and was there on time. It rained so hard only half the players were there, so we experimented with light and looking glasses to make moonbeams and lightning. I chewed some of Audrey Bryant's bark, of all things. I surely spit…

Tuesday, April 9, 1929

We went to the church this afternoon to practice. Dewey McKnight is taking his part in the play, all right.

His mother surely felt bad about him talking to me as he did. The people are surely good to make us quilt blocks. I rushed home and had a bath before we went over to Sister Cumming's. Sister Bailey surely gave me some beautiful roses of all colors. We went to Mutual, and the Boy Scouts invited the junior girls to a play in the church to be given Thursday night.

Wednesday, April 10, 1929

I have been giving exams today. Oh my, I can hardly get Syril Hamberlin and Bennion Perry to read Romeo and Juliet. I fear they will never get their credit in English, but I worry more than they do. I let both girls' classes meet in domestic science, and each made what they wanted to. The cream puffs were really good, but we had to make a filling, and the cream would not whip. We had a good practice up to the church. They know their parts quite well.

Thursday, April 11, 1929

We went to town today. Laura and Emma went with us. I wanted to get a pair of light shoes, so I tried everything they had in town but didn't buy any. After I got home, I wished I had bought the last pair I tried on. I saw some beautiful dresses too. I would like one of the rose georgette ones. We came home but visited Sister Bradshaw on our way. Sister Wade had asked us to go sit with her a while. Went to the Boy Scout party for the junior girls. They had six gallons of ice cream.

Friday, April 12, 1929

We were going to the Athenian Club meeting over to Med Buckley's, but Sister Boyle had our car and did not come for us. When she did come, the back tire was flat. We pumped it and went to borrow things for the play. Then we went to Henderson's for supper. I had to be at the church to practice at 7:30 but didn't get there until eight o'clock. Our tire went flat and we couldn't get it fixed, so Sister Boyle and Stewart were parked there until 10:30 or after. When I came home, they were not here so I took the lantern and went out in the rain to find them. Met them coming home.

Saturday, April 13, 1929

Went to Boyle's to write in all the books we bought with the proceeds of the play June Time. It was too rainy to wash. Went to town with Elder Boyle in our car. Sisters Jones, Alexander, and Loretta. I bought some light shoes and decided to take the rose dress but did not take it out. They reduced it $4.50. We went with Boyles to the Hill and Dale Booster Club meeting. When I gave my farewell talk, I cried several tears. President Bennion came down in his car and brought Lelia and Elder Bennion.

Monday, April 14, 1929

Sister Stewart would not give the lesson because Lelia Bryant was there. I played the piano until Sister Cornelia Hamberlin came. We went to Jones's for dinner. Just came home and started to study when Elder Bennion came. He gave us a picture and wrote in our books. We were going to Enoch, but a terrible storm came up. The Boyles and I went up there to church. They didn't have any church, and we just got home in time to avoid a drenching rain. Elder Bennion stayed here.

Monday, April 15, 1929

The Athenian Club gave us a party. I helped with the games. We played a game where we had to run with feet spread out; the next one they ran with their feet turned in (too funny). Prizes were given for the best one of each.

They had judges. They got two even lines—part men and part women in each one. The ones who were the best they had to try over again. Moroni Hamberlin laid an egg. When he had finished, they were given slips of paper so they would know whether they were to cackle or crow. Brothers Alexander and Jones wrestled. I shall never forget Brother Jones's green bloomers. Maurice and Bennion wrestled too. Had the surprise of my life; the club gave us the cutest apron and picture, and Sister McKnight gave me an incense burner. Sister Stewart wouldn't talk first, and I know I made a mess of what I said. Elder Bennion was there, and that made me feel even sillier.

Tuesday, April 16, 1929

We went to town today. Elder Bennion drove, and Sister Stewart and I sat in the back. I got $2 more knocked off my dress so I bought it. Saw President Bennion in town, and he wanted to know if I was wearing a diamond. He told me we could go anyplace we wanted to. We had a practice after Mutual. Vera Wade went to the oil well and didn't come to practice.

Wednesday, April 17, 1929

Today is the last day of school. I can hardly realize it. Oh my! The work. When I came home from practice, I had to sit up and correct papers, and today, I feel the effects. President Bennion came up to school, and making our reports. I rode up and Sister Bennion.

Thursday, April 18, 1929

Oh dear, I can hardly move today. I have felt so terrible. I do not know whether it has been the strain of this closing program, but I feel terrible. Elders Beardall and Cheney came to tell us goodbye. Then they went to Enoch with Brother Pritchett. President Bennion left this morning. We made reports all day, and I didn't get to take my quilt over to Sister Dixon's. Now they won't get to quilt it for me. We went to a dance over to Sister Grantham's. I had so much fun I forgot I was sick.

Friday, April 19, 1929

We went to the schoolhouse and worked on reports. Then went to town and sent a long telegram to President Bennion asking for addresses. We rushed home and did a two-week wash, then went to Sister Dixon's to the Athenian. Didn't get there until five o'clock. Visited for a minute and then went to Wade's for supper. They gave us a balling out for being late and for eating before we went there. We went with them to the oil well. Vera rode in our car. We didn't stay long. We were too tired. We came home and ironed then went to bed.

Sunday, April 21, 1929

We woke with a start at the sound of someone calling, "Girls." We were up and out of bed before we were fully awake because we knew the Boyles were nearly ready to start on our trip, but we were ready when they called. We reached Waco at nine o'clock tonight. We had intended to stay with Belle, but Elder Boyle didn't know the city, so we went on the streetcar out to Farley's and stayed all night. Mary had us surprise her mother and father. They seemed overjoyed to see us, treated us royally, called Sister Reeves, and she came down and talked until midnight. We slept fine until breakfast was ready, then we got up and called Mrs. Spindle and the missionaries.

Monday, April 22, 1929

After breakfast, Mr. Farley took us out to Elder Boyle's. We left Waco in good time, but when we got out eight miles, we discovered we had a broken spring, so we had to come back into Waco to have it fixed. I called the missionaries, and Elder Widdowson and Sisters Lindbergh and Woolley came down and talked to us. I was much disappointed at not seeing Belle, but it couldn't be helped. We reached Austin tonight and stayed in a tourist camp—first one in my life. We saw the city by night.

Tuesday, April 23, 1929

We went through the capital. Oh my. It is four hundred and some odd steps from the basement to the dome. It was so hot we nearly suffocated. Elder Boyle accomplished what he wanted to at the capital, and then we went to San Antonio. We found the missionaries all right, but they had given us the elder's address. After we visited them, they took us down to the girls and I was glad to find Sister Kindred and Sister Hixson. We went to Mutual, then out to Sister Turley's, and stayed all night. We lay there in the bed and listened to the radio.

Wednesday, April 24, 1929

It was raining this morning when Mrs. Turley took us home in their car after she had given us a very good breakfast. We went downtown and shopped there. Brother Wickwire took us in his car all over the city. Then we went to the Aztec Theater and saw The Showboat. It was so different from most of the shows. We sat on the lawn and listened to the band, and then got a free seat to see the Pioneer Parade. After the parade, we ate and came home. The girls went to Turley's.

Thursday, April 25, 1929

After we got up this morning, we went to town with Turley's and then to the Palace to see The Goose Hangs High. Then we went home and went out to the Spanishspeaking where President Pratt talked. It was very interesting, if not very instructive. Songs and all were carried on in Spanish. We were going to leave tonight, but Turleys didn't come soon enough. Sister Hixson came for us, and we went to Turley's for dinner. Then they took us to the parade of the fiesta. It took one hour and twenty minutes to pass in front of us.

Mrs. Turley took us home, and the girls went to a street meeting. We left at 11:30 p.m. on the Sunset Limited. We had a chair car but didn't sleep much. Got off the train at Houston and looked around the city but didn't see anything so impressive as the mounted police. We looked for the missionaries on the street, but in vain. Left that night for New Orleans; we had a chair car but slept better. Sister Stewart had a pillow.

Sunday, April 28, 1929

We reached New Orleans at 6:40 a.m. after the unique experience of crossing the Mississippi on a ferry. We found the elder's address, and they took us to the girl's place. They went to Sunday school, but when we had our baths, we went too. They had us preach, then we went through the Saint Charles and Roosevelt Hotel, down to the park, came back, and went to street meeting. It seems strange. Went home and had pie and ice cream.

Monday, April 29, 1929

We got up to class and really enjoyed quoting scripture again. We went on a sightseeing trip in the Gray Line. Canal Street is 172 feet wide. Five streetcar tracks on it separate Spanish and French settlements from American. Gave us a sample of magnolia perfume made out of the state flower. We went to Thompson's and had lunch, then met Sister Stringham. We were too late to go with the first group, but when they found we were missionaries, they took us through with a special guide. We all went to the Saenger Theater and saw Nothing but the Truth. It was clever. That is by far the most beautiful theater I have ever been in. It is filled with French statuary. They took us through and showed us all the heating and cooling apparatus and how the clouds move in the moonlight garden with many novelties in lights, flowers, and water; I shall never forget them unloading bananas.

Tuesday, April 30, 1929

I worked a quilt block for Sister Reich of Hurricane, and then Elder Giles came in and said his mother had had a stroke of paralysis. He felt so bad, and we tried to comfort him. Then we all went down to the loading docks on the Mississippi River, but no boats were in. Went back to the French market, which covers two blocks. Every vegetable I have ever heard of was there, and some I never knew grew. We bought a bunch of bananas for us, and I bought a basket to put them in so we could bring them home to Brother Alexander.

We did some shopping then came home, had dinner, went to the train, and at 9:10 started our journey to Shreveport.

Wednesday, May 1, 1929

We reached Shreveport at seven o'clock after having spent a miserable night on the most bumpy, jerky train in the US. We had breakfast and then went through the town and to the Parish Courthouse. It is all built of white marble and very pretty. We were tired out, so I didn't see much of the town. We went back to the station and slept and wrote letters. We had a layover from 7:00 in the morning until 12:40 p.m. Then we took the train to Marshall, where we had to lay over forty minutes after we got on the train. Oh, how it rained. We were afraid Alexanders wouldn't be there, but they were, and we enjoyed our trip home. It seemed like we had been gone eleven weeks instead of that many days. We had ice cream. Oh, it was good. Then we went to bed. We had lots of mail when we came home. A box of candy too.

Thursday, May 2, 1929
We wrote letters today and cleaned up our house, then tonight we went to the oil well and saw the grave where lies the last scout who crossed over the fence. We had a puncture on our way down, and Donnie and Brother Alexander fixed it for us.

Friday, May 3, 1929
We went to the club over to Eva Dixon's, and they gave us our quilts. They are surely pretty. We went down to Edgar's and spent the night. We promised them we would come all winter long, but we never got there until tonight. She had quilts with the tiniest blocks I've ever seen.

Saturday, May 4, 1929
We came home early, and I did two weeks' wash. We got ready and took Sister Ava Dixon, her daughter Faye, Sister Alice Alexander, and her daughter Loretta. We brought some ice and strawberries home, and of all the good ice cream I have ever eaten, it was then. We had a very bad rain.

Sunday, May 5, 1929
We went to Enoch to Sunday school, and when they found we would be there, they had a meeting right after Sunday school and turned it over to us, and it was very much of a surprise. I taught the Book of Mormon class, we had dinner at President Lindsey's, then we came home, slept, studied, and got ready for the meeting, but

they had a program, so we didn't have to preach. We took Brother and Sister Dotson, along with Carl, home in the car tonight. It seemed good to see everyone. We came home and had supper here. They want us to wait long enough for the "M" men to give us a party.

Monday, May 6, 1929

We didn't get any mail today. I guess no one knows where we are. It was so hot this afternoon we felt we would suffocate. We went to Sister Taylor Smith's to visit. Sherwin had just had a chill. Went to Henderson's, then to Bradshaw's, where Stewart and I made ourselves sick eating mulberries. After supper, we danced and did all kinds of stunts.

Tuesday, May 7, 1929

Got up this morning at 5:15 a.m. and had breakfast. Ate mulberries, picked peas, got new potatoes, and then came to Muckleroy's. Rex had had a chill. Said goodbye to Sister Perry and Sister Shore and then had lunch at Sister Wade's. Took Vera on our ward teaching as far as the oil well. Paul set them up for us. We came home and mended our clothes. Sister Cummings came over and nearly talked to her head off. We took her home in the car. Went to Mutual. Sister Myers had the girls, so then I gave the lesson. The M men planned a party for us tomorrow night. We were to stay at Myrtle's, but she wasn't home.

Wednesday, May 8, 1929

Today, we got all our things packed to leave in the morning. They, especially Brother Alexander, were trying to get us not to go. We went to town, posted our quilts and my picture home, and then rushed back to

President Green's for dinner. He forgot to tell them we were coming so they had finished dinner, but they gave us some. We visited Sisters Perry and Jones there, then we went to Benders to see if you could have a party in the schoolhouse. He said since it was us who is asking, we could have it. It rained all afternoon. We made two freezers full of ice cream at the party. I surely did enjoy it. We brought strawberries home tonight. Alexanders got ice and made ice cream. Came home with Ben Dixon, and Brother Alexander was still up. He said he could not sleep. He said he surely did hate to see us go. We talked until nearly 1:00 a.m. then went to bed.

Thursday, May 9, 1929

It was still raining when we got up. Herber Jones would not come up after the milk and was late taking our trunks. Brother Alexander had asked him to come up after our trunks tomorrow. I slept all morning. Sister Shore, Beatrice Bell, and her mother (Loretta Dixon) were there. They popped corn and gave us popcorn balls, sweetened popcorn, and peanut brittle. Maybe it was brittle. Then we went to Sister McKnight's, Sister Whitehead's, Brother Shirley's, Myrtle Hamberlin's and then Edgar's. They wanted us to stay all night, but we wanted to stay all night "at home." This morning, Brother Alexander told us how much he hated to see us go. He talked by the kitchen stove, and he almost surprised me by what he said. Loretta (Alexander Burnett) and Sister Alexander gave us some sofa cushion tops.

Friday, May 10, 1929

This morning, we visited with the Alexanders. Oh my, one of the hardest things I have had to do in this life has been to tell the people here in Kelsey goodbye.

Loretta wouldn't tell us goodbye; she went to the garden. Brother Alexander's lip quivered, and Sister Alexander, Sister Stewart, and I cried. Then we bid Moroni Hamberlin and Sister Lindsey's folks goodbye. We all cried; we went to Bradshaw's, bade them goodbye, then onto town and said farewell to our "little old" Ford. The ticket agent let us bring 420 pounds of freight on our clergy tickets. We should've brought only one hundred pounds. We saw Brother Jones and Ralph Whitehead and waved goodbye as the train pulled out. We had to wait in Big Sandy from 12:40 to 4:13. Then we rearched Dallas at 7:45 and came out to the girls' rooms. I had a sick headache so did not talk much, even to Elder Saurey. I went to bed early.

Saturday, May 11, 1929

We had a priesthood meeting this morning. I washed too. Brother Brown brought his family and came in. They are having a party out to his place for us next Saturday. We went shopping, I took my wristband to be fixed, and two drunk men talked to me or tried to as I came down on the elevator. We had a street meeting, but I did not have to talk. We came home, and the seven of us had four bricks of ice cream. We had a good time.

Sunday, May 12, 1929

The elders came, and we all went to Sunday school. Everyone seemed to be glad to see me. They said they'd been waiting for me for three weeks. I had to give something on Mother's Day. It was such a surprise. I read from the Liahona "A Mother's Love." It was very appropriate. We went out to Sister Serilda Lukin's for dinner. Rena was over there too. A lot of people asked us to go home with them. Sister Ellett said her husband said, "All that is the matter with the church is that they didn't have enough peppy missionaries like Sister Dalton." We came to the priesthood meeting at night and then planned for Tuesday night refreshments and a party.

Monday, May 13, 1929

We were going tracking, but it rained too hard, so the elders came over and brought their albums, and then oh, how we laughed. In the afternoon, we went to Dr. Jay's office and had our teeth fixed, then caught a bus and went out to Davis's, where we stayed until nine o'clock. When we came home, some of the streets were filled with water. Davis treated us royally.

Tuesday, May 14, 1929

I left the house early this morning and went downtown to visit investigators. Went first to see about my wristband, then to Dr. Jay's, and then all out in the south part of Dallas. Had lunch at Shriver's, saw Mrs. Smith, went out to see Karen Williams, then helped

Sister Knight get the punch and ice cream ready. Then I went out to President Knight's and met Sister Stewart, Chappell, and Tanner. We had dinner and then went to the church for the one hundredth anniversary of the founding of the Aaronic Priesthood. They served ice cream, cake, punch, and buttermilk. We girls sang "Neapolitan Nights," then for the encore, we sang, "I Love You Truly." We lost our pitch on that one. We had to leave before the party was out to take Sister Stewart and Chappell to the train. And they left for Tulsa at 10:45 tonight. The elders gave them a box of candy. We cried and came home. Sister Brinkerhoff was married to Henry Carroll today.

Wednesday, May 15, 1929

We went tracking the first house I went to. It just seemed that I never had tracked before. I couldn't even remember my scriptures, but I sold a Book of Mormon and three little books. The lady gave me a dollar for them. She had been very nervous for years and had lost all hope of the hereafter, but she said she felt so much better when we left. Then at another place, I sold three little books. We came home, and I left Beardall, reading the meaning of different ways of sticking postage stamps. I went over to the elders to see about getting our tour of the city tomorrow. While I was there, the elders had supper, and I ate some combination salad with them. Carl Dotson came in during that time, and I came home. The Booths came while we were there. Brother Booth kissed me, and I blushed for four hours. Sister Booth said, "Well, Sister Dalton, you are surely good for sore eyes." She said they just weren't going to let me go off at conference. They needed me here too badly. They took us down to Carpenter's, where I surely enjoyed myself. They asked me if I would like to go to Kelsey for conference and then come back that same night, and of course, I was just overjoyed. The elders were here when we came home so we talked for a while, and then they went home. I wore my new hat, and Elder Beardall said I surely looked nice.

Thursday, May 16, 1929

Mr. Falcon called for us, and we went sightseeing: the Elders, Saurey, Cherney, and Beardall with Sister Tanner and me. We went through a recently remodeled part of the city, then the Munger Edition, and then out in East Dallas to see all the new land and hear the agents rave. The land here has surely gone up in price. If I had been going to live here, I might have bought some land. We had lunch out there, then went to Ellis's for dinner and to spend the evening, then down to Duncan's, where we met Carl Dotson and Elder Saurey. We had a meeting and then went over to Collin's. She invited us out to dinner on Sunday. Received a huge box of vegetables from Alexanders.

Friday, May 17, 1929

We tracked for four hours today, but I didn't even sell a Book of Mormon. We came home and had dinner, then went to Primary out to Mrs. Hall's and had seventeen there. I took a class of boys who seemed to enjoy Primary and begged me to teach them "Old MacDonald Had a Farm." A real cloud came up, and oh, how it rained. Mrs. Hill took us over to Lukin's, where we met Elder Saucy and had a cottage meeting. Then we waded from the streetcar to the house. I received a book of poems from Sister Morgan.

Saturday, May 18, 1929

We could not wash today because it rained too much. We made plans to go out to Sister Elliot's and then to Brother Brown's and then to street meeting. As the weather came and changed suddenly, we finally ended up going out to Brother Brown's after we had eaten a huge lunch. After we got out to Brown's, they had us eat again; then I talked to Brother Rupert, and Sister Tanner washed he dishes. The elders froze the ice cream, and after 9:00, we had a cottage meeting; there were twenty-one there. I talked on faith and works. At our party afterward, Mrs. Crothers said she was afraid I wasn't going to talk, and that is what she came for—just to hear me talk. We had canned milk ice cream.

Sunday, May 19, 1929

We got up at about 5:30, but oh, I was so sleepy. We didn't get to bed until 12:30. Brother Brown brought us into Sunday school, but we had to get ready and come home first. After Sunday school, we went out to Collins on McDonald Street, then hunted Mrs. Tidwell and went to meeting. Brother Carpenter and Carl Dotson talked, and I sat easy, and then I had to preach, but I did not have time to develop my subject. We went to find Mark Kennison. Mrs. Tidwell brought us home in her car.

Monday, May 20, 1929

We did some revisiting. I went with Sister Tanner and tried to sell a Book of Mormon for her, but another lady came in, and I sold her one. Sister Tanner came home, and I tracked alone. I came home and washed; I surely did have to hurry. The elders and Mark Kennison came here for supper. I had to hang some of my clothes out after dark. We went out to Elliott's and had ice cream.

Tuesday, May 21, 1929

Elder Beardall and I went to town, and then Sister Tanner and I went with Sister Leinbach to see Mrs. Miller at the Elite Costuming Company. From there, we went to a Relief Society meeting. Then Sister Tanner and I went with Sister Knight out to Mrs. Gibson's, found she had moved, and went to see Mrs. Tidwell. Arranged for a cottage meeting to be held Monday night at her place. She took us to find Mr. Gibson. I hurried and found a present for Loretta Burnett, then came home. Got dinner for we had to hurry out to meeting, but when we got there, they weren't home, so we came back. Elder Cheney played the violin, and Elder Beardall played the mouth organ.

Wednesday, May 22, 1929

Elder Carlson and Smith went over to class. We tracked individually for four hours. Elder Beardall, Sister Tanner, and I went out to Sister Bullock's. She has a sincere testimony of the Gospel, and her sincerity strengthens my testimony.

Thursday, May 23, 1929

We were very much surprised to have Presidents Hugh C. Bennion and Pressler here in class. It seemed good too. We tracked for four hours and came home long enough to change our dresses, then out to primary we went; thirty-three were there. I read "Franz" and "Betty at the Baseball Game."

We played games, and Mrs. Hill served refreshments. Then we went out to Weil's to dinner. They seemed glad to have us come. Mr. Legio was going to take us to Duncan's to meeting, but when we got in his car, he had a flat tire, so we walked. Found Beardall and Bingham waiting for us, held our meeting, and left. Called at Collins for our cake but didn't get any. Beardall bought me a toothbrush at the drugstore and treated us all to ice cream cones. Booths were here to tell us we would go to Kelsey in the morning.

Friday, May 24, 1929

I got up at 3:30 and was ready to go to Kelsey when Booths came for me at 4:00 a.m. It rained a little, but not too much. We had breakfast. Yes, a hamburger at Mineola. Then got to Bradshaw's at 9:30, went to Alexanders, and stayed all day. I had a wonderful dinner and lay down to rest for a few minutes. Imogene insisted on shooing the flies off. They surely hated to see me come back. We had dinner tonight at Sister Bradshaw's. Everyone enjoyed it immensely. We were late to meeting. I had to talk. Everyone seemed overjoyed to see me, and I was mighty happy to be back. President Bennion came home with us. We had candy and soda water, stopped for gas, and found a bat in the car. Got in Dallas at 5:30 and went to bed with few preliminaries.

Saturday, May 25, 1929

After sleeping two and a half hours, I got up. We had breakfast at Booth's and went to Priesthood meeting. I had a good talk with President Bennion after Priesthood meeting, then I went with Sister Lottie Knight to gather refreshments for tonight. We had pudding and cake at Sister Lukin's. Elder Beardall felt discouraged I tried to cheer him up. Oh my, I can hardly realize that this is my last conference. It seems only yesterday since the first one I helped serve supper. Goldie Schrader wants me to be sure and write to her we had a good meeting; Elder Widdison and Sister Woolley were the only missionaries who preached. They served ice cream after the meeting. They gave us the salad, the sandwiches, and the cakes that were left. It was raining when we came home so we surely did run. Everyone seems to be very disappointed because I'm transferred; we have plans to go to Fort

Worth tomorrow. I surely am tired tonight. I have been up forty-three and a half hours.

Sunday, May 26, 1929

We went to Sunday school in the rain. President Knight didn't come early, so we had to stand in the rain. It was too rainy to go to Fort Worth, so Goldie Schrader came home with us, and they gave us the food that we got at the church last night. Yes, that's what we had for dinner. Elder Bennion spent the afternoon with us.

The journal ends here. Six and a half blank pages remain, and another month and a half of mission before her release and her trip east. Could there be another lost journal somewhere?

Reva Virginia Dalton is the daughter of Charles and Virginia Peterson Dalton of Circleville, Piute, Utah. After her mission, she married Silas Mardell Topham in the Salt Lake temple on May 16, 1933. She was married a month and five days short of five years when she died from complications after the birth of her third child. She accomplished so much in her short life and impacted many lives for good. I will be forever grateful for this extraordinary journal she left behind.

CHAPTER 26

The Conclusion

After researching records, reviewing the histories, and the journal, I have come to know much more about the joys and hardships of these ancestors. I will never in this life truly understand all that they endured just to survive.

They all went through hardships, and many struggled with the word of wisdom that was new to them. They were set in their ways but learned to rely on each other for support as they worshiped their God in this new colony they called Kelsey.

Clara, like many of the sisters, did write her history. She wrote about how wonderful her grandparents were, how much she loved and appreciated het parents, how they taught her all the correct principles, and how strong her testimony was of the Church of Jesus Christ of Latter-day Saints. She knew Joseph Smith was a prophet and that her children had been blessed by the power of the priesthood many times. She said the greatest blessings in her life were when her five sons were placed in her arms at birth.

She gives no insight into what the rest of her life was like in her history. Her son, Glenn, stated that they had two homes burned by the time he was eight.

They were in an area that had no electricity or running water. A fire would have been an enormous concern to them over their safety. How did the quilt survive the house fire?

The only documentation on the fires I found was a story from thirty years ago saying P. A. Hamberlin's year-old house burned, printed in the Gilmer Mirror and published in 1965. So the last fire was in 1935.

Glenn's daughter Liz said her father told her that during the oil boom of 1929, Percy went to work in the oil fields because of failed crops. This strained the marriage, with him unable to help her with the boys and the farm. I don't know what made her so unhappy with him.

My husband, Jim, had always said when he was six, he visited his grandparents' home in Salt Lake City; his grandpa lived in the basement. The story always was that something had happened, and even though he asked her to forgive him and stayed with Clara and his family until he died in 1952, she never could forgive him. She even went so far as to have her sealing to him canceled after his death.

When we started working on family history in 1980, Glenn told me she made him promise never to seal them back together. I told him I felt like she had to have loved him to be that hurt, and I knew she had a strong testimony of Christ's teachings.

Forgiveness is something that we receive only when we forgive others. I knew that when she died and could look at everything more Christlike, she would forgive him and want to be with him and their children. I said I hadn't promised her.

It was not me that sealed them back together but someone who lived close to the Dallas, Texas, temple. A family member there who loved them and wanted to make things right. I have no idea who, though I am sure they lived in Kelsey.

Events in her life caused her to build a wall of protection around herself and maybe even her sons. I think it happened at the time of the quilt. Reva's journal mentions Percy Hamberlin, Clara's husband, but never Clara. Then after seeing how close all the sisters in the journal were to Reva and that she was the teacher of the young sisters Faye Dixon and Bee Lindsey, who had "to my teacher" embroidered on their orphan blocks, I thought the blocks could have all been for her. Carrie Hamberlin had put her mailing address on her block in the quilt like she wanted the receiver to write her and keep in touch. Then when Reva talks about not getting her blocks to Ava Dixon in time to be quilted, it made me think that these blocks and the quilt were made for Sister Dalton.

At first, I thought Clara must have intentionally hidden the quilt. The more I thought about that, the more it didn't feel right. She would have thrown them away or even let them burn in a fire if it were intentional.

My daughter, Courtney, reminded me that recently she came across a quilt she started in high school. It was to be her Celestial Quilt, all-white eyelet. It had never been put together and finished. She had forgotten about it until she saw it. I then realized that I had started and never finished more things than I could count. Out of sight, out of mind.

That is not counting the things I never finished because I couldn't find them when I looked for them. I am sure the sisters in Kelsey and Enoch made the blocks again, and they were able to send Sister Dalton home with two quilts.

She says at the end that she packed her quilts in the trunk she sent home. I wonder where those quilts are today. After her death, where did they go, and who kept them? Did they know the love that she had for the Kelsey sisters? Probably not.

Clara most likely had no idea that by losing them, she saved them for a time of computers and technology that made it possible to preserve the history and testimonies of so many faithful sisters to be shared with everyone. I am so thankful for all the joy I found in learning about these women and how it has strengthened my testimony of my Savior and the Atonement.

This story had to be told to remind us how important it is to learn about our ancestors. To read what others have written and write what we know about them. Share our life stories for our posterity so they may learn from our mistakes and learn that we have gone through all the same things they are experiencing. I am thankful I have learned to love them all, especially Clara.

I think that we must forgive others and forgive ourselves. Maybe now Clara can forgive any wrongs done to her and let the truth set her free to find eternal happiness because she is a daughter of God.

Kesley Connections

Alexander
Imogene A
James Buford
Loretta Mae
Norma Gwendolyn
Rawleigh Bee
Willie Hamilton

Amonette
Lillie

Arrington
Denzil
Wilhelmina Gertrude

Ault
Joshua Stephen
Mary Medomosile

Bailey
Benjamin Franklin
Bessie Alverine
Charlotte
Ethel Mae
Gussie
James Arthur
James Duran
James Erskine
Joseph Jason
Luther Kennedy
Newie Adelbert
Shirley Erskine
William Jehu

William Milton
Zora

Baker
Martha Laura

Barksdale
John Jackson

Barney
Ann Pomeroy
Kimberly

Bell
Charles Vinson
Evelyn Beatrice

Belnap
Flora
Wallace J

Bennion
Samuel Otis

Bierce
Charles
Elizabeth

Bodine
Jerry
John Jay
Warren Oliver
William Thomas Oliver

Bonebrake
Harold

Bowers

Patrice

Bradshaw
Auto Delois
Elton Bennion
Elvin Thomas
Gaylon
Glenna Adline
Maureen Odean
Silas William
Thomas James Judson

Brinkerhoff
Maurine

Bryant
Audrey
Carl
Earley Bell
Laura Pauline
Emmons Church
Lelia Irene
Myron B
Robert Emmons

Buckley
Abby
Arthur Maurice
Arthur Lee
Guy Maurice
Mar Jo
William Thomas

Burnett

Beverly Juanell
Donald Buford
Donnie Odell
Marvin Forrest
Wade

Cagle
Sarah Francess "Sallie"

Caldwell
James Joel

Cannon
George Quale
Mary

Chevalier
Oni
William

Church
Margaret Nomie

Click
Matilda Elizabeth

Compton
Ronald 'Ron"
Ronald Gilbert

Corley
Joe Terry

Craig
Martha Catherine

Crouch
Isabelle Joseph
James Rice
Martha Ann
Samuel Benjamin

Cummins

Lona Elizabeth
George Washington Sr

Dalton
Charles R
Reva

Davis
Hazel Laurie
Hugh
Tom Ellis
William T

Dawson
Luther
Shane
Rusis Susie Bessie
William King

Defreese
Charles Howard
Charlie
Bobbie

Denton
Carol Lynn

Dickason
Clara Annie
John Wesley Sr
Mary Estell
Susie Maggie
Emma Elizabeth

Dilly
Benjamin William
Elvie Willene
Joseph Norman
Carrie Lamarshard

Dixon

Anna Belle
Benjamin Cluff
Clyde Edward
Emma Smoot
Harold Maurice
James Franklin
John
Mathew Henderson Jr
Oletha Faye
Reva Eldeen
Richard Joseph
Tazwell Jackson
Van Smith
Vera Mae
William Thomas

Dotson
Alfred C
Carl Christopher
Wilma

Duffin
James G

Ellett
Albert Hayden
Arthur Odell
Ava Christine
Eleanor Winifred
Isaac William
Katie Oletha
Robert Owen Sr
Ruby Nell
William Walter

Ellsworth
Thurza

Ennis
Calvin Richard
Iva Viola

Farley
Marion C
James Toney
Lucy Lucile

Farnsworth
Sylvia

Flake
Osmer Dennis
Kellir

Fox
Myron

Futrell
David Childress
Earl Eugene
James Braxton
James Edward
John Whitaker Jr
Travis Preston
Virginia

Grantham
Ennis Edward
James Edward

Green
Charles Nathaniel
Charles William
Daisy Eleana
Earnest Love
George Franklin
Irene
John Benjamin

Katy Doy
Leon Nathaniel
Martha Catherine "Kitty"
Robert J
Sharon Ann
Viola
Weldon M "Thatcher"
Woodfin Grady

Grizzle
Billy Earl
Danny Paul
Gary Lloyd
Mark Allen

Grover
Lenard Crouch
Maggie Arminta
Olive Bell
Samuel Banks

Grubbs
William

Hamberlin
Ancel Enos
Artie Alton
Courtney Louise
David
Debra
Doyle Carlos
Effie Fayrene
Elizabeth
Flossie Frankie
Forrest Richard
Frances Lena
Hettie Ina
Marlee

Intha Ophelia "Toni"
James Doyle
James Ridge
James Wesley
Julia Amanda
Lena Ovena
Leland Glenn
Letha Irwin
Lorenzo Tracy
Lucious Lamar
Martin Alonzo
Mary Alma
McKenzie
Melvin Rudger
Otis Lamar
Percy Alton
Retha Vaughn
Scyril Berwis
Sidney
Victor Carl Sr
Virginia Josie
Walter Moroni
William Angus
William Moses

Hardman
Rhaunal Arthur

Hefley
Olive Louise
Ava Nell

Henderson
Carol Daron
Flavius Carlyle
Glenna E
Gwendoline

Linda Gay
Sandra Diane
Sharon Kay
Wallace Reed
William Robert

Henry
James Edgar

Hobby
Ida Crook
James Crook

Hunt
Evelyn Grace

Hunter
Carrie Effie Dove
William Wesley

Iglinsky
Avoid Louis Jr

Irwin
Effie Lavinia
Ida Adella
Julia Helen
Sophronia Mary

Jackson
Royce

Jewkes
Kent Dixon
Kim Lorraine
Richard Dale
Richard Rollo

Johnson
Katie Elizabeth

Jones

Andrew Jackson
Blenda Noreen
Chauncey Lee
Cornelia Gladys
Dorothy Jean
Earnest Stuart
Emil Obie
Horace Heber
John L
Lenora Myrtle
Samantha Evelena
William Harrison

Kendall
Mary Elizabeth

Knight
Bernice
Blynn
Della O
Frederick Homer
H Madison
Homer Arnell
Peggy
Reagan Grant
Rowan Dean

Layton
Ida Dora

Leake
Berta Adeline "Birdie"
Moses Asbury

Lee
Chester Arthur
Gracie Bell
Katie Ella

Wesley Hector
William Hector "Heck"

Lewis
Docia Elizabeth

Lindsey
Arthur Emmett
Archie Willie
Blanche
Connie
David Michael
Don Carlos
Edna Laurine
Frances Ella
Geneva
Harold Hubert
Horace Joseph
Hubert Hefley
Irene Ethel
Jessie Beatrice
John Bryan
John Wayne
Joseph Milam
Mamie Arnold
Marilyn Elaine
Mary Faye
Maude
Myrtle
Parley Jenson
Paul Jeffery
Pleasant James
Raymond Amory
Sadie
Sarah
Steven Edward

William Jasper
Zelma Fern

Luna
Minnie Bell
William C

Luton
Mary Blanche
Martin
Mary Josephine
William P

Mattox
Wendy Elaine

McKnight
Edward Doyle "Dewey"
Erma Blynn
Maurine
William "Will"

Means
Bonnie Donnetta
Leo Virgil
Naomi Jill

Meyers
Dana Larry
Giles Randle
Laquita Ann
Wallace Harold
Mildred

Michels
Harriett

Miller
Dorothy LaVerne
Wade Hampton

Mitchell
Beatrice Othella
Sheldon William
Welton D.C.
William Joseph

Motes
Margaret

Muckleroy
Belita
Dolly Jo
Grace Juanell
Martin Alan
Robert

Mull
Martha
Emma Christina Lucinda

Perry
Bennion Leroy
Charlotte
Thomas Harrison
Joseph Aden Sr
Nathan
Tempie Arminta
William

Pritchett
Jamie
Lelia Flora
Tommy L
Vickie J

Rich
Benjamin Erastus

Riding
Todd

Roberts
Sarah Virginia

Rowley
Dawna Lynn
James A
Janice
Patrick Lindsey
Scott David

Sanders
Benjamin Milton
Ella Theodocia "Docie"
Ercell Maud
James Arthur
Joseph Milton
Julia
Oni Rosebud
Ruth Marie
Amanda Florence
Agusta Theodocia
Jonathan Travis

Shore
Charles Hamilton
Cora Alice
Etta Loretta
Floy Bee
John Henry
Roy Lee

Shulps
Stanla Sue

Simmons
Albertine
Doris Faye
Robert S

Smith
John B Taylor
Lacoleon
Robert Franklin
Velda Maleese

Strasburg
George Bryant
George Taylor
Laura Pauline

Sullivan
Effie Ziella

Tefteller
Samuel Monroe
Lawrence

Tocconi
Darlene
Peitro "Pete" Moretti

Thrailkill
Rebecca Jane

Topham
Dale
Mardell
Silas Mardell
Virginia

Tusler
Margarett Ann

Vice
Beatrice Jane
James Milton
Byron Ashbury
Chester King
Clyde Sexton

Ethel Letha
Jasper Carolina
Linnie Shirlene
Mamie Adeline
Pearl
Vera

Walters
Lillie Fair

Webb
Canace

White
Danny
Wilford "Wizzer"

Whitehead
Elizabeth Lucinda
David Lafayette

Whitlock
Connie Sue
Enola Marie
Jacob Isaiah

Wilson
Mary Magdalene

Wofford
Charlotte Lucinda

Woodruff
Willford
Abraham Owen

Woodhouse
Anna Ruth

www.ingramcontent.com/pod-product-compliance
Lightning Source LLC
Chambersburg PA
CBHW051134120626
46547CB00012B/803